ANCESTRAL LINES

ANCESTRAL LINES

THE MAISIN OF PAPUA NEW GUINEA AND THE FATE OF THE RAINFOREST

Second Edition
John Barker

UNIVERSITY OF TORONTO PRESS

LIBRARY AND ARCHIVES CANADA CATALOGUING IN PUBLICATION

Barker, John, 1953–, author
Ancestral lines: the Maisin of Papua New Guinea and the fate of the rainforest / John Barker.—Second edition.
(Teaching culture: UTP ethnographies for the classroom)

Includes bibliographical references and index.

Issued in print and electronic formats.

ISBN 978-1-4426-3593-7 (bound).—ISBN 978-1-4426-3592-0 (paperback).
—ISBN 978-1-4426-3595-1 (pdf).—ISBN 978-1-4426-3594-4 (html).

1. Maisin (Papua New Guinean people). 2. Maisin (Papua New Guinean people)—Social life and customs. 3. Maisin (Papua New Guinean people)—Economic conditions. 4. Rain forests—Papua New Guinea. 5. Logging—Papua New Guinea. I. Title. II. Series: Teaching culture

DU744.35.M32B37 2016   305.89'912   C2015-907492-4
                                               C2015-907493-2

We welcome comments and suggestions regarding any aspect of our publications—please feel free to contact us at news@utphighereducation.com or visit our Internet site at www.utppublishing.com.

North America
5201 Dufferin Street
North York, Ontario, Canada, M3H 5T8

2250 Military Road
Tonawanda, New York, USA, 14150

ORDERS PHONE: 1-800-565-9523
ORDERS FAX: 1-800-221-9985
ORDERS E-MAIL: utpbooks@utpress.utoronto.ca

UK, Ireland, and continental Europe
NBN International
Estover Road, Plymouth, PL6 7PY, UK
ORDERS PHONE: 44 (0) 1752 202301
ORDERS FAX: 44 (0) 1752 202333
ORDERS E-MAIL: enquiries@nbninternational.com

Every effort has been made to contact copyright holders; in the event of an error or omission, please notify the publisher.

The University of Toronto Press acknowledges the financial support for its publishing activities of the Government of Canada through the Canada Book Fund.

Printed in the United States of America.

For Anne, Jessica, and our Maisin families

CONTENTS

ILLUSTRATIONS

COLOUR PLATES

PREFACE

This book emerged from teaching anthropology to undergraduate students. For most students, an introductory course may be the only experience they have of the hugely diverse and lively discipline of anthropology. In North America in particular, instructors tend to use large introductory textbooks usually accompanied by a volume of readings and/or a book-length ethnographic study of a single people. There are excellent books available. Yet, more often than not, they fail to match up with each other. Most ethnographic monographs, even those explicitly written for undergraduates new to anthropology, are not designed with introductory textbooks in mind. They focus upon an aspect of the community under study of particular interest to the author, only dealing with one or two of the general topics covered in the accompanying textbook, or they are written more or less as autobiographical accounts, forcing students to sift out general themes from the personal stories. This book is first and foremost an ethnography, but one constructed in a way that conforms to the sequence of topics found in most introductory textbooks. Hence the chapters of this study deal with, in turn, fieldwork, economics, social organization, religion, political and legal organization, and the application of anthropology to social problems. While the chapters build upon each other, I have written them so that an instructor, if she or he chooses, can easily stretch out the reading of the book over an entire term or quarter, in tandem with a textbook. Rather than dealing with a new culture for each new topic, students can return to a culture that becomes increasingly familiar over time as they study it from successive angles.

As an ethnography, this book provides an introduction to the cultural and historic experience of the Maisin people of Papua New Guinea, organized around the theme of tapa cloth (decorated bark cloth), culminating in an exploration of the community's rejection of industrial logging on their ancestral lands in the 1990s. It also includes personal vignettes. Anthropologists love to tell stories from the field; when told well, they enliven lectures and convey important truths about the nature of learning about foreign cultures. Much of the text, however, follows the conventions of traditional ethnography in seeking to provide readers with a sense of the way of life in a remote Melanesian village and an interpretation of the key values and orientations that provide the basic frameworks that govern its people's lives.

Because the primary audience for this book is introductory-level undergraduates, I keep specialized language and references to a minimum. Today's textbooks and readers, often supplemented by a website, provide students with a huge list of recommended sources and references that can be daunting. I see no reason to add to this. Thus, I have tried to limit references to those directly relevant to this work, along with some to guide students with particular interests in Melanesia or who are just curious about the Maisin and their neighbours. Students wishing to learn more about, say, legal systems or art will find plenty of excellent references in their textbooks and from their instructors.

This book is also intended for students taking courses on the cultures of the Pacific Islands, on Indigenous people's art, and on the environment in an age of globalization. Using tapa cloth as a metaphor for culture, this study examines a small society that is facing challenges common to all of us. The Maisin provide a fresh perspective and, to borrow the words of David Suzuki, "good news for a change" (Suzuki and Dressel 2002) in a world very much in need of it.

Most importantly, this book is intended for the Maisin of today and future generations. This is not the kind of book a Maisin would write and, I hope, one day soon will write. This is an outsider's account; yet it is one based on a long acquaintance with and respect for the Maisin people. I hope, in a small way, it will contribute to their struggle to maintain control over their lands and honour their ancestral heritage. At the very least, it provides a record of their society as I observed it during a time of momentous change.

A NOTE ON THE SECOND EDITION

The first edition of *Ancestral Lines* was well received by colleagues, students, and my Maisin friends. When the Maisin and their allies in Collingwood Bay won a second victory against loggers in the National Court of Papua New Guinea in May 2015, it struck me as an opportune time for a second edition. My initial intention was to correct a few errors and clarify wording here and there. The main change would be a new concluding chapter to bring the story up to date. Once I got going, however, the temptation to tighten the language, rearrange for clarity, and update key arguments proved impossible to resist. While the ethnographic description follows the same course of development found in the first edition, I have thoroughly revised the text as a whole. I want to thank my students, Dr. Anna-Karina Hermkens, and, in particular, Dr. Tad McIlwraith and his students, all of whose criticisms and suggestions guided my approach to revising the book. I am especially grateful to Dr. Anne Marie Tietjen for her close reading of the text, which led to many improvements and saved me from several embarrassments. The final text, of course, is my full responsibility.

The research on which this book is based was supported by the Social Sciences and Humanities Research Council of Canada, the National Geographic Foundation, the Wenner-Gren Foundation for Anthropological Research, the Overseas Ministries Study Center in New Haven, and the Hampton Fund of the University of British Columbia. In Port Moresby and Popondetta, I received much practical support from the Australian National University, the Institute for Papua New Guinea Studies, the Anglican Church of Papua New Guinea, the University of Papua New Guinea, the National Research Institute, and Conservation Melanesia. My thanks as well to the very helpful research staff members of the Australian Museum in Sydney, the New Guinea Collection at the University of Papua New Guinea, the National Library of Papua New Guinea, and the National Archives of Papua New Guinea. In the United Kingdom, I am grateful for the kind assistance of curatorial staffs at the British Museum, the Cambridge Museum of Archaeology and Anthropology, the Pitt-Rivers Museum, and the Horniman Museum in locating Maisin objects and related documentation.

While in Papua New Guinea, I enjoyed the hospitality and benefited from the sound advice offered by many people. I wish to thank in particular Archbishop David Hand, Bishop Isaac Gadebu, Archbishop George Ambo, Sister Helen Roberts (MBE), Bishop Paul Richardson, Father Timothy Kinohan, Paul Sillitoe, David and Betty Buchan, James and Achsah Carrier, Maev O'Collins, Father Wellington Aburin, Father Giles Ganasa, Sian Upton, Gary Trompf, John Waiko, Benson Gegeyo, Lester Seri, and Arthur Moi.

Many colleagues have contributed to my understanding of the Maisin, Melanesia, and anthropology. I wish to acknowledge in particular Kenelm Burridge, Cyril Belshaw, John LeRoy, Martin Silverman, Bill McKellin, Dan Jorgensen, Bronwen Douglas, Ann Chowning, John Horne, David Marsh, Anna-Karina Hermkens, Elisabetta Gnecchi-Ruscone, Jan Hasselberg, Liz Bonshek, Lafcadio Cortesi, David Wakefield, Marisa McHenry, and Joanna Frampton. A warm thanks to Bruce Miller, who more than once saved my sanity during the Maisin-Stó:lō exchange in June 2000. I owe a special debt of gratitude to Roger Lohmann and Joel Robbins who painstakingly read through the original manuscript and offered many excellent suggestions for improvement.

Thanks as well to my students, both undergraduate and graduate, who have been subjected over many years to my stories from the field. Your curiosity, challenging questions, and determination to make the world a better place are very much part of this book.

My wife, Dr. Anne Marie Tietjen, was my companion and colleague in 1981–83, 2000, and 2007, conducting pioneering research on developmental and social psychology in a Melanesian society. She appears several times in this account, as does our daughter, Jessica, who experienced her own memorable visit in 2000. Less visible, but no less real, are the results of Anne's careful reading of the first and second editions of the manuscript. Her insights and suggestions—and corrections to my sometimes creative memory—run through this book.

I have also had the good fortune to work with the wonderful "Teaching Cultures" team at Broadview Press and the University of Toronto Press. My sincere thanks in particular to Anne Brackenbury for her encouragement and wise guidance through both editions and to Betsy Struthers and Eileen Eckert for their careful copyediting of the first and second editions respectively.

My greatest debts are to the Maisin people—my friends, my teachers, and my adopted family. Many of those we sat with and learned from in earlier years are now departed, but fondly remembered. I begin by recalling three men who were more than teachers, insisting that I call them my fathers: Adelbert Sevaru, Frank Davis Dodi, and Jairus Ifoki. I am also grateful to all those who worked as research assistants and translators, particularly MacSherry Gegeyo, Willie Sevaru, and Roland Wawe. It is not possible to thank all of those who assisted me over the years, but I do want to mention George and Mary Rose Sevaru, Franklin Seri, Romney Gegeyo, Father Kinsley Gegeyo, Lester Seri, Julia Seri, John Wesley Vaso, Gideon Ifoki and Frieda Numa, Sylvester Moi, Rebecca Gegeyo Moi, Agnes Sanangi, Lambert Gebari, Deacon Didymus Gisore, Deacon Russell Maikin, Copland King Ganeba, Nigel Bairan, Macdonald Rarama, Holland and Maggie Kania, Naomi Sakai, Guy Kimanu, Frederick Bogara, David Beyo, and Ross Kania. In Sinapa, I'm grateful to Christian Karebi for friendship and guidance; likewise to Andrew Ofare in Yuayu and Cephus Dave in Airara. To all the others who have shared their lives with Anne and me over the years, I say: *Au natofo, tekyu bejji.*

Royalties from this book will be donated to the Maisin elementary schools in Uiaku and Airara villages.

CHAPTER 1

FIELDWORK AMONG THE MAISIN

14 August 1982. We expected a small party. We had been living in Uiaku for almost nine months and had reached the dreaded moment when my wife Anne's leave from her university job ended, requiring her return to Canada. Anne would return to the village for three months at the end of the school year, but that was a long eight months away. The village councillor had told us that the people were organizing a goodbye dinner. We had been to many community gatherings and had a good idea of what to expect. Late in the afternoon, women gathered by the shelter near our house with baskets of food, firewood, and blackened clay cooking pots. Young boys husked and scraped coconuts while the women sat peeling taro. They filled the pots to the brim with large chunks of the grey tubers along with plantains, squash, sweet potatoes, wild pork, and fish, topped by edible greens. They then poured in water sweetened by squeezing it through coconut shavings. They covered the pots with banana leaves and laid them out in a long line, each atop a pile of firewood. As the food cooked, the men sat on the shaded shelter platform, chewing betelnut,[1] smoking, and discussing the events of the day.

Anne came attired for the occasion in a finely decorated bark cloth ("tapa") skirt and top that the church women's group, the Mothers' Union, had made for her. As I took pictures, Anne pitched in to help the women, who greeted her with a chorus of jokes and laughter. Eventually, we were requested to sit at the place of honour on a large, gorgeously designed tapa cloth at the head of the shelter. Women forked food into bowls and then climbed onto the platform, crossing it on their knees to place the food before the seated men. Once the deacon had said the grace, Anne rejoined the women on the ground and we all tucked in. After the feast ended and the women had cleared the bowls away, the senior men made speeches thanking us for our work in the community. There was a pause for more betelnut chewing. An elder called out to the crowd around the shelter, "Has anyone gifts to give our sister?" Then the most

1

Figure 1.1 The farewell party, August 1982. Anne is greeted by Ilma Joyce Gombi and a little girl. Note the line of women waiting to present tapa cloths. (Photo by J. Barker)

amazing thing happened. Women, children, and men came forward to place shell ornaments around Anne's neck and tuck flowers and fragrant leaves into the coconut husk bracelets adorning her arms and legs. They brought an abundance of tapa, opening each folded cloth with a flourish and then placing it before Anne or on her lap.

This event marked one of those moments that occur periodically in the course of anthropological fieldwork and serve to define a culture, illuminating what makes it special and unique. Over the course of six visits extending over three decades, I have come to think of the Maisin who inhabit Uiaku and neighbouring villages as "tapa people" because their distinctive, beautiful cloth figures so centrally in their history, interactions with each other, and dealings with the outside world. This book is about how the Maisin make a living, organize social interactions, conceptualize the spiritual world, and meet the opportunities and tragedies of life. It is about the ways they have adjusted to the encroaching colonial and post-colonial worlds. And it is about the fateful decision the Maisin made in the early 1990s to refuse commercial logging on their ancestral lands.

Much has changed over the years, not least during recent times when the Maisin have faced grave threats to the rainforest and waters that sustain their lives. Maisin tapa cloth, adorned with rich red geometric swirls and curls, has also sustained the people. It connects them to a still vital ancestral past; it defines gender roles and the modes of sociability; it provides income where there are very few opportunities to make money; and it stands as an iconic symbol of identity within the cultural mosaic that is Papua New Guinea. It is appropriate, then, to approach Maisin culture and history through the medium of tapa.

Tapa is the common name for cloth made from the pounded inner bark of the paper mulberry (*Broussonetia papyrifera*) and some varieties of ficus trees. Prior to European colonization, most of the inhabitants of the South Pacific Islands manufactured bark cloth, ranging from the delicately coloured *kapa* worn by nobility in the Hawaiian Islands (from which we get the word "tapa") to simple unadorned loincloths worn by men in parts of Melanesia (Neich and Prendergast 2005). Across the region, people experimented with a wide variety of trees, dyes, tools, and techniques, resulting in a kaleidoscope of styles as varied as the cultures themselves. Tapa served many purposes: clothing, wealth, a symbol of authority and divinity, a canvas for decorative designs or the face of an ancestor. European visitors admired tapa for its beauty and practicality. The incorporation of the islands into global commercial networks, however, opened the door to the import of cheap and durable mass-manufactured cotton and, later, synthetic clothing, hastening the demise of tapa. Today, tapa is regularly made in only a few places such as Samoa, Fiji, and Tonga, chiefly for the tourist trade and for ceremonial purposes (Kooijman 1972). Where tapa has survived, it is associated with people's cultural identity in an increasingly mobile and interconnected world (e.g., Addo 2013; Ewins 2009). The Maisin are one of those people.

The people of Uiaku and neighbouring villages call themselves the Maisin (pronounced "My-seen"). Numbering around 3,000 people, many of whom now live in distant towns, the Maisin form one of the more than 850 linguistic groups that make up the nation of Papua New Guinea. The cultural diversity of Papua New Guinea has long been a beacon for anthropologists. Although the land and population are relatively small (as of 2013, around seven million people live on its 462,840 square kilometres of land spread between several islands), few places have been as intensely studied by ethnographers—leading to the old joke that the typical New Guinean family consists of a husband, a wife, children, a pig, and an anthropologist. Anthropologists originally went to faraway places to document exotic cultures before they were transformed by the juggernauts of Christianity, commerce, and Western "civilization." It cannot be denied that the area continues to exert a romantic allure, but anthropologists working in Papua New Guinea today seek mainly to understand present-day experience. We have much to learn from people like the Maisin, not just about the diversity of human culture but, just as importantly, about the ways in which people in the far corners of the globe are dealing with problems that confront us all. This book is concerned with two of those challenges in particular: first, how a people can retain a sense of cultural identity in the face of the homogenizing influences of the global system that has so greatly eased the mass movement of people, products, and ideas; and second, how they can create and maintain a decent standard of living without destroying the environment in which all life is ultimately sustained.

All people face these challenges, but the stakes appear far more consequential and stark for some Indigenous cultures due to their small size, lack of economic and political clout, and, in many areas, direct dependence on the natural environment for their survival. By the time that Anne and I arrived late in 1981, Maisin culture had already been inalterably transformed by outside interventions. A school and church had existed in Uiaku since 1902. All of the people were Christian, all had attended at least the village school, and a quarter of the population resided outside the rural villages. Yet for all of the changes, Maisin villages retained a strong connection to a distinctive ancestral past, including their language, key traditional rituals, active local kinship and exchange networks, and, not least, a sense of pride in their cultural achievements, most notably tapa cloth. It seemed to us that people had found a mix that combined some of the best features of the old and new. The balance, however, was fragile. Most villagers considered themselves shamefully poor and eagerly sought opportunities to make money. In the early 1980s, the best option appeared to lie in selling off timber rights to the nearby rainforest. The cleared land would be replaced by profitable commercial plantations of oil palm, providing the people with a steady income. Many people were aware of the risks; even at that early date, word had reached them of the environmental damage caused by industrial logging elsewhere in the country and the unfulfilled promises made by the logging companies and their political backers. Yet people felt that their isolation from markets and shameful poverty left them with little choice.

Many Indigenous peoples have made such choices or, more often, had their lands and resources taken from them in the name of "development." Knowing this, Anne and I left Uiaku in July 1983, quietly lamenting that, even if the opportunity arose to return, the village we had come to love might well be changed beyond recognition. But the people had a change of heart. Doubts about the wisdom of clear-cutting the rainforest had, by the mid-1990s, hardened into a determination to keep out commercial loggers. Villagers fought off a series of projects pressed upon them by urban-based promoters and logging companies. Their quixotic campaign attracted the attention of international environmental organizations and, soon after, museum curators and the international media. Maisin delegations visited North America, Australia, and Japan to promote their cause. Maisin tapa was exhibited in art galleries in Berkeley, New York, Philadelphia, and Tokyo.

I had the good fortune to return to the Maisin villages in the midst of these developments for a couple of brief visits in 1997 and 1998. In July 2000, Anne and our 12-year-old daughter, Jessica, came as well. We were met with a joyful celebration in which Jess was taken through the first stages of the initiation ceremony for a first-born child. Physically, the villages and their surroundings looked much the same as in the early 1980s. The changes that had occurred were less visible but perhaps more significant. More people could speak English, and villagers appeared more affluent. They had better clothes and owned more store-bought goods. There was now a biweekly market at which people sold garden produce for cash. As we met with old friends and got to know younger folk who were babes-in-arms during our first visit, we detected a remarkable sense of confidence that had largely replaced the shame people had expressed over their "poverty." People spoke proudly of their ancestral traditions and contrasted their subsistence way of life favourably against the daily struggles of relatives to make enough money to survive in the towns. They eloquently told of the need to preserve both their distinct traditions and the environment for future generations. Tapa cloth had become the key symbol of that determination. Yet tapa had also become a major source of income for villages, alleviating the pressure to find money. At the time of our last visit, in June 2007, the boom in tapa sales was over and Maisin were again struggling with the choices of how best to foster local economic development without losing the most cherished aspects of their culture.

Tapa inspires my approach to this ethnography of the Maisin. Ethnographic fieldwork is based largely upon participant-observation or, as anthropologists occasionally joke, "deep hanging out." One learns not just through asking questions or observing but by getting involved directly, trying things out oneself. Making my own piece of tapa enabled me to better appreciate the skills involved and the wider significance of the cloth to the Maisin. Making a tapa involves several discrete stages, each building upon the other while employing distinct techniques and procedures. A human culture is a bit like that. You encounter a way of life as a seamless whole at first, but in time you learn to distinguish among the general processes and domains that sustain it. Each chapter of this book thus opens with a short section concerning tapa cloth as an introduction to differing facets of the society as I observed it during the latter two decades of the twentieth century. The introductory sections of Chapters 2 through 4 trace the making of a piece of tapa from the cultivation of the tree that provides the bark to the finishing application of red dye. These sections, in turn, introduce three of the fundamental domains of social life: economic activities, social organization, and religion. Chapter 5 opens with a survey of the various ways Maisin use tapa for community purposes and as a source of income, leading into a discussion of the legal and political aspects of community life. While not ignoring change, the first five chapters focus mostly upon the enduring fundamentals of Maisin society. Chapter 6 focuses on the Maisin campaign to save their rainforest in the 1990s. It opens with the visit by a four-man delegation from Uiaku to the Berkeley Art Museum in California to celebrate a major exhibition of Maisin tapa cloth. While Maisin culture retained its distinctive shape, the decision to reject commercial logging significantly increased the involvement of Maisin with outside agencies. These entanglements, in turn, encouraged the people to rethink their relationship to their own ancestral roots and the world outside their villages.

The first edition of *Ancestral Lines* ended in 2002 when the Maisin won a major victory in the National Court blocking logging on their lands. Since that time, the people have faced continuing pressure to allow logging and, more recently, mining in their ancestral territory. During the same period, the land faced a new threat when flooding from Cyclone Guba destroyed the gardens, a harbinger of the threat global climate change poses to low-lying regions. The closing of the local grass airstrip leaves the area even more of an economic backwater than 30 years ago, yet cheap cell phones have made communication with the outside world vastly easier. A new conclusion in Chapter 7 discusses these changes, bringing the account up to May 2015 and the Maisin's second victory against loggers in the National Court.

Before turning to these topics, it will be helpful to provide some background, beginning with an account of how Anne and I came to live and work with the Maisin. I then turn to the physical world within which Maisin live, and finish with an overview of the historical changes that have occurred in the area since first contact with European colonials in 1890.

FIELDWORK IN UIAKU

As is the case with most anthropologists, a twisting path led us to Uiaku. I first became interested in the South Pacific Islands while studying for my BA in anthropology at Western University in London, Ontario. In 1978, I landed a Commonwealth Scholarship that took me to Victoria University of Wellington in New Zealand for graduate studies under Ann Chowning, one of the great figures in Melanesian anthropology. I was excited about my proposed project: a study of the impact of multinational corporations upon the self-image of Pacific Islanders. This turned out to be impractical, given my tiny research budget and the difficulties of gathering scattered information in the days before the Internet. I spent my mornings in the Alexander Turnbull Library scanning ads in newspapers from its marvellous collection of Pacific Islands documents, my spirits steadily sinking as the impediments to the project became obvious. From time to time, my attention wandered to the Library's famed collection of early works on the Pacific Islands, many of which had been written by pioneering missionaries in the period prior to formal colonization. I was soon captivated. The books were not the stiff-necked "preachy" tracts I had expected (although they contained many expressions of piety and more than a little ethnocentrism)—they were more like the Victorian adventure stories by the likes of H. Rider Haggard, the author of *King Solomon's Mines*, which I had enjoyed as a child.

In the end, I wrote my MA thesis on the social history of three missions that operated in southeast Papua New Guinea between 1871 and 1930 (Barker 1979). This in turn led me to the topic for my PhD research. I had read widely in the anthropological literature on Melanesia by this point and was surprised by how little attention anthropologists paid to the impact of the missions and the presence of Christianity (Barker 1992). The most recent national census figures from Papua New Guinea indicated that an overwhelming majority of the people, more than 90 per cent, considered themselves Christian.[2] I also learned that most of the old missions had been succeeded by national churches headed by Papua New Guineans. Yet you would never know this from anthropological works, which focused almost exclusively upon Indigenous religious practices and ideas (Barker 1990a, 1992). What happened when people became Christians? I had some ideas from my MA research, but almost all of the assessments had been done by European missionaries writing decades earlier. I wondered what Papua New Guinean Christians themselves made of their Christian faith and its relationship to their ancestral cultures.

To pursue this topic, I decided that it would be best to study a community where the church had been an accepted part of ordinary life for generations and missionaries were a fading memory. This limited my choices to a coastal area. I also wanted to work in the southeast of the country so I could make good use of the historical research I had already done. Of the three missions I had studied, I was most intrigued by the Anglicans who, in contrast to the stereotypes many hold about missionaries, had been ardent defenders of most village traditions and fiercely critical of industrial society (Wetherell 1977). This narrowed my search to the northeastern coast of the island of New Guinea where the Anglicans were long established.

In 1979, I returned to Canada to take up PhD studies at the University of British Columbia under the supervision of Kenelm Burridge, another great

Melanesianist scholar best known for his writings on religious movements and, more recently, missionaries. I had about 500 kilometres of coastline to consider for possible field sites. Two events led me to the Maisin and Uiaku village. The first was falling in love and marrying Anne Marie Tietjen. Trained as a developmental psychologist at Cornell University, Anne was keenly interested in cross-cultural research, having carried out her dissertation fieldwork in Sweden. She developed a project to study the development of social cognition and behaviour that required a village with lots of children (Tietjen 1986). I came across an old census of the region and found that the two largest villages along hundreds of kilometres of the New Guinea coast lay within 12 kilometres of each other on Collingwood Bay: Wanigela and Uiaku. The second event was a fundraising visit to Vancouver by the Right Reverend David Hand, the Archbishop of the Anglican Church of Papua New Guinea. He had begun his missionary career in 1946 working as the priest-in-charge for the area and greatly admired the Maisin, who he told us had achieved a remarkable balance between their ancestral ways and modernity.

Bishop David suggested I contact Father Wellington Aburin, the parish priest for southern Collingwood Bay who resided in Uiaku. I dutifully wrote, outlining our research plans. I didn't receive a reply. This was worrisome, but Anne and I pushed on, writing grant proposals and applying for research visas. Soon everything was more or less in place. In October 1981, I set off ahead for Australia, where I carried out archival research, and then to Port Moresby, the capital of Papua New Guinea, where Anne caught up with me about six weeks later.

At the time of my departure, all we knew about the Maisin was the names of some of their villages, the approximate size of their population, and some aspects of their unusual language gleaned from a few brief articles. I reasoned that they shared cultural features and a similar experience of colonization with better-documented coastal peoples, but it was disconcerting to be going in so blind. Once in Port Moresby, I managed to pick up some details about Uiaku. I met my first Maisin—Father Kingsley Gegeyo, then a chaplain at the University of Papua New Guinea. He was friendly and encouraging, praising the village way of life and making suggestions on where we might stay until we arranged to have a house built. We stocked up with provisions before flying to Popondetta, the capital of Oro Province, to meet with government and church officials. We then flew out in a tiny prop plane, passing over heavily forested mountains and swampland before circling around the cloud-shrouded volcanic peak of Mount Victory and landing on the grass airfield at Wanigela, located two kilometres inland from Collingwood Bay. We were greeted by Sister Helen Roberts, a missionary nurse who had lived in Wanigela since 1946. She was a font of information on the local people, who held her in the highest regard, and quickly became a close friend. We also met David and Betty Buchan, a New Zealand couple managing a small rubber plantation on the lower slopes of Mount Victory, who also became fast friends during our stay.

Within a few hours of our arriving at the airstrip, Sister Helen introduced us to several women who had come up from the Maisin villages to sell tapa. They spoke little English so mostly we smiled at each other. A couple of days later, Father Wellington appeared. As it turned out, he had received our letters and told us that we had been expected to arrive two weeks earlier. He was friendly but quiet, and I worried that this was less from shyness than annoyance with our tardiness. Father Wellington returned to Uiaku in the afternoon. We really did not know what to expect at this point, but the next morning several young Maisin men appeared at the mission house ready to take us and our gear down to the beach to be loaded on a dinghy for the trip across Collingwood Bay to Uiaku. We had reached the final stage of our journey.

As the dinghy swung out from the beach into open water, we were dazzled by the dramatic scenery—the broad sweep of rainforest rising from the coast, the immense mountain wall to the south, and the line of volcanic peaks to the west. An hour later, we approached Uiaku. The boat operator pulled up the little outboard motor and we surfed across a low sandbar into the mouth of a broad river, shaded by high coconut palms. We landed at what we were told was the "mission station." Father Wellington was there along with the community school headmaster and dozens of curious children. Father Wellington took us up to his house—a commodious, cool building constructed of bush materials, with a broad verandah looking out over the river.

As we sipped heavily sugared tea, we were relieved to learn that a house had been made available for our use. A small bush house had recently been built to serve as an office accommodating a radio-telephone promised by the Bishop. When we materialized instead of the radio, the village leaders decided that it would serve as our home. The house was small, but more than suitable, with an extension that would serve as our kitchen, a bedroom just large enough for our mattress and mosquito net, two small offices with rough tables, and an alcove that we adapted for a bucket shower and wash area. As we walked to our new home, we were relieved to find a group of men hard at work constructing a latrine to the side (we had been contemplating the station latrines with some dread—they were little huts built over the river at the end of long rickety bridges).

After moving in our suitcases and boxes, we took a walk through the nearby part of the village. We felt a bit like royalty on parade, with cheerful people lining the sides of the path to see us and the children calling out "hello, hello" and breaking into hysterical giggles every time we replied. White people rarely visited the area, and so we were quite a novelty—so much so that the smaller tots burst into terrified screams at our approach. Around dinnertime, Gideon Ifoki appeared at our door. Gideon and Ilma Joyce Daima served as our first research assistants. They were our age and spoke excellent English. Both had left paying jobs elsewhere in the country to return home to care for aging parents. At the moment we met, Gideon was leading the first of a succession of groups of women who over the next two days brought string bags full of garden produce, which they unloaded just inside our house. The mounting pile of food, we were told, was a gift. We were not to pay for it.

We could hardly have dreamed of a more welcoming reception, with a house, food, and research assistants all pre-arranged by the people themselves. We were grateful but also overwhelmed. Why were they doing this? What did they expect of us? The morning after we arrived, Father Wellington introduced us to the community after the church service. I took the opportunity to give an explanation in simple English of our research goals and to invite questions (all this was translated for the congregation by Gideon). Later I repeated the speech at a community meeting called to discuss our project. In succeeding weeks and months, I often repeated my speech as I made the rounds of the villages. I think that most people understood the basics of what we said we were up to, yet they simply couldn't credit that white people would come all that way to live among them just to study their culture. Some people assumed we were missionaries who had come to translate the Bible, perhaps Pentecostals seeking to challenge the long-established Anglican Church. Others hoped that we would make use of our (supposed) connections to "American businessmen" to bring "development" to the area. Many years later, we learned that there had been whispers among some of the old people that we might be ances-tral spirits returning to our old home.[3] I doubt that we were able to entirely scotch the rumours that attended our arrival, but after a time when nothing miraculous happened, most people seemed to accept that we really had come to learn about their lives.

Living in Uiaku required adjustments. First of all, there were the physical discomforts. We had arrived at the start of the rainy season, and the combi-nation of heat and high humidity left us exhausted. We found it impossible to remain clean for long. During the day we had to slather ourselves repeatedly with strong insect repellent, to fend off swarms of tiny sandflies that rose as the air heated up, topped with additional layers of sunscreen. In the evenings, we lathered on more repellent and donned extra clothes despite the heat to protect ourselves from the anopheles mosquito, the carrier of malaria. Grit got into everything—our clothes, our skin, our hair. At first, the lack of running water and electricity seemed romantic, like camping out. The novelty quickly wore off. Everything took longer: hauling and boiling drinking water, lighting the stubborn wicks on our kerosene stove, adjusting and mending our mosquito net in a vain attempt to keep the bugs out, and on and on. Fortunately, we liked the local food. The staples of taro, sweet potatoes, and cooking bananas were starchy and bland, but there was plenty of fruit from the gardens, and we had brought spices and tinned sauces to add some variety. Periodically, visitors offered fish or game. This was always a treat.

The lack of privacy posed another challenge. The thin sago-ribbed walls of the houses did little to muffle sounds and so we, along with everyone else, got to listen in whenever voices became raised in our neighbourhood. We ourselves were objects of intense curiosity, especially to children, who often hung around and under our house, hoping to catch sight of us. It is rather unnerving to glance down and see a pair of young eyes staring at you through a crack in the floorboards. We had brought scrapbooks with pictures of animals and places around the world cut from magazines and invited the children into the house, where they sat mesmerized for hours at a time. The kids living closest to our house soon got used to us, but whenever I ventured to the further reaches of the village, I would be followed by curious children, shouting out "Bye! Bye!" or "Bariyawa!" (Whiteman) and squealing with laughter whenever I replied.

Over time, we adjusted to our new home. I suspect that the Maisin were just as unsure of how to deal with us as we were with them. In the early days, people continually brought us food whether we needed it or not and, just as insistently, requested things from us. We knew that they were treating us as one of their own, but we did not have gardens and realized quickly that we had to carefully pace our gift-giving of tobacco, rice, and other goods because of both the expense and the difficulty of getting new supplies.[4] Eventually we worked out a balance. People brought a more reasonable amount of food, and we learned how to negotiate a more balanced rate of return in store goods (see Chapter 2). Perhaps the most welcome and useful thing we did was to provide some basic first aid for our neighbours. Each morning began with Anne treating a line of men, women, and children with bandages for cuts and scrapes and care for other minor ailments.

Ethnographic Fieldwork

Anne and I arrived in Uiaku to pursue specific research projects. We knew, however, that the path to learning about the contemporary religious ideas and the psychological development of children ran through the culture as a whole. We would not be able to gain more than a superficial grasp of our research

11

topics without the broadest possible understanding of Maisin historical experience and cultural orientations. Ethnographic research draws on a holistic perspective, a basic assumption that "the various parts of a culture must be viewed in the broadest possible context to understand their interconnections and interdependence" (Haviland et al. 2013:3). Ethnographic fieldwork is thus intimate and slow. To fully understand the impact of Christianity on the Maisin, I would need to do much more than attend church services and conduct interviews. I would need to become familiar with the language, daily routines, social organization, and care of the young and elderly—the minutiae of life. I would witness crises and conflicts, celebrations and debates, all of which would shed light on deeper social patterns. Through this, I would gradually enculturate, become increasingly familiar with Maisin ways and expectations. The more Anne and I learned, the more our projects took new and often unexpected directions. They became less our own and more a collaboration with our Maisin hosts.

Learning about a culture requires engagement and gaining a degree of competence in its ways. Here's an example. From our reading on other Melanesian societies, we knew that reciprocity would play a central role in social relations. This was confirmed by the school headmaster moments after we stepped out of the boat on our arrival. He advised us not to pay money for any services or food. "We live by the 'Melanesian Way,'" which he explained meant that people share their resources rather than buying and selling them (see Narakobi 1980). This confirmed what we had read, but we quickly learned that understanding a social system intellectually and dealing with it practically are two very different things. We received our first of many lessons in the complexities of reciprocity that first afternoon in Uiaku as we watched the pile of garden produce deposited in the centre of our empty "kitchen" mount. We couldn't possibly eat more than a tiny amount of it. And if we reciprocated in kind, the small store of rice and tobacco we had brought to use as gifts for those who assisted us in our research would vanish before we started. By the afternoon of the second day, the taro, bananas, sweet potatoes, and squash were beginning to rot, but still people kept bringing us more. What should we do? If we refused these gifts, wouldn't the people be insulted? Yet throwing it out would be worse. We decided to ask Father Wellington, who we noticed eying the food on his frequent visits to our house. His suggestion was simplicity itself: "Give it to the priest." Under the cloak of darkness, he relieved us of our burden. Later I learned that, within the hour, the food had been redistributed across the station, to the three teachers and church deacon, with the excess eventually returning to families in the village. We had been initiated into the local exchange network.

We thus began a process of cultural immersion that anthropologists call "participant observation." The basic idea is that one can learn a great deal about a society by joining in ongoing activities. Fieldwork for me has involved garden work, making tapa cloth, tying roof thatch, traditional dancing, attending church services, and endless hours chewing betelnut on verandahs while sharing the gossip of the day. "Being there" is often challenging. Whenever I work with Maisin, I am reminded of my relative physical weakness and incompetence at even the most basic tasks. Anne and I faced numerous obstacles, beginning with the language but also including Maisin assumptions about proper behaviour. We made mistakes and did our best to learn from them. The Maisin were gracious, although we certainly must often have tested people's patience.

If participant observation only involved engagement in local activities, however, fieldwork would amount to little more than adventure tourism. Anne and I immersed ourselves in community life with a serious purpose in mind— to further our research. This required maintaining good fieldnotes. I carried a notebook everywhere I went, jotting down observations. These could be very detailed, especially for events like village business meetings, funerals, or disputes. In the evenings, I reviewed and reordered my notes, filling in gaps and noting questions to pursue further. I also kept a daily journal for more personal reflections. As I reviewed my notes, I gradually began to see patterns of behaviour and thought emerging. These, in turn, led into more informed lines of investigation.

I used participant observation in conjunction with a variety of other research methodologies. The day after we arrived, I walked the length of Uiaku with Gideon, sketching a map indicating the location of houses and major features such as the mission station and the river and two creeks that formed natural divisions. Where I saw uneven lines of houses, Gideon identified clusters belonging to different clans, their boundaries subtly marked by trees or bushes. A couple of weeks later, I devised a basic household census. Gideon translated the questions into Maisin, and, with his help as an interpreter, I proceeded to visit all of the houses in the village. The census provided information about household composition, education, marriage, languages spoken, and a variety of other basic matters, giving me an overview of the social makeup of the village. I practised my small Maisin vocabulary as I read each question haltingly, to the great amusement of all, and spent time with every household in the village. Census work could be tedious, but I was surprised by how much I enjoyed myself. The questions often led to free-ranging conversations on the people's lives, traditional customs, culture, and local history. I gave participants gifts of packaged rice and oily tobacco sticks. Interviews always ended with smoking, in which I did not indulge, and a chew of betelnut, for which I rapidly developed a fondness.

Soon after completing the census, I arranged group meetings with members of the different clans to record genealogies. While not without their difficulties—few Maisin remember their ancestors back further than two to three generations—the genealogies provided useful details on kinship relations and marriage alliances, the basics of the local social system (described in Chapter 3). Later, I conducted surveys probing understandings of death, attitudes towards leaders, the frequency and contents of economic exchanges, and understandings of Christianity. In my second year, I carried out a census and other inquiries in the Maisin village of Sinapa, a coastal village about six kilometres to the east, to broaden my knowledge of the Maisin beyond Uiaku.

Most days, I interviewed individuals about a wide range of subjects. I tried to engage with as wide a circle of people as I could on most matters, but inevitably I found myself frequently consulting a small number of people who were especially knowledgeable and helpful. In anthropological parlance, such people are known as "key informants." The term does not adequately describe the reality. I first visited elders such as Adelbert Sevaru, Frank Davis Dodi, and Agnes Sanangi intending to interview them, as they were very active in the church and respected for their knowledge of Maisin traditions. It didn't take long for them to define our relationship. They were the authorities, the elders, the teachers. They listened patiently to my questions but more often than not talked about what they knew to be relevant. Eager to get on with my work, I was at first impatient. With time, I calmed my urge to direct the flow of conversation and just sat, hour upon hour, listening quietly, asking the occasional question. I dimly realized I was being offered a gift. My "informants" became my mentors and, as my knowledge grew, my collaborators. At the most intimate level, as trust grew, they drew Anne and me into their families.

Learning the Maisin language posed the greatest challenge.[5] Bronislaw Malinowski (1922), a superb ethnographer who worked on the Trobriand Islands to the east of Collingwood Bay between 1915 and 1918, argued that fluency in a native tongue is a precondition of good fieldwork. It is, alas, one of the worst kept secrets that many anthropologists fail to measure up to Malinowski's high standards. In my own case, I diligently studied the Maisin language through my first season of fieldwork, driving my teachers to distraction as I struggled to shape my mouth to pronounce Maisin words and stumbled over (to me) complicated verb formations. I developed a good working vocabulary and learned to "hear" spoken Maisin—as long as it wasn't spoken too quickly or by more than a couple of people at a time—but my ability to speak the language was limited to simple sentences. Fortunately, many younger

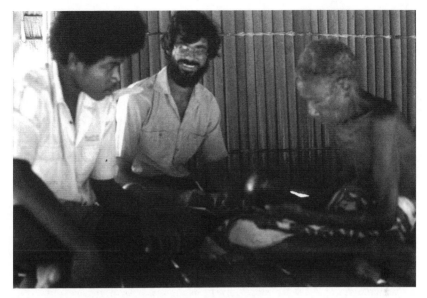

Figure 1.2 Conducting an interview with Nita Keru (holding a lime gourd), with my research assistant, MacSherry Gegeyo, in 1983. (Photo by A.M. Tietjen)

villagers were fluent in English, and I found it possible to get by in most situations with a mixture of English and Maisin, assisted as needed by translators. The time I spent on the language was far from wasted. Early in my fieldwork, I began recording folk stories on tape and transcribing them as a way of building my vocabulary. I eventually amassed a working lexicon of the language while developing a passion for the Maisin's rich oral traditions. Over the years, I've recorded nearly 200 *kikiki* ("narratives"), including stories and histories of elders now long passed away. For future generations of Maisin, these tapes—now digitized—may be the most lasting contribution of my research.

The work was not without frustrations. A few people were suspicious or scared and refused to talk with me. Sometimes villagers were too busy with gardening or other chores to bother with my endless questions. Anne and I had a hard time keeping good research assistants. Some got bored with the work, but most quit because they couldn't cope with endless badgering by relatives who suspected them of amassing a fortune from the wages we paid them. Most trying was the sheer difficulty of making sense of what was going on around us, especially during the early months. Yet even at the end of my fieldwork, I was acutely aware that there were questions I had not thought to ask, many aspects of Maisin experience that remained a mystery to me. I had amassed several thousand pages of notes, hundreds of hours of interviews and stories on tape, and countless photographs and films of people engaged in ordinary activities and ceremonial events. As I reviewed this material, rich as it was, I came to appreciate that I was barely scratching the surface.

Departures and Returns

Anne and I loved living in Uiaku. We learned to cope with the difficulties, and each day presented something new and remarkable. We compared notes on our projects during the evenings and were encouraged that we were independently experiencing the same basic cultural and social patterns. We became very close to some people, some of whom adopted us into their families. In August 1982, Anne returned to Canada while I remained in the village. She returned to a boisterous welcome the next May for three final months of fieldwork. The final push was very productive but also a time that brought us closer to our Maisin friends. Finally, the time came to depart. We spent a day visiting and dividing our gear amongst different families, in a way reciprocating for that huge gift of food that had welcomed us. With many tears all around, we left as we had come, by dinghy, up to the Wanigela airstrip. It was July 1983.

Three years later, I returned on my own for two months to research tapa cloth and women's facial tattooing. I found that our neighbours had torn down our old house and taken an axe to the surrounding coconut palms, treating our departure as a death. So on this visit, as on most subsequent ones, I lived with a family in the village, which gave me a different vista than we had experienced from the mission station. The return trip was very productive, but perhaps its main importance was to establish for Maisin as well as ourselves that our mutual bonds would not be easily broken. As it turned out, however, this was the last fieldwork I was able to carry out in Uiaku for some time. I moved from a post-doctoral research position at the University of Washington to a teaching post at the University of British Columbia. Soon after this, Jessica was born, and I looked for fieldwork possibilities that would not require long absences from home. I began to work with the Nisga'a and Nuxalk First Nations of British Columbia on different projects.

Of course, Anne and I did not forget about the Maisin. We continued to publish academic papers, mailing copies to friends in Uiaku along with tapes and notes we had recorded in the 1980s. We received the occasional letter in response, informing us of deaths and other events. In late 1994, we received an unexpected letter from our dear friend Franklin Seri. He and four other men were travelling to Berkeley, California, to put on a museum exhibit of tapa cloth and talk about the rainforest. This is how I first learned about the Maisin's decision not to allow commercial logging in their territory and their alliance with Greenpeace, which had co-sponsored this trip with the Berkeley

Art Museum (see Chapter 6). Anne, Jess, and I went to Berkeley where we had a wonderful reunion with the Maisin delegation. Franklin stayed behind with us for two months during which time we produced a reader of stories, in Maisin and simple English, for the elementary schools in Uiaku and Airara (Barker and Seri 1995).

This event renewed our ties to the Maisin. I returned to Uiaku in February 1997 for six weeks to study the community's attitudes towards rainforest conservation and the impact of their partnerships with national and international environmentalists. My role was now changing. In the past, I had studied the community while remaining detached from politics. People appreciated the records I made, especially of traditions that were fast disappearing. But now I wanted to make a contribution to improving social conditions and defending Maisin rights. My knowledge of Maisin history and culture was useful to some of the non-governmental organizations (NGOs) working with the people, for whom I served as a consultant.

I also developed a new project of my own. I returned briefly in 1998 with two Canadian filmmakers to discuss the possibility of setting up an exchange of delegations between the Maisin and the Stó:lō First Nation in British Columbia. The visits would be filmed as documentaries to highlight the Maisin's fight to save their rainforest from commercial loggers and to witness two very different Indigenous peoples working out solutions to common problems. The concept intrigued Bruce Miller, a colleague in my department with long experience working with First Nations communities in southern British Columbia and Washington State, and he agreed to join in. Following a frenzy of fundraising, recruiting, and planning, Bruce, five Stó:lō delegates, and I arrived to a glorious welcoming ceremony in Ganjiga village in June 2000. The film crew had already arrived and for the next two weeks proceeded to document the exchange.[6] While exhilarating, dealing with the often conflicting needs of the delegation, the film crew, and the Maisin left me exhausted. It was with some relief that I travelled to Port Moresby to see Bruce and the Stó:lō off to Canada (the film crew had already departed) and to greet Anne and Jessica, who had arrived on the same plane. As our dinghy touched the shore in Uiaku, we were met with a boisterous reception from Anne's adoptive family who, to our amazement, swept up Jess to a shelter and then adorned her with shell necklaces and tapa marking her initiation as a first-born child (see Chapter 3).

In June 2007, Anne and I returned for a month's stay. Anne carried out interviews recording the life histories of three generations of Maisin women while I focused on what turned out to be possibly the largest end-of-mourning ceremony in Maisin history (described in Chapter 7). Physically, the village looked much the same, and we were cheered by the sight of familiar faces. Yet we noted many changes. The population had greatly expanded. Some people had left jobs elsewhere in the country and moved their families, sometimes with a non-Maisin spouse, back to the village. Because of poor job prospects, many more young people were staying in the village. While Maisin remained the main language for most, we heard far more English than in the past. A few houses, including the one we borrowed, had solar panels, and here and there fluorescent lights appeared in the evening. We too had changed, of course. For most of the youthful population, we were now "grandparents" associated with a period of Maisin history that was rapidly receding from memory as the older generation—our teachers—passed. It was an exhilarating visit and a physically trying one. When we left, we wondered if we would ever return.

Anne's and my association with the Maisin now stretches back more than 30 years. Much has changed over the decades. While the regional airstrip at Wanigela is now closed, in some ways the Maisin villages are not as isolated as they once were. The area is served by a small passenger boat that cruises the coast each week between Alotau and Lae. Although reception is poor, cell phones have also reached the area. The large Maisin diaspora, scattered across the country and in Australia and New Zealand, are connected by e-mail and Facebook. Yet, despite the passing of time, much in the local communities remains the same—the subsistence basis of life, adherence to Christianity, strong kinship ties, and an ethic of moral egalitarianism—values all exemplified by that central emblem of Maisin identity, tapa cloth. Above all, through determined resistance, the Maisin have so far been able to protect the forests and waters that sustain them.

THE PHYSICAL SETTING

The Maisin live in a breathtakingly beautiful place. From a canoe or small boat in the midst of Collingwood Bay, the southern shore stretches out in a vast arc. The coast is outlined by a dark green line of mangrove swamps. Behind this, a sweep of dense forest spreads upwards to the mountain wall of the Owen Stanley range, about 20 kilometres inland. In the early morning, before heavy clouds set in, one can often see the 3,676-metre peak of Mount Suckling (Gorofi). The mountain wall is torn at places by the scars of massive landslides and broken by waterfalls plunging from high basins. From the beach, one has a clear view of the dormant volcanic peak of Mount Victory (Kerorova) and its now extinct sister, Mount Trafalgar.

As one approaches the Maisin villages from the sea, houses slowly emerge as glimmering brown aggregates of cubes suspended between the sea and the forest. Drawing closer, the cubes separate and take on sharper outline, as

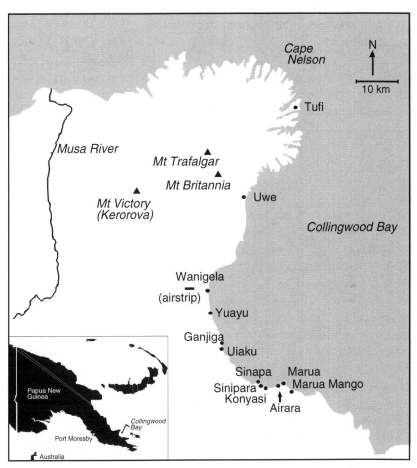

Figure 1.3 Location map of Collingwood Bay and the Maisin villages

groves of coconut palms also emerge into focus. Finally, a dark beach comes into view, lined by greying outrigger canoes of varying sizes and the occasional aluminum dinghy. The Maisin villages are long and narrow, situated along sand bars between the surf and the swampy bushlands behind. They are vulnerable to erosion and flooding. The Vayova River that runs through Uiaku, for instance, has broadened and shifted in the past decades, forcing some of the villagers who used to live on the south side to relocate their houses to the north.

On the mission station and scattered in the villages, one finds a few buildings with rusty corrugated iron roofs, but even most of these "modern" houses are built largely of materials gathered from the nearby bush and forest. Village houses are simple in design but very appealing. Built on posts, rising one to

three metres above the ground, many have broad open verandahs or underlying platforms where residents eat their meals and socialize with neighbours.
In most villages, the houses are arranged in uneven parallel lines, facing across
an area of bare packed earth that serves as both central path and plaza. In a
few places, the houses spread apart to enclose much broader plazas, usually
to the side of the main village pathway. The ground under and around the
houses, paths, and plazas is kept completely bare of grass. One often wakes
up in the morning to a gentle rhythmic sound of women and girls sweeping up
dead leaves, twigs, and bits of refuse with palm filament brooms. The Maisin
plant areca palms, small shade trees, and flowering plants around their homes.
The villages are clean, open, and breezy, forming an attractive contrast to the
contorted mix of tall grasses, palms, and jungle that commence immediately
behind the interior row of houses.

At the geographical centre of Uiaku lies a large grassy sports field bordered
by neat croton shrub-lined paths. Classrooms, the church, houses for the
priest and teachers, shelters for visitors and special occasions, and, since 1986,
market stalls line the edges. Graceful mango trees planted a century ago by
Melanesian teachers mark the site of the first church. Although decades have
passed since the last Anglican missionary worked in the region, Maisin refer
to this space as the "mission station."

Maisin have only a single word for a settlement (wa'ki), but they nonetheless recognize several encompassing levels. At the broadest level are four
village clusters along the southwestern shores of Collingwood Bay. These are,
going from the north to the southeast, Yuayu, Uiaku, Sinapa, and Airara. The
last three are made up of smaller villages. The Uiaku cluster is composed of
Ganjiga on the northern side of the Vayova River and Uiaku on the south.
Uiaku proper is further divided into Vayova, Maume, and Yamakero. Two
of the villages making up the Sinapa cluster are occupied by single clans.
Everywhere else, however, the villages are multi-nucleated: home to two or
more clans each with its own hamlet. These are often contiguous, although
everyone knows where the boundaries lie.

Beyond the swampy area behind the village houses lies a zone of secondary
forest radiating out four or five kilometres; this is where people make their
gardens and harvest sago. Further inland, one finds areas of extensive grassland and primary rainforest. The lush jungles, swamps, grasslands, and forests
of the Maisin environment nurture a rich diversity of flora and fauna. The
forest is home for a profusion of birds: cockatoos, hornbills, and birds of paradise, among many others. Hunters track bandicoots, wallabies, cassowaries,
and wild pigs in the bush and grasslands. Giant pythons, monitor lizards, and
dangerous saltwater crocodiles inhabit the low-lying swamps and rivers. Insects

of all descriptions, even the rare Queen Alexandra butterfly—the largest in the world—thrive in the area. As in other parts of Papua New Guinea, the lands around Collingwood Bay are rich breeding grounds for the anopheles mosquito, the carrier of malaria. The dark sands under the villages provide a home for billions of sand flies, infinitesimal insects that, until the invention of Deet-based insect repellents, probably did more than anything to discourage anthropological research along these coasts.[7] The shallow waters and coral reefs of southern Collingwood Bay teem with a diversity of marine life.

When breezes fail to blow in from the bay, the combination of hot tropical temperatures and high humidity can be oppressive. The annual rainfall ranges between 1,800 and 3,300 millimetres, increasing as one moves inland towards the mountains. The Maisin speak of distinct "rainy" and "dry" seasons. The rainy season generally runs between November and April, marked by short but heavy downpours most days, including dramatic tropical thunderstorms. The rains taper off in the dry season, with afternoons marked by strong winds from the north and east. Temperatures average 27.5°C annually, but may rise to higher than 32.2°C during the wet season. Nights in the dry season can actually feel quite cold. Local climatic patterns have been greatly disrupted since at least the early 1980s by global shifts, especially the El Niño phenomenon. Along with the rest of Papua New Guinea, the Maisin lands have recently suffered through extended periods of drought followed by rainy seasons lasting several years. In November 2007, the villages and garden lands were flooded during Cyclone Guba along with much of the rest of Oro Province—an indication of how vulnerable the low coast is to rising sea levels and the extreme weather events associated with global climate change. In 1997 and 2015, the entirety of Papua New Guinea experienced profound drought, causing severe water shortages and crop failures.

The Maisin have always lived close to the land, which furnishes them with food, medicines, and building materials. Yet, as we shall see repeatedly in these pages, the land is far more than a source of resources. It is, for most Maisin, alive with historical memories and ancestral spirits. It is the key to their identity and survival as a people.

THE CULTURAL SETTING

Evidence of human settlement in New Guinea dates back 40,000 years, but there must have been much earlier movements, as the ancestors of the Australian Aborigines journeyed through New Guinea from Asia at least 55,000 years ago (Moore 2003). During that long early period, humans gradually spread to the furthest reaches of New Guinea's vast interior and offshore islands, diversifying into hundreds of distinct cultures and languages, referred to collectively by linguists as Non-Austronesian or Papuan. Around 9,000 years ago, some groups learned to cultivate taro as a supplement to foraging and hunting. The last group of Asian migrants was Austronesian speakers, who settled along the coasts and islands of Papua New Guinea around 4,000 years ago. From these jumping-off points, further waves of Austronesian migrants pushed eastward. Their descendants crossed vast expanses of open ocean to discover and colonize the far reaches of the southern Pacific, from Vanuatu to Rapa Nui (Easter Island) and from Aotearoa (New Zealand) to Hawai'i (Kirch 2000).

Collingwood Bay was a cultural and linguistic meeting place in the centuries before the arrival of Europeans (Egloff 1979). The 10,000 or so people who make the bay their home speak five distinct languages. Korafe and Onjob belong to the older Papuan group, while Ubir and Miniafia are Austronesian. When Maisin was first studied, it was immediately seen as anomalous, possessing both Non-Austronesian and Austronesian grammatical features (Ray 1911; Strong 1911). Linguists now consider it to be basically Austronesian with borrowed non-Austronesian elements (Frampton 2013)—interesting given that Maisin traditions relate that the people migrated from a Papuan-speaking area near the Musa River to the west in the mid-nineteenth century. Prior to the enforcement of colonial control, incessant warfare and raiding led to much movement, resulting in a confusing linguistic situation on the ground. While most Maisin live along southwestern Collingwood Bay, one group shares the village of Uwe on Cape Nelson with Miniafia speakers and a remnant of Maisin speakers lives near their origin place deep in the Musa swamplands. When not fighting, Collingwood Bay people traded shell valuables and stone axes among other items, arranged marriages, and engaged in competitive feasts. Ethnographic research on the bay indicates that all of the language groups share similar forms of social organization, cosmology, and ritual, suggesting an extended period of mingling and cultural co-development (e.g., Gnecchi-Ruscone 1991). The decorative culture is also largely shared: dance forms and costumes, women's facial tattoos, and tapa clothing. Given such commonalities, Maisin and their neighbours are often called "Tufi people" by outsiders, after the sub-district station on Cape Nelson.

This rich mix of distinct languages and overlapping customs is typical of much of lowlands Papua New Guinea. Confronted by such linguistic diversity, outsiders often wonder how people manage to communicate and share in customary practices. In colonial times, government officers, traders, and missionaries encouraged the spread of several simplified trade languages, either based upon a native language, like Motu spoken by people living near Port Moresby, or using mostly European vocabulary with a simplified Melanesian grammar, like Pidgin English, also known as Neo-Melanesian or *Tok Pisin*. Today, English, Motu, and *Tok Pisin* are the official languages of the country. Many Maisin speak all three, but most adults also speak or at least understand the other languages spoken in the Collingwood Bay area, and this must have been the case in the past as well.

A BRIEF HISTORY[8]

We will return frequently in this book to the dynamics of continuity and change. At the onset, however, it will be helpful to sketch out a historical chronology of the main changes and challenges the Maisin have faced since the first contact with European outsiders in 1890. We cannot know for certain what Maisin culture was like before this time. The histories related by elders, however, describe the Maisin as recent migrants to the bay, expanding their territory through warfare and by absorbing other groups before being checked by the arrival of the colonial government.

In May 1874, Captain John Moresby sailed across the northern reaches of Collingwood Bay. He was so impressed by the dramatic scenery that he turned to the memory of the great English naval hero Horatio Nelson for suitably grand names for the main features: Cape Nelson, Mounts Victory and Trafalgar, and the name of the bay itself (Moresby 1876). A small number of missionaries and gold prospectors settled along the southeastern coast of New Guinea, but no one ventured into the bay again for 16 years. In 1884, Britain and Germany divided the eastern half of New Guinea and offshore islands (the western half had long before been claimed by Holland). Four years later, Dr. William MacGregor took up the post of Administrator of the British possession with the mandate of exploring its reaches, establishing the rudiments of government control, and bringing some semblance of British civilization to the Queen's newest subjects. This was all to be accomplished on the most minimal of budgets. MacGregor was a resourceful innovator who set up the basic structure of the colonial state in what became Papua, after the newly independent Australian government assumed control in 1906 (Joyce 1971).[9] The government took upon itself the task of exploration and pacification of local tribes. This was accomplished by establishing a network of district stations under Resident Magistrates who, with the aid of a native police force, set out on regular patrols first to contact tribes and then to control fighting, enforce ordinances meant to improve village life (at least, as the Europeans perceived it), and eventually integrate villagers into the emerging colonial economy. MacGregor encouraged white entrepreneurs to establish plantations and mines in the colony, creating a system of labour recruitment from villages to provide them with an inexpensive work force. Finally, the Administrator strongly supported the work of Christian missionaries, not only because he was himself staunchly Presbyterian but because missions were able to reach the native peoples in their villages in their own languages and provide, at no cost to the government, basic schooling and medical services.

In late July 1890, on one of his first patrols along the northeastern coast of the possession, MacGregor steamed into Collingwood Bay on the small government launch the *Merrie England*, landing at each village in succession. The Maisin were wary of the strange newcomers; no women or children were to be seen, and the men who did venture forth to meet them ran away terrified when one of the landing party lit a match. The men were reluctant to accept gifts of tobacco or iron, unaware of their use. Still, the short visit was friendly. The *Merrie England* returned several times over the next decade, always to a boisterous reception from the Maisin, who quickly developed a hunger for steel axes, knives, cloth, and other trade goods. The Maisin continued to raid their neighbours, but it was only a matter of time before their autonomy was brought to an end. In 1900, the government built a district station 40 kilometres to the north at Tufi on Cape Nelson under the control of C.A.W. Monckton, a brash, often violent New Zealander (Monckton 1922). After receiving news about a number of Maisin raids, including a planned ambush of one of his own patrols, Monckton set his police loose on Uiaku where they destroyed several canoes and shot three men dead, wounding an unknown number of others. Following the fracas, a large party of Maisin men voluntarily travelled to Tufi, accepting a short period of confinement in return for peace with the new power. Monckton appointed two of the leading warriors as village constables and, over the next few years, recruited more into his fledgling police force. The Maisin were now "pacified."

MacGregor had been accompanied in 1890 by a young Anglican priest, Albert Maclaren, who was scouting out possible headquarters for a new mission for the northern part of the possession (Synge 1908; Wetherell 1977). He chose Dogura, a high plateau over Bartle Bay, about 80 kilometres to the southeast of the Maisin. The mission got off to a rocky start. Maclaren died four months after arriving, worn out by malaria, a poor diet, and physical exhaustion. His partner, the Reverend Copland King, kept the mission going with a tiny staff and meagre support from the Australian parishes. In 1898, on the verge of collapse, the mission received a boost with the appointment of a British clergyman, John Montague Stone-Wigg, as its first bishop. Although frail in health, Stone-Wigg was an effective fundraiser and administrator. Expansion into Collingwood Bay became his first priority. His initial choice for a head station at the Maisin village of Sinapa had to be rejected because it was too swampy. Wanigela, located just north of Maisin territory, instead became the residence of the district missionary in 1898 and, in later years, a district school for advanced students and a small hospital (Chignell 1911).

In 1902, Percy John Money—an Australian lay missionary then in charge of the Wanigela district—travelled down to Uiaku to supervise the building of an enormous mission station using only native materials, including a school that could accommodate upwards of 210 pupils and a church that could seat 550 (close to the entire population of the village at the time), with a dormitory for boys, a house for teachers, and a lovely two-storey residence for himself (Barker 2005b). The Anglicans intended to place a white missionary in charge of the Maisin because of their relatively large population and their reputation as a "recalcitrant" people who required the "strong hand" of a European. Eventually, a recruit was found, but A.P. Jennings proved too sensitive a soul to abide the dirt, pigs, and all night drumming accompanying major feasts that could last for weeks at a time. He suffered a nervous breakdown and fled Uiaku in 1920, less than three years after his arrival. The first generation of teachers was made up of men from the Solomon Islands and New Hebrides (now Vanuatu) who had converted to Christianity while working as indentured labourers in the Queensland sugar fields. Barely literate, almost all died while labouring in the mission fields of Papua. Their ranks were soon augmented by better-educated Papuan converts, trained by the white missionaries at Dogura. Villagers thus learned about Christianity as well as the "three R's" at the feet of Melanesian teacher-evangelists who looked very much like themselves.[10] Under the direction of the teachers, with periodic visits from the white missionary at Wanigela, a group of young men and women received baptism in 1911. By the late 1920s, a Christian majority had emerged in Uiaku, made up mostly of the younger people who had attended village schools.

Throughout the colonial period, Collingwood Bay remained an economic backwater, the handful of whites in the area limited to government officers, missionaries, and an occasional trader. All the same, the Maisin were steadily integrated into the emerging colonial system. Regular labour recruiting began around 1910. By the end of the decade, it had become routine for young unmarried men to spend one or two 18-month stints working on copra[11] or rubber plantations or on the gold fields elsewhere in the territory, and people had come to rely upon the calico cloth, tobacco, and steel knives and axes workers brought back to the villages. The government became more intrusive, enforcing a series of decrees meant to improve village health such as the construction of latrines and the replacement of traditional houses—windowless shelters entered via ladders in the floor, literally smoked over the cooking fires below—with a standard coastal design of simple rectangular houses on low posts with window openings. In 1918, the government imposed a head tax and ordered villagers to set up separate coconut plantations from which they could make and sell copra to pay the tax. The Maisin resented and resisted these changes at first, but by the 1930s they had accommodated to the new regime. Soccer tournaments became the rage, and Maisin villages regularly won small prizes from the Resident Magistrate in the annual contest for the most attractive village in the Tufi region.

World War II was a watershed moment here as elsewhere in the Pacific. On 22 July 1942, Japanese troops landed near the village of Gona to the northwest of Collingwood Bay. Facing little resistance, they marched to the treacherous Kokoda Track in the mistaken belief, based on a poor map, that it was a road providing a direct route over the Owen Stanley Range to Port Moresby. A month after the landing, the Australians sent boats to Collingwood Bay, which remained outside of the occupied area, scooping up every available able-bodied man who could be found to serve as labourers in the war effort. The Maisin were assigned to a large force of Papuans slogging heavy loads of supplies up the northern end of the mud- and blood-soaked Kokoda Track and carrying the broken bodies of Australian soldiers on the return trips, as the exhausted Japanese forces fell back. Once on the plains, Australian and American troops fought a horrific campaign against Japanese forces entrenched on the coast, which left hundreds of soldiers on both sides dead (Mayo 1974). Amazingly, only one Maisin was killed, shot by a Japanese soldier while investigating what he supposed to be an abandoned tunnel. As bodies piled up and rotted in the coastal swamps, the Maisin carriers saw many horrors.

Forty years later, the veterans broke down in tears as they told me of their experiences. Yet the war revealed other more positive truths to Papua New Guineans. They were surprised by the friendliness of the Australian and American soldiers, their willingness to share food and cigarettes, and their frank criticisms of the Papuan colonial regime. The war, older Maisin often told me, "changed everything." They had met white men who treated them as equals, and they heard speeches from army commanders promising a new era of economic prosperity once the fighting was over.

Following the defeat of Japan in 1945, however, the Australian government proved slow in meeting its promises and, in the eyes of many Papua New Guineans, appeared more interested in restoring the old colonial system. Local people were not content to wait. So-called cargo cults broke out in several areas, particularly parts of the former German colony of New Guinea that had been administered by Australia since 1914.[12] However, here, as elsewhere in long-contacted coastal areas of Papua and New Guinea, would-be prophets proclaiming the return of ancestors delivering the coveted wealth

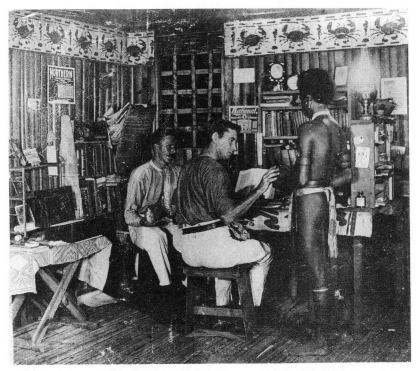

Figure 1.4 Percy John Money in his "den," Uiaku, c. 1905. The names of the two men on either side are not known. Note the tapa cloth covering the tables. (Courtesy of the State Library of New South Wales)

of white men failed to stir their audiences. On the other hand, news of an economic experiment at Gona village spread like wildfire across the region (Dakeyne 1966). The Reverend James Benson, an Anglican priest who had survived three horrific years of internment in a Japanese prisoner camp on New Britain, returned to his ruined mission station to establish a Christian cooperative society in Gona. Benson was influenced by the Christian socialist movement in Australia and hoped that a combination of new types of crops, prayers, and commitment to sharing work and its profits would improve the lives of villagers. Soon Christian cooperatives were springing up all over the Northern District.

The Maisin experimented with a series of cooperatives from around 1946 to the mid-1980s (Barker 1996). The cooperatives sought out local commodities that could be sold to traders—such as sea cucumbers, trochus shell, panned gold, copra, coffee, and cocoa—and opened small trade stores offering a selection of commercial goods to locals. Few of these ventures made money, and, when they did, it was soon spent. They faced several obstacles, including the distance to markets, the people's unfamiliarity with keeping financial records, and local politics. All the same, the cooperatives profoundly affected the way that the Maisin thought about and organized their community. At the founding meeting for a Christian cooperative held in September 1949, representatives of different Maisin clans publicly broke war clubs, symbolizing an end to internal divisions. Like the church upon which it was modelled, the cooperative sought to unify the entire community. The Maisin signified the close ties they saw between Christianity, social unity, and economic success with their single most important cooperative project. With the aid of the district priest at Wanigela, who blessed the project and managed the bank account, villagers in Uiaku began selling copra with the intention of buying materials for a permanent church. They succeeded, erecting an attractive church with twin towers and an iron roof on the Uiaku mission station in the late 1950s. At the consecration of St. Thomas Church in 1962, Bishop George Ambo installed a Papuan man from Buna as the parish's first resident priest since Father Jennings's abrupt departure in 1920.

When Anne and I arrived in 1982, the Maisin looked back on the consecration of the church as a golden moment, a crowning achievement against which the apparent failings of the present—the cooperative store teetering on the edge of collapse, incessant gossip, fears of sorcery, the difficulties of getting people to work together on community projects, and so forth—stood out in sharp contrast (Barker 1993). Other changes occurring through the same period had even more profound social effects. Here again the mission played a major role. Maisin had attended mission schools since 1902. Most had two or three years in the classroom, where they learned the rudiments of "A-B-C" and "1-2-3," as they described the favoured methods of rote learning used by the Melanesian teachers. Only a small number of male students had been able to further their education under white priests at the district station in Wanigela and the small theological college at Dogura, as they trained to become teachers themselves. Following the war, the Anglicans worked to improve the village school system and to expand options for advanced learning. In 1948, they opened the Martyrs Memorial School for boys at Sangara in the central part of the Northern District, named in honour of 11 Anglican missionaries and native teachers killed by invading Japanese soldiers in 1942. Three years later, Mount Lamington exploded in a volcanic eruption, destroying Sangara and nearby villages and killing more than 3,000 people. Fortunately, students were home on holidays at the time of the disaster, but neither the staff nor the school was spared. The Anglicans rebuilt an expanded school at Agenehambo, a safe distance from the volcano, opening its doors in 1953. Maisin boys began to enroll regularly soon after. In 1956, Holy Name School for girls opened at Dogura. Meanwhile, the mission improved the quality of the village schools, gradually adding fourth, fifth, and sixth years. Those students successful in completing final exams in the village school could attend the residential high schools.

The missionaries intended that graduates of the new high schools would go on to staff the mission's expanding national system of churches, schools, and medical centres. Many did, but shifts in administrative policy opened other opportunities. During the 1950s, the Administration had intervened in the mission education system to set basic standards, especially the promotion of English, and had tentatively begun to establish its own secular school system. In the early 1960s, stung by a United Nations report criticizing Australia's tardiness at preparing its colony for independence, the government suddenly stepped up its involvement, investing heavily in education, the civil service, and the economy. New secondary and tertiary schools were opened across the country, including the crown jewel of the system, the University of Papua New Guinea in 1966. The government's Department of Education now set the standards for the training of teachers and the curriculum in the community schools and assumed responsibility for salaries. The frenetic efforts of the Australians to prepare Papua New Guinea for independence created a boom in relatively well-paying jobs for better educated Papua New Guineans, especially in the burgeoning civil service. Maisin were in an excellent position to take advantage. Many of them landed positions scattered around the country as priests, teachers, nurses, doctors, civil servants, and other professionals. Meanwhile, the colonial government beefed up its outreach programs in rural areas with improvements to transportation, the establishment of an extensive system of village aid posts offering basic medical care, and expertise on cash cropping, among other programs.

In 1973, the Anglican Church of Papua New Guinea succeeded the old missionary diocese. By 1982, all but one of its parish priests were Papua New Guineans, as were two of the five bishops. Papua New Guinea itself gained independence in 1975, a scant 13 years after the United Nations report. Most of a generation of Maisin had left the villages to work elsewhere. I was amazed to discover, after completing my census of Uiaku, that people in their 60s greatly outnumbered the combined totals of people in their 20s and 30s. Indeed, the 270 people living in Uiaku proper included only one man in his 30s. This exodus had profound effects upon village life. The drain of younger folk meant that villagers found it difficult to maintain large gardens and to mount traditional life-cycle ceremonies. At the same time, people had become increasingly dependent upon remittances from working relatives.

The Maisin's integration into the wider Papua New Guinea society and economy has steadily increased in the years since independence. While villagers spend much of their days engaged in subsistence activities, everyone relies on an ever-increasing range of manufactured goods such as clothing, steel pots, and packaged rice. Villagers also require money to cover transportation costs to visit relatives in town, to pay the priest's stipend and school fees, and for medicines for their families. Finding and keeping sources of money have always been challenging. In the years since independence, the Maisin have lost many of their educational and employment advantages as ever more high school graduates compete for scarce jobs in the towns. Village populations have swollen as unemployed young people have returned home. During the same time, government services to Collingwood Bay and other rural areas have virtually disappeared. By the late 1990s, the local postal service had ceased to operate, teachers often went for months without receiving pay, and village medical aid posts had closed down for lack of supplies. The Maisin now find themselves urgently searching for new ways to support themselves and their children.

The Maisin, no less than the rest of us, live in an increasingly interconnected world. This carries a cost, most noticeably an alarming loss of traditional knowledge. Far fewer Maisin today know and can narrate the histories and stories I recorded in the early 1980s; they have ceased to tattoo the faces of adolescent girls; and no one knows how to construct the ceremonial shelters once required for intertribal feasts. Even the language is not the same as it was, as younger people mix *Tok Pisin* and English with Maisin words and more subtly modify the cadences of their speech. Change, of course, has always occurred, but it seems to be accelerating. All the same, were you to visit the Maisin villages in the early years of this new millennium, I suspect you would be struck by the "traditional" appearance of the houses and the rhythms of daily life. The Maisin have little choice but to maintain a lifestyle based upon subsistence activities. They cannot shop for food at the local supermarket or hire carpenters to construct their homes. Yet they are also products of a culture that leads them to perceive the world and organize their social life in particular patterns. Those patterns are apparent even in the mundane activities of making a living. They are among the lines that continue to connect the Maisin to their past in a rapidly changing world.

A NOTE ON TENSES

Ethnographies are historical documents. They are based on research that occurred in a particular time and place. Yet the convention in anthropology is to write ethnographies in the present tense, the so-called ethnographic present. Because of this convention, an ethnography can give an impression that the society under study is stuck in a time warp; the older the study, the more this impression is accentuated. The lives of the Nuer of Southern Sudan or the Trobriand Islands of Papua New Guinea today are very different (although not entirely different) from the ways they appear in classic studies most familiar to anthropologists, yet those older ways often get referred to in the present tense as if they are eternal and unchanging. This has led some anthropologists to argue that ethnographies should be written in the past tense to signal that they are the equivalent of snapshots taken at a particular time.

Yet to say that ethnographies are historical is not to say they are *histories*. The use of the present tense signals the anthropological attempt—always partial and incomplete—to create a holistic image of a community as experienced at a particular time. This is a very different purpose from a history and, I think, a useful one, as it allows us to see patterns that while certainly shaping historical developments may not be as apparent in accounts of sequences of events and changing circumstances.

Here is how I use tenses in this book: Chapters 2 through 5 provide a portrait of Maisin society as I observed it in the last two decades of the twentieth century. I use the present tense in describing aspects of that society that I perceive as foundational, generally shared, and enduring—modes of subsistence, kinship terminologies, perceptions of ghosts, and so forth. I make no claim that any of these generalizations still continue to hold true (although as of 2015, most have). I use the past tense to relate specific events I observed and participated in. Chapters 6 and 7 shift to a more historical mode, to describe the events of the anti-logging campaign of the 1990s and subsequent developments in the region. Here, I mostly use the past tense. The earlier chapters, however, provide a framework within which I attempt to explain Maisin attitudes, motivations, and actions as well as to assess the nature of change as we move closer to 2015, the endpoint of this book.

Notes

1. Betelnut is a mild intoxicant, widely used across South Asia and the western Pacific. When chewed with the leaves of the betel pepper plant (*Piper betle*) and lime, the husked nut of the areca palm releases alkaloids and produces a very bright red saliva that is eventually spat out. It has a bitter flavour that takes some getting used to, but it is chewed almost incessantly by Maisin, young and old.

2. In the national census of 2000, over 96 per cent of adults in Papua New Guinea declared themselves members of one or another of the more than 200 Christian denominations established in the country (Gibbs 2006). Papua New Guinea now ranks as

one of the most thoroughly Christianized nations in the world, matched only by a few Latin American countries such as Ecuador.

3. The appearance of white-skinned men bearing immense wealth and powerful weapons caused much speculation among Melanesian populations. Many initially thought white people were ancestral spirits, returned from the dead (Schieffelin and Crittenden 1991). Maisin today refer to Europeans as *bariyawa* (a loan word from further up the coast that means "spirits" in its original language), but have long understood that Europeans are as human as themselves.

4. Tobacco was unknown prior to European contact, but like most Melanesians, the Maisin were quick to pick up the habit. Tarry sticks of cured tobacco leaf were used as a kind of currency during the colonial period and were still a common form of tobacco smoked by Maisin in the 1980s. Smokers shaved bits of the tobacco onto a strip of newspaper, producing a foul-smelling type of cigar. "Black stick" has long disappeared from the market. Today, some Maisin grow and cure their own leaf but most prefer fast-burning cigarettes marketed by global tobacco corporations, a type of tobacco delivery that is far more damaging to health than the older form. I ceased giving gifts of tobacco after 1983. Despite educational campaigns and government restrictions, Papua New Guinea suffers from one of the highest rates of smoking in the world (Marshall 2013).

5. In my defence, Maisin is acknowledged amongst Collingwood people to be a challenging language. The difficulties are partly to do with Maisin's unusual grammatical features that have been debated by linguists for a century now (discussed later in this chapter). The language also has an unusually large vocabulary of synonyms: different words with identical meanings. This partly has to do with a taboo against mentioning the name—or even a word sounding like the name—of an in-law. As a result, the Maisin have generated two and often three words for many things, including ordinary items like coconuts. Malcolm Ross (1996) argues that, as warriors who invaded and displaced people on Collingwood Bay in pre-contact times, Maisin may have deliberately developed a variant vocabulary and odd grammatical forms as a kind of in-code to exclude outsiders, a process of "esoterogeny" that has been reported from other parts of Papua New Guinea. It appears to have worked!

6. The documentary *Changing Ground* aired on *The Nature of Things* science program on the Canadian Broadcasting Corporation (CBC) television network in Canada in early 2001. In July 2001, seven Maisin paid a return visit to the Stó:lō Nation in British Columbia. This was also the subject of a documentary, *Years from Now*, televised on the CBC in 2002. The Maisin were also one of the subjects of an earlier film, *Anthropology on Trial*, which includes a ten-minute segment on my fieldwork in Uiaku. It appeared on the *NOVA* science series on the PBS network in the United States in 1983. The films are visually arresting and very supportive of the Maisin but unfortunately are not very informative about their culture or history. For a detailed critique, see Barker (2004b).

7. So suggested the pioneer ethnographer, F.E. Williams, who preferred to brave the mosquito-infested interior villages of the Orokaiva than cope with sandflies "whose irritating bite is out of all proportion to their size" (Williams 1930).

8. This section summarizes a number of much more detailed studies of Maisin history (Barker 1987, 1996, 2001, 2005b). For a good general history of Papua New Guinea through the colonial and early Independence periods, see Waiko (1993).

9. In 1914, Australia seized the German territory, which it ruled separately from Papua during the interwar years. Following World War II, the two administrations were merged into the colony of Papua and New Guinea.

10. Most missionary work in the Pacific region was carried out by islanders under the often loose supervision of a small number of Europeans (Lange 2005). One of my reasons for choosing Uiaku over Wanigela was because I wanted to study a community that had been evangelized mainly by islander converts (Barker 2005b).

11. Copra is made from the dried inner flesh of coconuts. The oil is later extracted for use in commercial soap, cosmetics, and food products. It has been one of the major exports from the South Pacific islands since the mid-nineteenth century.

12. Cargo cults are the most studied and debated of the many forms of religious and political movements arising across Melanesia in the wake of colonial penetration and control (Burridge 1969; Lindstrom 1993; Worsley 1968). While there are many variations, the classic form of cargoism rests on a belief that Europeans gained their immense wealth and power due to events that occurred in ancestral times. The rituals engaged in by cultists are meant to undo this condition and result in the return of ancestors bearing copious quantities of manufactured goods and thus restoring dignity to Melanesians.

CHAPTER 2

MAKING A LIVING

In October 1986, I came to Uiaku to spend two months studying tapa cloth and women's facial tattooing. I immediately sought out Mildred Gayave. Mildred had been a great friend of Anne and mine; she was flamboyant, with a wickedly funny sense of humour. Like most adult Maisin, she had no idea of her birth date, but I estimated her to be in her early to mid-40s, as her first child was then a young adult. Mildred was a superb tapa maker who had developed a unique style, producing thick large cloths decorated with detailed geometric designs that rather reminded me of Persian carpets. While the designs were wonderful, I was more curious to know how she managed to consistently produce outstanding fabric—thick and near white, with very few holes. I thought that I could best learn the first steps of turning raw tree bark into fine cloth by accompanying Mildred to her tapa garden.

Maisin make tapa from a semi-cultivated, fast-growing tree they call *wuwusi*, which is likely a type of paper mulberry (*Broussonetia papyrifera*), the most common source of bark cloth in the Pacific Islands. They declare, however, that *wuwusi* is unique to southern Collingwood Bay and far superior to the types of trees used elsewhere in Oro province. Indeed, villagers worry from time to time that outsiders might steal cuttings from the local trees, threatening their dominant position in tapa sales in Papua New Guinea. In respect for these concerns, I will use only Maisin vernacular terms for the various plants that provide the bark and dyes used in making tapa.

Mildred and I were accompanied by her adopted son, Clarence, a cheerful 10-year-old. I always enjoy visiting the gardens. After leaving the village, you plunge through dank swamplands of mangrove and pandanus trees, emerging into a wide band of secondary bush and garden land. Networks of paths crisscross stretches of jungle and grassland. During the rainy season, the paths become stream beds, and you often have to struggle through ankle-deep mud. The dry season lingered in October, however, and the path was as

34

hard as concrete under a perfectly blue sky. Mildred walked ahead, machete in hand, a large empty string bag hanging from her forehead and flopping across her back. We crossed a log fence, a barrier to marauding wild pigs, to enter Mildred's garden which presented the usual frenzy of life: verdant broad taro leaves, tall banana trees, purple-edged sweet potato creepers, bright flowers, butterflies, and white cockatoos calling raucously from the trees at the edge of the clearing.

Much of the land around the Maisin villages is low-lying and swampy, ideal conditions for taro—the main staple crop—but not for *wuwusi*, which requires drier sandy loam. All village women make tapa, but those who do not have access to the right kind of land must trade for *wuwusi* from others. Mildred had a thick clump of saplings growing at the edge of her garden. The plantation was nearly two years old. The tallest trees had been transplanted from an older garden—a simple matter of pulling a sapling out of the ground with roots attached, lopping off the top with a machete, carrying it to the new garden, and plunking it back into the ground. *Wuwusi* grows very quickly, sending up shoots from the root system that become new saplings. Once planted, the base of the tree needs to be cleared of weeds for a month or two. After that, cultivation is a matter of periodically checking the growing trees and snapping off twigs to prevent the growth of branches that would leave holes in the finished cloth. As the patches of trees spread out, they form thickets of willowy, silver-coloured saplings. A trunk 50 to 100 millimetres in diameter is perfect for tapa, yielding one to two average-sized tapas. Most of the trees attain the proper girth within a couple of years, but older trees may be harvested to make larger cloths. These tend to be darker and rougher in texture and traditionally were used as blankets.

Wuwusi is ready to cut right around the time that garden productivity declines. People periodically return to the old gardens for a year or so to harvest fruit trees and sweet potato patches and to get cuttings for transplanting to new sites. They harvest *wuwusi* during this time, but gradually the old garden becomes covered by creepers and trees, returning to jungle. It frequently happens that after people return to clear an old garden site a decade or two later, *wuwusi* springs up in the new clearing.

The saplings looked pretty much the same to my untrained eyes. Mildred, however, touched one after another, naming some *koefi*—the term for a male's loin cloth—and others *embobi*, a woman's skirt. The *koefi* trees were slightly narrower in diameter, but I was not able to find out whether it was because of this or some difference in the appearance of the outer bark that Mildred knew these trees would produce the thinner cloth men wrap around their loins.

Figure 2.1 Mildred Gayave holding a *wuwusi* sapling in her garden surrounded by taro and banana plants, 1986. (Photo by J. Barker)

As opposed to identifying a good tapa tree, which requires a practiced eye, harvesting is an easy business of lopping off the base and the leafy top of a sapling with a machete, leaving a nicely rounded thick stick, two to three metres in length. Once harvested, the *wuwusi* sticks may be bundled and carried back to the village. If kept in a cool, dark place—usually under a house—they can be left for up to a month before becoming too dried out to make cloth. If a woman plans to make cloth immediately, however, she saves herself the bother of carrying the sticks and strips off the bark on the spot. Mildred demonstrated the process: she cut a strip of bark from a tree too old to be suitable for cloth, using it to lash discarded sticks together into a firm frame to serve as a brace against which she rested a fine *wuwusi* sapling. She efficiently scraped off the outer bark with a knife, made a slit down the length of the stick where the bark was thinnest, and carefully pried off the thick, milky-white inner bark. She folded the bark strip lengthwise upon itself, with the scraped outer surface exposed, to protect the glistening sticky inner surface from dirt, securing the bundle with another strip of *wuwusi* bark. A half hour later we were on our way back to the village, Mildred's string bag bulging with a load of firewood, bundles of *wuwusi*, and vegetables for the evening meal balanced on top.

The bast (inner bark) dries quickly and so needs to be beaten into cloth within a couple of days. As in most Pacific Island cultures, traditionally a gendered division of labour corresponded to the materials used in the production of objects (Teilhet 1983). Women worked mostly with pliable "soft" materials to make cloth, mats, and string bags. Men worked with wood and shells to make body ornaments, drums, canoes, and houses. While some of these objects are no longer made and some men today design tapa cloth, generally this division of labour continues to hold. Men make the primary tools for beating tapa. The anvil (*fo*) still forms a standard piece of furnishing found on most verandahs, under the taller houses, and in garden shelters. It is a large hardwood log, squared and smoothed by hand, to form a suitable surface for beating out cloth. Men also carve two types of mallets, made from the dense, fibrous wood of the black palm. The smaller, called a *fisiga*, is narrow with two sharpened edges. The larger—like the anvil, called a *fo*—resembles a small cricket bat with broad, slightly rounded edges. Most mallets are left plain, but in the past a few men of artistic bent carved patterns on the flat sides, which they brought into relief with white lime powder, similar to lime spatulas used for chewing betelnut. Mallets and anvils last generations, but several women have replaced the old wooden *fisiga* with large steel files or bars with cloth grips provided by men working in the towns, finding these more efficient tools.

Mildred belonged to the old school and used only wooden mallets. Whether using wood or metal, however, the process of beating is the same. One begins

Figure 2.2 Josephine Arauveve beating tapa cloth with a *fo* mallet, 1982. (Photo by A.M. Tietjen)

by trimming away any dry edges and ends of the bast and then cutting the strip into two or more smaller pieces, depending on the size of tapa desired. Using the sharp edge of the *fisiga* mallet, the maker then systematically pounds the length of the strip on both sides, a process that loosens the fibres and slightly expands the cloth. This takes a lot of energetic beating and much care to make sure that the bast is evenly pounded. Once she is satisfied that the bast has been sufficiently softened, the maker folds the bark tightly several times over itself, lifts up the heavy *fo* mallet with both hands, and wallops the bast with the rounded edge, gradually progressing up its length. Each time she completes a length, she unfolds and refolds the bast to make sure all of the surfaces are evenly beaten. The pounded bark spreads very quickly. Towards the end of the process, the maker will hold up and inspect the cloth. Once satisfied, she folds the cloth one last time and gives it a satisfying slap with the flat side of her mallet.

The bast widens and shortens slightly in the course of beating. The degree of spread varies, depending on the quality of the bast and the desired thickness of the final cloth. Roughly speaking, the male *koefi* bast doubles in width, while the thicker bast used for *embobi* skirts may widen by a factor of eight to nine. At a rough estimate, a 150 cm by 8 cm bark strip should result in a standard sized *embobi* measuring 130 cm long and 70 cm wide and take an hour to 90 minutes for a skilled tapa maker to beat (cf. Hermkens 2013:77; Regius 1988:11). Thicker and wider strips result in larger cloths (maxing out at around 165 cm long and 105 cm wide), but require considerably more time, strength, and skill to produce the desired evenness and thickness. Because male loin cloths wrap around sensitive genitals and upper thighs, they are produced from younger trees to yield a thinner, more supple cloth; less care is taken to prevent holes from overbeating.

Freshly beaten tapa is immediately hung up to dry inside or under the house where it will not be exposed to direct sunlight. Sometimes makers miss a bit of outer bark when first scraping the tree, which shows up as a stain on the finished cloth. Stained cloths are gently rinsed in the river and then rebeaten with the *fo*. The cloths are checked carefully and removed from the clotheslines while still a little damp, folded and placed under sleeping mats (made from pandanus strips), and slept upon for a night, which smoothes surface wrinkles. The larger *embobi* are folded twice, creating four flat panels between the creases, while the *koefi* are folded three times, creating eight panels. After the first night, the cloths are hung in direct sunlight and allowed to dry thoroughly to prevent mold from forming. Once dry, they are stored under sleeping mats until it is time to apply designs.

Naturally, I was eager to try my hand at beating bark into cloth. I turned again to experts for help—Lottie Ororogo and Martha Maiyova, who gave me a small strip of bast to practise on. As I pounded away, I discovered that my body was not built for this kind of work. The muscle power required for hefting the heavy mallets was one thing, but what nearly did me in was the sharp impact of the mallet hitting the anvil. After a half hour my arm felt like it would separate from my shoulder socket, and my whacks became steadily more feeble and uneven. It was a minor compensation to know that my antics provided entertainment for a rapidly growing crowd of giggling women and children. When Lottie and Martha declared my cloth satisfactory, after about an hour of pounding, I was pleased to see that while by no means a masterful bit of work, it was big and smooth enough for me to apply a design, a far less physically demanding job that I would attempt in a few days. With a quiet sense of accomplishment, I hung up my little tapa sheet to dry under a house and later folded it under my mattress for the night.

The experience of beating a tapa, like so many I have had with Maisin, helped me to appreciate how their lives centre around basic physical pursuits—subsistence activities like gardening, fishing, and manufacturing material necessities like canoes, mats, and houses—and the skill and grace with which they undertake such labours. Manufacturing cloth from *wuwusi* bark is one of the basic activities by which Maisin people make their living. Such activities are usually glossed as "economic" and seen as providing the foundation for social organization and cultural worldviews. Yet, as we shall see in this chapter, they involve much more than simple survival. The Maisin "make their living" in the fullest sense of the phrase.

SUBSISTENCE ACTIVITIES

Although Maisin are increasingly dependent upon store-bought goods, they continue to rely primarily upon the lands and waters around them for their basic needs. Steel axes, nylon fishnets, and shotguns have replaced some of the tools used by their ancestors. Still, were an ancestor to return, they would find the basic techniques used to produce food, to make canoes, or to put up a house essentially unchanged. In Papua New Guinea as a whole, at least 70 per cent of the population continues to rely on small-scale gardening, fishing, and gathering for much of their food.

The Maisin spend most of their waking hours involved in the food quest, as gardeners, hunters, fishermen, and gatherers. As in other small-scale cultures, they organize work along gender lines. In general, men take on tasks that require relatively brief bursts of energetic activity, such as pig hunting and clearing bush. Women take on more repetitive jobs that require sustained effort, such as carrying produce, weeding gardens, and gathering shellfish. If asked, Maisin justify this division of labour on the basis of the relative strength of men and women. Still, cultural expectations are clearly at work. Fishing, for instance, calls for less strength than chopping and hauling wood, yet only men fish and only women chop and carry firewood. In some other Melanesian cultures, women traditionally fish alone or alongside men.

Anne and I received a lesson on the gendered division of labour soon after we began living in Uiaku. Finding clean water for washing required a daily trip up the muddy river beyond the last village houses and into a side creek, where we filled four buckets with clear water and returned. One day, we had just begun the trek back to the mission station, each of us lugging two heavy buckets. Normally people were away in the gardens at this time of day, but on this occasion a group of women had remained behind and were chatting some distance ahead of us. They saw us and shrieked. One of them rushed up to relieve me of my buckets, putting one on her head and giving another to a companion. Anne, meanwhile, was left with her burden and a lesson, at least from the Maisin point of view, in the proper duties of a wife. In recent years, some younger people have eased up on the restrictions—you occasionally see a husband helping a wife carry food, for instance, or chopping wood—but generally the Maisin continue to follow the old ways. I have often been told that a man lacking a sister or a wife to do the essential garden work would face starvation (although I very much doubt the community would allow it).

Only men hunt. The Maisin greatly relish meat and require it for feasts. A few households keep domesticated pigs, which are always reserved for a major event such as a bride wealth payment for which a fat village pig is a requirement, but most meat comes from game killed by hunters in the bush and forest. A few villagers own shotguns, but shells are expensive and hard to obtain so guns tend to be reserved for shooting crocodiles when they get too close to the villages.[1] Maisin hunt mainly for bush pigs, using steel-tipped black palm spears and packs of dogs. Tracking and spearing a pig requires great skill, patience, and bravery, as a cornered pig is extremely dangerous. The best hunters work alone at night, often crouching silently for hours in the swampy areas favoured by pigs, enduring swarms of mosquitoes before making their kill. If he is successful, the hunter guts the pig on the spot, binds its legs, and hoists the heavy carcass across his back to bear to the village, usually several kilometres away. The Maisin are opportunistic hunters and will spear wallabies, cassowaries, and other game that cross their paths. In the past, they also employed a variety of bird and pig traps, but knowledge of these has largely been lost.

Fish and shellfish provide important supplements to the diet. While the number of dinghies with outboard motors has been steadily increasing, most people still rely upon outrigger canoes for coastal travel and for fishing. Making a canoe requires great skill. One must find a good "canoe" tree in the forest, chop down, and then roughly hollow it with an adze so that it is light enough to drag down to the coast without risk of splitting. Once in the village, the hull is shaded from the hot sun. An expert canoe-maker finishes hollowing out the hull with an adze, carefully chipping away at the sides and bottom, to make the craft as light as possible without punching a hole. Once the hull is completed, the canoe-maker lashes together the outrigger super-structure and, in the case of larger canoes, a platform. The task of building canoes, like constructing houses, falls entirely to men. Maisin canoes tend to be rather small, capable of carrying three to five persons. A few men are skilled enough to make larger canoes capable of extended trips on the ocean, but the Maisin acquire most of their seagoing canoes from Miniafia villagers on Cape Nelson, who trade them for cash and tapa cloth. Men fish from canoes using spears and nets. They also spear and net fish found in shallows close to shore.

Women do most of the gathering of wild foodstuffs as well as firewood and water. They collect crabs and shellfish from mangrove swamps and reefs near the shore. When they are in season, they also bring home delectable and protein-rich okari nuts (*T. kaernbachii*) from the forest. Both men and women gather building materials for houses as well as medicinal plants and tapa dyes. Men and women work cooperatively in harvesting and preparing sago. Sago is made from the inner pith of a type of semi-cultivated palm tree growing in swamps behind the village. While a husband and wife can handle a small sago, often men form work groups. They begin by cutting down the palm and splitting off the harder outer bark, revealing the white pith inside. Sitting with their legs resting against the trunk, the men rhythmically pound the pith with adzes, to the accompaniment of boisterous songs. Meanwhile, the women take a length of the bark and set it up near a stream in a frame-work to produce a kind of funnel with a mesh filter at the lower end. They scoop the pulverized pith, soak it in water, and then squeeze the mash against the filter. The soapy residue is caught in a plastic-lined pool. This is repeated until the pith is used up and the sediment settles to the bottom of the pool. When the water is drained off, one is left with a pure white starch. The Maisin consider sago a "famine food," to be eaten when garden produce is running low. It has the advantage of growing in swampy areas not suitable for gardens and, once prepared, does not spoil quickly. Maisin prepare sago either by mixing it with water to produce an orange glue-like porridge or by baking it into large white chunks with an interior texture that reminded me of plaster of Paris. It is, to say the least, an acquired taste. Flavourless, sago is one of only a few foods produced by the Maisin that I have never gotten used to; I dreaded the sight of a visitor coming to the door with a tell-tale leaf-wrapped packet. The Maisin quite like it and consider it a treat.

The Maisin get most of their food from gardens cleared and planted within a zone of secondary bush radiating three to five kilometres from the villages. Groups of brothers and closely related patrilineal kin co-residing in hamlets claim specific areas in which they make their gardens and which they pass to their sons. People also frequently make gardens on lands owned by maternal

Figure 2.3 A newly cleared garden with logs marking paths between the plots. (Photo by J. Barker)

relations and in-laws. They must always ask permission and should give a gift of produce from the new gardens to the owners. Maternal relatives sometimes will gift land to one of their sisters' sons, especially if their own numbers are declining, but this is rare. While land should remain within the patrilineal group, fruit and palm trees are owned by those who plant them even when on another's land. The rules concerning land use and ownership are thus quite straightforward, but in practice they lend themselves to periodic disputes. People remember boundaries based on the placement, among other things, of trees and rivers. Yet trees die and rivers shift. Sometimes people have differing recollections of where their ancestors first planted gardens and whether maternal relatives merely gave temporary rights to plant or ceded ownership.

The Maisin practise swidden horticulture, clearing and using garden sites for two to three years before abandoning them to the bush and moving on. Ideally, a former garden should be left for a period of 10 to 20 years before being re-used, long enough to allow the site to be covered by a lush growth of jungle and trees. Areas gardened too frequently will eventually become grassland and never recover their previous fertility. Most households maintain at least three dispersed gardens in different stages of production at any one time. This assures a steady supply of food, while offering some insurance against flooding, drought, and marauding pigs.

The basic technology of gardening is little changed from pre-European times. Imported steel axes and machetes long ago replaced locally fashioned stone tools, greatly easing the work of clearing brush and weeding, but Maisin continue to use fire-hardened digging sticks for planting. They make no use of composting or irrigation techniques. Villagers replant and extend their gardens throughout the year, but the most intense work of creating new gardens takes place in the dry season. Clearing a garden space is done entirely by men. They cut trees, laying out trunks and larger branches in lines to mark plots and pathways, gathering and burning the remaining brush after it's had a few days to dry. One of the typical signals of the onset of the dry season is the sight from out on Collingwood Bay of plumes of smoke rising from dozens of new gardens dispersed behind the villages. Tree stumps are left in place; along with larger logs, they provide a useful source of firewood. Once a garden has been cleared, men must turn their attention to two further tasks. The first is the construction of a garden shelter for sleeping and storing tools. The second task is the construction of a fence to protect the garden from pigs. Bush pigs are a constant worry. Entering gardens under the shelter of darkness, the animals rapidly destroy large areas as they root about for tubers. Some men leave smouldering fires on the edges of the clearing to scare pigs away, but the only sure defence is a sturdy fence of small logs roped together to enclose the cultivated area.

Once the garden clearing is prepared, women will fetch taro tops, banana suckers, and other seed plants from older gardens. Men and women share the work of planting, which entails pushing a digging stick into the soil and shoving in the cuttings. The low floodland plains of Collingwood Bay support a wide variety of crops of which taro (sp. *Colocasia*) is the most important. As in other parts of Melanesia, the Maisin grow a large number of varieties that differ only slightly in the shapes or coloration of the tuber, stalk, or leaf. In 1983, I recorded the names of 21 varieties from one master gardener, although most were indistinguishable to my eye. Other staples include varieties of sweet and plantain (cooking) bananas, sweet potatoes, and yams. A Maisin garden also typically contains a wide range of native and introduced secondary crops such as squash, manioc, sugar cane, tomatoes, cucumbers, beans, maize, watermelons, and pineapples. Gardeners also plant trees, most of which come into production after the garden has been abandoned—papayas, coconuts, areca (betelnut) palms, and, less often, guava or mangos. People finish off their gardens by planting fragrant and ornamental bushes and flowers. These add to the attractiveness of the space and provide materials for dancing costumes.

Once the planting is completed, the bulk of garden work falls to women. Areas around the new plants are weeded two to three times to give the crops a chance to grow. Women carry out the routine tasks of harvesting and hauling crops and firewood. In the late afternoons, one sees groups of women trudging back from the gardens bearing heavy loads of firewood, crops, and sometimes an infant in large string bags strapped across the forehead and suspended down the back. In total, the burden may weight up to 25 kg, although 10 to 15 kg is more common.

The thin soil rapidly loses fertility as crops mature. Gardeners usually can get a second planting, mostly of sweet potatoes, which demand fewer nutrients than taro or yams, but most gardens are abandoned after two years. Owners will occasionally return over the next few years to gather bananas and, once they mature, coconuts and betelnuts if they have been planted. Long after a garden has returned to bush, palms and other cultivated trees stand as markers of prior activity.

The Maisin enjoy spending time in their gardens. Often people live for days or even weeks away from the village, sleeping in open-sided garden shelters which, like village houses, are raised on posts to catch cooling breezes. I also enjoyed spending time in the gardens. Although very hot during the day—the surrounding forests block cooling breezes—the gardens present a lush profusion of shapes and colours. The best moments are early morning and late afternoon when it is cool and flocks of small parrots and white and black cockatoos descend to feed on fallen papayas and rotting fruits. The garden shelters provide a lovely place to socialize, share gossip, listen to folk tales, or simply enjoy the sounds of the jungle.

Most visitors to rural communities in Papua New Guinea get no further than the villages. Because most of us are urban dwellers who "forage" for food at grocery stores, it is easy to assume that villages form the centre of social life. After a few days in a garden, however, you realize that this is misleading. For the Maisin, gardens are about much more than just growing food.

To begin with, gardens are spiritual places. In the recent past, well after most of the people had become Christians, people initiated new gardens by placing a small amount of betelnut and tobacco on a makeshift platform at the centre of the area to be cleared. This sacrifice assured that the ancestors who had previously worked that land would not be upset by the noise and disruption of garden work and would reciprocate for the gift by increasing the fertility of the soil. Few Maisin do this today, but several will ask the priest to bless new gardens, and everyone is conscious of the continuing presence of the people who used the land in earlier times. Older people remember being cautioned as children by their parents not to be too rowdy in the garden lest the noise disturb the ancestors. Maisin today often credit ancestors for a good crop and blame failures due to insect infestations, floods, or drought upon angered ghosts. Recently deceased fathers and mothers often appear in dreams to tell their children where to plant, hunt, or fish. The Maisin regard none of this as extraordinary or spooky. The ancestors are *just there*, as real as the trees or the butterflies.

Gardens are also key locations of moral and social development. As soon as a child receives a name, usually when they are nine months to a year old, their parents assign them a garden plot and plant and harvest crops in the child's name. Everyone gardens as soon and for as long as they are able. The good man or woman, in the Maisin's estimation, works hard and is rewarded by an abundance of good crops, which they should then generously share. Parents will size up a prospective spouse for their son or daughter by virtue of their skill as gardeners and their willingness to share labour and food with their kin. Most of the rich folklore elders share after the evening meal involves scenes in gardens, the action turning upon the interactions between siblings, spouses, and in-laws working out their relationships through growing, exchanging, and consuming food.[2]

Gardens also lie at the centre of everyday politics: the formation of alliances and vying for influence. When a man clears a garden on his father's and paternal grandfather's land, he demonstrates a claim against others who may also believe they have an ancestral right to part or all of that land. Gardens thus physically affirm a person's genealogical identity. At the same time, individuals build influence through their actions in the gardens. Prominent senior men encourage clan mates and in-laws to join together to clear a large area within which each household develops separate garden plots. Such cooperation eases the burden of clearing and cultivating gardens while providing participants with welcome opportunities for socializing. It also serves as evidence of a leader's ability to influence and coordinate the labour of others. Managing a large group garden is usually the first step towards the sponsoring of a major ceremony such as the initiation for a first-born child, which requires large quantities of raw food to give away as gifts and cooked food for feasting.

Gardens form the very heart of the local economic system. In the hot and moist conditions of the tropics, garden food begins to rot within a day of harvesting; slow-smoked fish or meat lasts longer, but by the second week begins to turn into an inedible tarry lump. With no reliable source of cash income, villagers rely upon a steady flow of food through daily subsistence activities to survive. Most of the food gets consumed by the households that produce it. Yet garden foods also yield the essential ingredients of wider economic and social relationships that bind households together. It is to this system we now turn.

HOUSEHOLDS AND RECIPROCITY

The daily round in Maisin village life centres on food. People spend most days clearing new gardens and cultivating and harvesting crops. As shadows lengthen in the late afternoon, people make their way back to the village, the women straining under their heavy loads of food and firewood. In the early evening, one's nose is greeted by the aroma of dozens of cooking fires. The basic cooking method is simple but effective. First, taro is peeled and cut into large chunks and placed at the bottom of a cooking pot. Depending on what is available, the pot is filled up with layers of yams, cooking bananas, sweet potatoes, squash, and fish or meat. As the women prepare the food, boys and girls scrape coconut meat and then squeeze water through it. The sweetened water is then poured into the pot, which is covered with a lid or, if a clay pot, banana leaves. The pot is then placed on a stack of firewood which is lit. The denser root crops at the bottom boil while the top food is steamed. Everything comes out with a slightly sweet nutty flavour. Dinner is the one big meal of the day. Breakfast consists of the cold leftovers. During the day, people snack on sweet bananas, sugar cane, or a leftover chunk of taro or sweet potato.

Compared to other cuisines, Maisin food is quite bland. They use no flavourings besides water sweetened with coconut. Yet, as with all human societies, the food Maisin grow, share, and eat is infused with cultural significance (Crowther 2013). Major community gatherings, for instance, are often marked with massive public exchanges of raw and cooked foods, followed by feasts in which people gorge themselves with food presented on banana leaves and eaten by hand. Maisin savour a wide range of foods, but taro (*kunkun*) is special. For Maisin, taro *is* food. With a symbolically significant gestation period of nine months, taro features in many Maisin narratives, sometimes as the name of characters. It is the first crop to be planted in new gardens and the first to be placed in the cooking pot. Its importance was brought home vividly to me in 1983 when a blight destroyed much of the taro crop. While there was no shortage of other garden crops, villagers complained incessantly of hunger during a time of "famine."[3]

Most productive activities in Maisin society are organized by individual households. A typical Maisin household is made up of a husband, wife, and children, but it is not unusual to also find elderly parents, cousins, or adopted children living together. Usually all of the members share a single building, but sometimes aging parents or a younger sibling may live in a small house near the main one, while men in polygynous marriages usually build separate residences for their wives and respective children. Members work together on most subsistence activities, donating the food they produce into a common pool. Households tend to be nearly self-sufficient. Some larger tasks, such as building a new house, require assistance. At such times, households belonging to the same clan or related through marriage will band together to form work parties.

A certain amount of sharing of labour and food is necessary for survival in any society. Maisin practice, however, goes well beyond basic necessity. Consider this: Maisin households produce exactly the same foods, varying mainly in the amount they can produce from the gardens, hunting, and fishing. Most easily produce enough food for their own needs and for the care of dependant infants, the old, and the infirm. There is rarely a practical need for people to share beyond their own household. Yet, each day, villagers give produce, betelnut, tobacco, and other gifts to kin and neighbours. Most evenings after the evening meal has been cooked, young children can be seen bearing small plates or pots of cooked food from house to house. More often than not, a household receives back from one or more neighbours exactly the same kinds of food as they sent out. During the early stages of my fieldwork, I went to several households every night for two weeks to record a log of their daily activities. I was impressed not only by the sheer amount of giving and taking that was going on but that people remembered even the smallest exchanges.

Anthropologists call this kind of arrangement a "gift economy" (Gregory 1982; Sykes 2005). It is the normal way of doing things in small-scale subsistence-based cultures in which money and commodities are often scarce. A principle of reciprocity lies at the heart of the system: Person A gives something to Person B, creating a debt and an obligation to make a return gift. Yet this very simplicity can be deceiving, for in practice the sequence of giving, receiving, and returning permits an extraordinarily broad range of variations. These variations turn on several interrelated factors: the intent of the partners who are exchanging things, the nature of the social relationships between exchange partners, the actual items exchanged, and the time lapse between the reception of a gift and reciprocation (Schwimmer 1973).

The virtue of giving is deeply engrained in Maisin culture. Children learn the habit of giving and receiving gifts by watching and interacting with older siblings and adults, developing a markedly more collectivistic social orientation than one finds in Western culture.[4] This is important to grasp because, as we shall see throughout this book, reciprocity provides the Maisin with a basic moral orientation to life. People expect reciprocity in their dealings with others. They share to help each other out, but exchanges more fundamentally provide the key means by which people create, assess, manipulate, and sometimes end social relationships. Everyone is involved in social relationships and so everyone exchanges. Like all things, exchanging can be done with finesse or gracelessly, with calculation or by habit. That said, the social environment in which Maisin are raised fosters behaviour based upon a keen sensitivity to interpersonal relationships. Anne's research on prosocial reasoning (people's explanations for behaving in ways that help others) revealed that the reasons Maisin children and adults give for helping others in specific situations are strongly oriented towards collective needs (Tietjen 1986). The kinds of appeals to abstract moral principles one finds expressed by many adults in Western culture—that is to say, principles governing *individual* behavior—were virtually absent among the Maisin adults she interviewed, who instead expressed "an empathic concern with the needs of others" (Tietjen 2006:56). For the Maisin, reciprocity is not simply a type of behaviour or a consciously held ideal; at a deeper level it reflects a worldview and disposition that, as we shall see throughout this book, fundamentally shapes Maisin understandings and actions in all domains of life.

Anthropologists have written extensively on reciprocity in Melanesian societies and elsewhere.[5] Prior to our fieldwork, we read this literature carefully. Still, reading and experiencing are two very different things. Nothing caused more strains in our early dealings with the Maisin than figuring out how to respond appropriately when people gave us gifts and requested things from us. We had to think about it and at first were slow on the uptake.

I wrote in Chapter 1 of how Anne and I received a huge quantity of food on our arrival in Uiaku. After we redistributed the produce the gifts tapered off, but most days at least one person would come to our door with some raw taro, bananas, other vegetables, and, occasionally, a fish or raw cut of pig meat. As they waited at the door, we pulled out a small bag of rice or a tobacco stick to give in return. Our most regular supplier was Rufus, a lively middle-aged man who lived with his three wives and children in the village next to the mission station. Rufus and I soon developed a kind of joking relationship, greeting each other with cries of *toma*! ("friend"), whenever we passed each other's place. Still, I soon came to dread and even resent his visits. Many days the offered food was tiny—a few scrawny sweet potatoes or a small fish—and yet we felt obliged to give the rice or tobacco regardless. It felt like extortion and, beyond this, terribly unfair to other villagers who brought more generous quantities of produce yet received the same return gifts from us.

One day, another regular visitor came with food. As usual, I thanked her and asked her to wait while I fetched a bag from our rapidly dwindling store of rice. When I returned, I was surprised and alarmed by her obvious distress. She refused the rice and went off in search of someone who could speak English. She came back with Ilma Joyce, who explained that she had not come to "sell" the food to us: it was a gift, offered in friendship. She had seen that we needed things, that we had no garden, and so had felt sorry for us and wanted to help.

The gift was offered in "love" (*marawa-wawe*). The implication was that by immediately giving rice in return, I was actually spurning her offer of friendship and treating her as one would a stranger.

We thus had our first practical lesson in "generalized reciprocity" (Sahlins 1972). Close kin should support each other through a steady give-and-take of gifts, labour, and advice. This is not done in a calculated way, by tracking what each person gives, receives, owes, or is owed. Instead, people demonstrate their mutual trust and support by allowing things to more or less balance out over time. This kind of sharing is a prime example of the Maisin value of *marawa-wawe*, a concept to which we will return often in this book. *Mara* refers to the physical sensation in the guts caused by strong emotion. Combined with *wawe*, "giving," the term suggests a state of sharing oneself with another. English-speaking Maisin often gloss it as "love," but, depending on the context, it can also mean "peace" or "social amity." As these glosses suggest, the Maisin see *marawa-wawe* as the ideal outcome of exchanges, the social goal that begins with the simple giving of a gift. This is how family and close friends should treat each other. Indeed, it is what makes family and close friends.

While the daily giving and taking of food and labour within and between closely related households appears free and uncalculated, the obligation to reciprocate is felt the most at this social level. What and how a person gives varies enormously depending on personality and circumstances, but generally reciprocal exchanges within the network of close kin fall into three types of relationships. Sisters and brothers, wives and husbands, engage in complementary reciprocity, with each making distinct contributions to the household. Their exchanges denote separate if not exactly equal status. Parents and children, older and younger siblings, engage in asymmetrical reciprocity. Their exchanges denote different statuses. The elder should "take care" (*kaifi*) of the child or sibling by providing general food and good advice; the child or younger sibling, in turn, should listen respectfully (*muan*) to the elder and obey his or her wishes; in the course of their life span, children should return the initial gifts of food and support to their aging parents or siblings, bringing the relationship into balance. Members of different households, clan mates, and "friends" engage in symmetrical exchanges of food and labour that remain more or less in balance, denoting their equivalence. As we shall see in Chapter 3, these three forms of reciprocal exchange reflect broader Maisin assumptions about the social order.

As I became more familiar with the workings of reciprocity, I applied my insights to my dealings with Rufus. I no longer gave rice or tobacco immediately upon receiving his gifts but instead occasionally sent a bag of rice or a couple of sticks of tobacco to his house. To my relief, and I expect his, our relationship greatly improved. I was at last behaving like a friend instead of a stranger.

BEYOND THE HOUSEHOLD

The Maisin often speak about their communities as if they were tightly integrated families. The rapid redistribution, across villages and beyond, of food given out at feasts or second-hand clothing brought in by a relative visiting from town during the Christmas holiday can leave one with the impression that the whole community exists in a kind of communal *marawa-wawe*, a state of generalized exchange. Yet this is not the case. The circle of neighbours and kin in which people typically experience a steady give-and-take tends not to extend much further than nearby households, which, as we will see in the next chapter, usually belong to close relations. These circles overlap, forming a dense interwoven exchange network that expands across the community but does not form into a unitary system.

There is no sharp boundary between those people one treats as intimate kin and more distant relatives, but there is a marked shift in interactions with social distance. The more distant people are, in terms of relatedness and physical residence, the harder it is to attain an ambience of easy give-and-take. Exchanges occur less frequently and tend to fall into a pattern of "balanced reciprocity" in which the exchanging parties are focused on the calculus of give-and-take. Exchanges are far less frequent, more carefully organized, and follow a conscious etiquette affirming that a balance will be struck. For instance, replacing a roof requires a large work party to cut sago fronds and to prepare and lay the thatch. The owner will first call upon neighbouring households because close kin help each other. The close relatives are treated fairly casually; the homeowner can and will help them out in return in a myriad of ways in coming days. When he invites more distant kin and friends to help, in contrast, they will expect a small meal at the end of the day including, ideally, generous quantities of the heavily sugared tea favoured by most Maisin. This doesn't finish the debt—a bit of cooked food and tea is not the equivalent of a day of hard labour. The proud owner of the new roof can expect in the future to help repair or replace the roofs of the various men who helped him out and who, in their turn, will provide a small meal with tea. And so on. This is a rather trivial example, however. Things get vastly more complicated when we come to the really big exchanges: those that mark the major transitions in individuals' lives—births, marriages, and deaths—and community feasts and celebrations.

Marriage forms the lynchpin of a series of life crisis ceremonies that mark one's passage from birth to death. Maisin speak of marriage as a kind of

Figure 2.4 Women bringing food to a feast. Note the "star" (*damana*) design on the tapa worn by the woman on the left in the photograph. (Photo by A.M. Tietjen)

exchange that begins when one clan provides a woman (including her labour and future children) to another clan. In accepting the woman, the recipients incur a huge debt that literally takes a lifetime to repay. They have a number of options: they may arrange for one of their young women to marry into the other clan; they may give the wife's clan a child for adoption; or they may present a large gift of food, goods (including tapa), and money after a few children are born ("bride wealth"). Regardless of what type of repayment they ultimately make, they must also "respect" the wife's people with frequent small gifts of food and labour and with larger prestations (presentations of gifts) when each child is born. Each of these gifts in turn triggers a reciprocal gift from the in-laws. The spiral of gifts and return gifts is ideally finally brought into balance after the death of the spouses, an event also marked by exchanges. The Maisin also refer to this idealized state as *marawa-wawe*, but here it has a different sense than generalized reciprocity: it refers to a perfect balance between clans that retain their distinct identities. Indeed, the act of exchange serves to define their identities (cf. Wagner 1967).

In the past, leaders of higher-ranking *Kawo* clans hosted feasts in their home villages that involved days and sometimes weeks of feasting and dancing, culminating in large prestations of raw food to their guests. These feasts were of two types: ones meant to end warfare and/or build alliances with outside groups, and competitive feasts rotating between allied Maisin clans that faced off as "food enemies," each one in turn trying to top the other with more splendid spectacles of generosity. A similar system of "fighting with food" persisted on nearby Goodenough Island into the 1960s (Young 1971), but was abandoned by Maisin a generation earlier. These older large-scale feasts have since been partly replaced by community-level events: feasts marked by traditional dancing to celebrate church holy days and visiting dignitaries.

These larger events illustrate an internal tension in reciprocal systems. On the one hand, reciprocity is all about equivalence and balance: you give something to someone who is obliged to make a return gift. Ideally, the exchange partners enter into the state of commensality that Maisin call *marawa-wawe*. On the other hand, reciprocal obligations create a temporary imbalance that gives an advantage to the giver, introducing an element of competition and power. Ambitious men in Melanesian societies prove their mettle by being more generous with gifts than others. They are quick to help with gifts of food or labour when a clan mate needs help with a bride wealth payment or to raise funds to pay school fees. Over time, if they are careful, they build up a network of obligations that can be called in when arranging a large event. As we'll see in Chapter 5, Maisin leaders cannot order people about; their authority rests on their personal reputations. An ability to persuade is crucial, but building a network of obligations is in itself a persuasive reason for people to support a leader as he works to manage the many moving parts of a large-scale feast. A successful event in which guests receive an impressive gift of food, tapa, money, and other things attests to the reputation of the leaders that manage it, while also making them a target of rivals who try to outdo them. Power rests not on personal wealth but on the ability of a man to organize his work and those of others in order to give away more than he receives.

As one moves further away from trusted family to exchange partners, one reaches the very edges of social relationships. "Negative reciprocity" occurs between parties that have little or no social connection and thus no moral obligation to each other. They are strangers or nearly so. People expect their exchange partners to try to take advantage of them and feel little compulsion not to seek advantage themselves; thus both sides watch the transactions very carefully, bartering for advantage. If one side does gain an advantage or is perceived to have done so, the other may retaliate—a reflex known throughout Melanesia as "payback" (Trompf 1994) or *vina* in the Maisin language. My early transactions with Rufus, described above, were of this sort. Because I (wrongly) assumed I had to pay immediately and at an inflated rate for the food he brought, I felt taken advantage of. Negative reciprocity is like that: there is little or no trust. Negative reciprocity thus tends to occur on the margins of the moral community in interactions with strangers or, more dangerously, encounters with sorcerers.

In sum, we find that in Maisin society there is a correlation between social distance and the sorts of exchanges in which people engage. Closely related people engage in a constant give-and-take that confirms and generates a sense of commonality. Further out, exchanges become less frequent and more public and formal. Social relationships at this level cannot be taken for granted: they are created, made visible, and validated through a series of formal prestations. As social distance increases, the antagonistic element of the reciprocal scenario becomes ever more prominent, arriving eventually in bartering with, stealing from, and—in the warrior past—killing social outsiders.

The model of generalized, balanced, and negative reciprocity developed by Marshall Sahlins (1972) from a comparative study of small-scale societies around the world, is very helpful. Yet reality is considerably more dynamic than such models suggest. They express ideals, while real life requires compromises. Taken to its extreme, generalized reciprocity would lead to the communal sharing of all property within a group. Yet Maisin recognize that some types of property—personal clothing and utensils, for instance—are individually owned and not subject to reciprocal demands. Further, there are polite ways of avoiding over-demanding kin. Garden shelters, for instance, provide a convenient place to store surplus food away from the eyes of other villagers. At the level of balanced reciprocity, appearance can be every bit as important as actuality. Consider, for example, a ceremony I witnessed in 1983 when a widow was released from mourning for her husband who had passed away some years earlier. Villagers spoke of two groups in balanced opposition: the wife's and the husband's "sides." This seemed neat enough until I discovered that a number of women who had provided and cooked food for the widow's people later received that very same food as members of the husband's side. During the first stage of the exchange, they were acting as close relatives of the widow. Yet they had married into her husband's clan, and so, when the time came, they formally received their fair share of the food distribution.

Reciprocity lies at the heart of the Maisin subsistence economy, but it should be clear by now that it is neither simple nor limited to the business of moving items between producers and consumers. Reciprocity provides the key means by which the Maisin create and sustain social relationships. The constant give-and-take of daily exchanges embodies an essential assumption that social relationships cannot be taken for granted. They must be created, affirmed, reproduced, and modified through giving and receiving. Reciprocity thus serves as a kind of language, communicating the moral precepts that make social life possible and comprehensible. Ask any Maisin, "What are the qualities of a good person?" and they will inevitably reply that he or she is generous with gifts and responsible in meeting exchange obligations. Maisin regard those who resist participating in exchanges with either scorn or fear. A man or woman who fails to meet exchange obligations because of a lack of ability or laziness is "rubbish," a source of annoyance to their families who can't depend on them to help out when needed. A person who *chooses* not to exchange is something else, for he or she stands apart from the common rules that make social life predictable, and thus threatens it. Outsiders pose one kind of threat, which is why the Maisin view them with suspicion. Yet a greater threat comes from insiders whose selfishness reflects a wilful defiance of the moral rules. Such is the nature of sorcerers. The Maisin believe that sorcerers, operating in secret, cause most major illnesses and accidents and are responsible for the majority of deaths. As we shall see in Chapter 4, however, the Maisin also believe that sorcerers tend to attack those people who have themselves breached morality by acting selfishly, non-reciprocally. The hope for social amity reinforces reciprocity in a positive way. The fear of a terrible death through sorcery adds a negative sanction against immoral behaviour.

It would be hard to exaggerate the importance of reciprocity to the Maisin. Yet this is not the whole story. As well as growing their own food and building houses from bush materials, the Maisin have also long lived in a world of cash and commodities, one that operates according to a different moral logic than reciprocity.

CASH, REMITTANCES, AND COMMODITIES: A CHANGING ECONOMY

Foreign visitors to Maisin villages are impressed that people grow their own food and manufacture much of their own material culture from the resources nature provides for them. Subsistence activities and reciprocity provide the foundation for village life, a foundation that was laid long before the arrival of Europeans. All the same, the Maisin are no strangers to money and what money can buy. Mass-manufactured commodities first entered Maisin society in the 1890s in the form of steel axes and knives traded by visiting missionaries and government officers. By the 1920s, villagers regularly purchased goods with money earned by young men working on plantations and mines elsewhere in the colony. Following World War II, Maisin actively sought ways of earning money locally, trying out a succession of cash crops and eventually finding a market for tapa. Beginning in the mid-1960s, most of a generation of young people left the villages to take up paid employment in the towns, sending home gifts of cash and goods to help their rural relations. Over the years, villagers have become increasingly dependent upon purchased commodities ranging from basic necessities, such as clothing and fish hooks, to "luxury" items such as soccer balls and cigarettes. Villagers frequently complain about the problems that money brings in its wake, but no one wants to return to a time when people relied solely upon local resources for survival.

The growing dependence upon money has had complex implications for Maisin culture. We will turn to this subject in the next section. First, however, we need to complete our survey of the local economy by examining the place of cash and commodities and the ways the Maisin try to secure them.

Prior to the early 1960s, only a limited range of commercial goods was locally available: machetes and knives, bolts of cloth for simple skirts, black stick tobacco, and so forth. This limitation was partly due to a lack of ready cash but also to the difficulties of getting commodities to the villages at a time when very few trade stores existed and infrequent coastal ships provided the only reliable source of transportation. Since this time, both the range of goods available to the Maisin and their ability to purchase them have increased enormously. When we arrived in the early 1980s, all Maisin wore Western clothing (mostly second-hand, imported from Australia and sold through dealers in the towns) and had become accustomed to a wide array of mass-produced goods, a trend that has continued to accelerate. Most people still cooked with traditional clay pots, purchased or traded for tapa from Wanigela, and ate with their fingers from tin plates or off banana leaves. By the late 1990s, steel cooking pots were in common use for all but ceremonial occasions, and most people in Uiaku, the richest of the villages, had metal, plastic, and in some cases china plates and steel cutlery. Many people now owned pressure lanterns. A few families with aid from employed relatives had purchased fibreglass boats equipped with outboard motors that were gradually replacing the larger outrigger canoes. While households still grew most of their food, many now supplemented their diet with rice, tinned fish, and other mass-produced foods purchased at local trade stores and from businesses located near the Wanigela airstrip. Radios had become common, although villagers often could not afford the batteries to keep them operating. Upon retiring from his job in town, one man had brought a generator and VCR to the village. In June 2000, two other returning workers introduced fluorescent lights powered by solar panels.

People need cash not just to clothe their bodies and supplement the local food supply, but to pay for transport to visit relatives in town, to get their children to and from distant high schools, or to deliver a relative to the provincial hospital. Community services also cost money. Since the late 1970s, the Anglican Church has required local congregations to pay the salary of the parish priest. Villagers are also responsible for the costs of church supplies, such as sacramental wine and wafers (both imported from Australia), as well as the building and maintenance of churches, classrooms, and housing for the priest and teachers. For much of the post-Independence period, parents have had to pay small school fees for students in elementary schools and far higher tuitions for those accepted into the private church or public high schools. Various village associations also regularly seek money in the form of government grants and donations from local people. The Mothers' Union, for instance, organizes occasional community meals to raise money for trips to conventions or supplies for the church, while youth groups hire themselves out to repair houses or work on gardens to raise money for sports equipment. The Maisin Integrated Conservation and Development organization (MICAD) organized tapa sales during the anti-logging campaign of the 1990s to purchase medicine on behalf of the community and cover the travel costs required to bring leaders from the different Maisin villages together for consultations (Chapter 6).

Opportunities for earning money locally are quite limited. Beginning in the 1920s, villagers periodically sold copra—dried coconut meat that can be rendered into oil—but this market had collapsed by the 1980s. Through the 1950s and 1960s, villagers planted thousands of cocoa trees under the guidance of government agricultural officers, but the lack of regular shipping in and out of Collingwood Bay made it too expensive to get the produce to market, and the trees were abandoned to the jungle. The most reliable local product has been tapa cloth. Maisin elders recalled their parents selling small quantities of tapa cloth to European traders in the late 1930s, but a regular market for tapa only came into existence in the late 1960s and early 1970s. Some Maisin travelling in the towns sold tapa to shops that, in turn, marketed them to the expatriate population as art and souvenirs. Around the same time, Sister Helen Roberts, a missionary nurse based at Wanigela, began to accept tapa as credit towards high school fees and transportation costs. Sister Helen actively sought out buyers across the country and overseas, gradually building a reputation for Maisin cloth in the artifact trade. During the same period, she built a market for Maisin cloth amongst Papua New Guineans, particularly in Oro Province, whose own traditions of tapa making were dying out but who needed decorated and undecorated cloths for ceremonial costumes. Finally, Sister Helen began a tradition of making clerical vestments from tapa for local and expatriate priests, one of which was presented to the Archbishop of Canterbury during the celebration of the centenary of the Anglican Church of Papua New Guinea in 1991.

In the mid-1980s, a skilled tapa maker could earn more than 200 kina per year—a considerable sum in those days—although most women made far less.[6] As the expatriate population in Papua New Guinea dwindled and the tourist trade slowed in the post-Independence years, however, partly in reaction to the growing theft and violence in the towns, tapa sales slumped. Maisin cloth enjoyed a major boost in the mid-1990s, when the environmental groups working with the Maisin actively promoted it as a sustainable form of locally controlled development (Chapter 6). These efforts led to a brief boom, but by 2000 tapa sales were again flagging.

Maisin often experiment with different ways to make money. Beginning in the 1990s, a few raised crocodiles for their skins or sold vegetables in the Tufi or Alotau markets. Some have experimented with insect farming[7] or planted small patches of oil palm. Other entrepreneurs open small trade stores or hire out their motorized boats to other villagers. Most of these enterprises soon go under, but a few men have managed to operate profitable businesses for a number of years. Generally, however, these attempts bring little money into the villages.

Since the early 1970s, the most important and reliable source of income for villagers has come in the form of remittances from working relatives. As related in Chapter 1, Maisin benefited from the massive expansion and localization of the Papua New Guinean civil service and private sector businesses during the late colonial period because of their early access to recently established secondary and advanced schools. Much of a generation of Maisin found jobs as teachers, nurses, priests, civil servants, and operators of various businesses. Despite its small population, Uiaku produced Papua New Guinea's first doctor (Dr. Wilfred Moi), one of the first dentists (Franklin Seri), and an ambassador to Indonesia (Benson Gegeyo). Once they gained steady employment, the first generation of graduates eased the path of younger siblings and relatives still in the villages by paying their high school fees, hosting them when they visited the towns looking for work, and recommending them for positions (cf. Carrier 1981). By the early 1980s, as much as a quarter of the population of Uiaku resided away from their natal villages and a new generation was growing up in the towns with little knowledge of their parents' culture or language. As I write in 2015, people of Maisin descent are spread across Papua New Guinea and some reside in Australia and New Zealand.

Villagers expect those who find employment to "not forget" the people back home. While life in the towns is expensive, most employed Maisin routinely put aside part of their salaries to assist their rural relatives in medical emergencies, bride wealth exchanges, funerals, and local business start-ups. They accommodate relatives visiting from the village and send them home with parcels of clothing and other goods. The biggest distributions occur when working relatives come home for the Christmas holiday, usually once every two years, bearing large suitcases stuffed with clothing and other gifts for their extended families. Employed Maisin do this in part because of their upbringing, reinforced by constant reminders from their rural relations of the reciprocal debt owed to those who raised them. They also do it to leave open the option of eventual retirement in their natal village. They help those who remain behind who, in turn, care for the land and protect the property rights of absent family members. The pattern of movement to and from the villages has had a profound impact upon Maisin society. Today almost all adult Maisin have lived for a time—and in many cases, for a long time—in the towns, either employed themselves or as the guest of an employed relative.

Even in the early 1980s, however, it was apparent that the Maisin strategy of exporting labour to the towns could not be sustained. Over the years, as high schools have opened their doors to more communities, Maisin have lost some of their advantage. While the high schools have expanded, the demand far outstrips their ability to absorb students, and so an increasing number of graduates from the Collingwood Bay village schools have been blocked from advancing their education. Meanwhile, employment opportunities have been steadily shrinking. Papua New Guinea's economy struggled in the early years after Independence and then lurched from crisis to crisis following the outbreak of a ten-year civil war on Bougainville Island and the closure of the country's most profitable gold and copper mine (Dorney 2000). Despite the rebound of the mining sector with the opening of massive (and massively polluting) projects around the country along with the expansion of other extractive industries, the number of high school and higher graduates greatly exceeds the jobs available. By 2000, villagers continued to look to remittances as the best source for cash and commodities, but the flow was far less reliable than in the recent past as the pool of employed Maisin shrank. As a consequence of these changes and a cultural preference for large families, the populations of Uiaku and other Maisin villages have been rapidly increasing since the early 1990s.

GIFTS AND COMMODITIES

Western visitors to rural communities in the Pacific Islands are often struck by the coexistence of old ways with new: subsistence activities alongside trade stores stocked with tinned fish and rice; robust exchange networks in which cash and traditional shell money pass between hands; stories of sorcery attacks shared after Sunday worship in the church. Today, most people under 60 speak some English, many fluently. Yet people live in thatched houses built by hand from bush materials, take great pride in the oral traditions of their ancestors, and feel intensely suspicious of neighbouring tribal groups. Tapa cloth epitomizes this mix of local and imported elements, for the Maisin use it interchangeably as a type of traditional wealth and ceremonial apparel and as a commodity that can be sold for money used to purchase, among other things, second-hand t-shirts, shorts, and skirts imported from overseas.

How do we make sense of this? Many observers see the presence of Western elements as evidence of a process of "modernization," a movement from a "traditional" past based upon loyalties to kin and an attachment to ancestral ways towards a "modern" society integrated into national and global financial, political, and social systems. They perceive this movement as inevitable, although they may celebrate or regret the changes. In 1999, for instance, a CNN film crew came to Uiaku to film a short news item on the Maisin's rejection of industrial logging of their forest. The segment features a lawyer explaining that "progress" was inevitable and generally benefited the people. For the most part, however, it conveys a sense of impending loss. The piece climaxes with a dramatic scene of Maisin "warriors" dancing in colourful traditional costumes. Yet the feeling one takes away is that another bit of cultural diversity is about to be crushed beneath the juggernaut of "development." The Canadian documentary *Changing Ground* (2001) conveys a similar theme. Here activities such as the preparation of sago, manufacture of tapa, and costumed dancing evoke a valiant traditional people resisting encroaching modernity, which in turn is represented as rapacious loggers destroying all in their path. The Maisin, we are told, have tasted the fruits of Western society and rejected them in favour of the ways of their own ancestors. In sum, modernity is represented in both videos as a choice between two incompatible worlds.

At the very centre of this contest, in theory, lies a conflict between an economic system built upon reciprocal exchanges and one dominated by money and the things and services money can buy ("commodities"). The shift from reciprocal gifts to purchased commodities would seem to have severe consequences. In reciprocal economies it is hard for any person to accumulate wealth, and thus traditional Melanesian societies are sometimes described as "egalitarian." It is not that inequality does not exist—certainly men generally dominate women, and some traditional societies had extremely powerful leaders—but they lack permanent socio-economic classes ranked according to wealth and privilege. Money potentially disrupts the obligation to return a gift in the simplest way possible: it can be stored away out of sight, whether under a mattress or in a bank account. At a deeper level, money and markets imply a different type of morality, one focused upon the individual who through hard work, good luck, or a combination of both succeeds on his or her own merits, with no help from others. Thus the introduction of money can be understood as the main engine of a series of transformations—from reciprocity between people to transactions mediated by abstract markets in which value is set; from self-reliance to dependence upon wages paid by employers; from a relatively egalitarian to an economically stratified society; from a moral emphasis upon one's obligations to kin and community to the celebration of the self-reliant individual (Akin and Robbins 1999; Bloch and Parry 1989; Burridge 1979).

There are signs of such a transformation in Maisin society. There can be little doubt that many imported goods have made life easier. No villager today would want to clear a garden using stone tools, even if they still possessed the knowledge to make them. Parents appreciate the medicines that have saved the lives of countless children, and builders praise the superiority of steel nails over bush twine in constructing the framework of houses. Yet a dependence on commodities comes at a cost. Few Maisin believe that they have enough money for what they need. The more that people become accustomed to things like tinned fish and rice, the more they perceive them as necessities rather than supplements. People thus spend a great deal of time and energy, in the household and in community meetings, discussing how to make money and diagnosing failed economic initiatives. A second cost is increasing divisions within the community. Unlike garden produce, money doesn't rot and can be kept secret from kin and neighbours. It permits a greater independence of households and individuals at the expense of wider kinship and exchange networks, introducing new inequalities into a society built upon an egalitarian moral ethos. Those people blessed with a large number of employed relatives or with highly skilled tapa makers in the family have a little more of everything than their neighbours.

At every stage, however, Maisin have modified their understanding and use of money and commodities according to their received assumptions about reciprocity and morality. I witnessed an interesting example of this process of localization during my second Christmas in Uiaku. A young man arrived from Port Moresby for a two-month holiday with suitcases bulging with clothes. I was sitting with his family when he arrived and took note of each piece as it was carefully unpacked. By the evening of the next day, I found that most of the clothing had been shared among close kin, but a good number of pieces had been delivered to more distant relatives across the village. The parents told me that while they would have liked to keep more for themselves, people would have considered them selfish had they not given away most of the clothes.

The requirement to reciprocate is a constant refrain in Maisin society, and it shapes the way that villagers approach money and commodities. Parents continually remind children fortunate enough to make it to high school and find employment of their debt to those who raised them. Employed Maisin often have complained to me of the unrelenting pressure from relatives who request cash for everything from small change to buy cigarettes to funds to stock a village canteen. Maisin in towns host relatives who drop in on them and live at their expense for months at a time. Those who return to the villages can expect a hostile reception if they fail to bring a generous quantity of gifts. Often they are criticized in any case. Those who opt out, who fail to support people back in the village, risk breaking ties completely. On a couple of occasions when doing the household census I would learn from one family of a cousin working in town who had not been mentioned by the person's own father and mother. Inevitably, when I returned to the person's immediate family to ask why they had failed to mention him, I was told that he did not support his village family with remittances. "My son is dead," declared one father sadly.

The pressure to share extends to villagers who earn income from tapa sales, from ferrying villagers in motorized dinghies, or as remittances from employed relatives. Many people keep some of their funds hidden in savings accounts in distant banks, saving up for school fees and other major expenses. In any case, it does not pay to make too obvious a showing of personal fortune. When we first arrived in Uiaku, we found only a single residence with a corrugated iron roof. A Maisin man then working as an agricultural officer at the provincial capital had built it for his elderly father. The father was proud to possess such a fine house, but he used it only for storage, sleeping instead in a tiny bush house beside it. "Were I to live in it," he told me, "people might get jealous; they might talk about me"—a common reference to sorcery. Other families told me that they had refused offers from working relations to pay for iron roofs for the same reason.

Such attitudes may come across to Western readers as calculating and harsh. Still, they are merely the flip side of the positive expressions of sharing, especially the key value of *marawa-wawe*, of "love" within a family and social harmony at large. The pressures and the threats, direct and veiled, are real enough. Yet most people share what they have because it is the normal thing to do. If they have more, they take pleasure and some pride at demonstrating their generosity, their willingness to "care for" others (*kaifi inei*), another key value. While privately complaining about the burden, most employed Maisin willingly support their rural relatives. By sharing and thus participating in the moral community, they demonstrate their continued membership and the right they and their children enjoy to return to their ancestral lands.

The money and commodities that come into the villages eventually get consumed, but at the point they are shared, they cease acting as elements of a market economy and instead take on the functions of gifts in an economy based upon reciprocity. This has a number of consequences. The first is that many (but not all) of the inequalities produced by the remittance system get levelled out through village exchange networks. The second consequence has been that, particularly since the 1960s, money and goods have entered

Figure 2.5 Market day on the Uiaku mission station, June 2000. (Photo by J. Barker)

exchange networks that formerly carried mostly locally produced items. In much of Melanesia, increasing availability of money and commodities led at least initially to an efflorescence of exchange systems, both in everyday reciprocity and formal exchanges (Gregory 1982). Maisin probably started using cash and mass-produced commodities for formal exchanges like bride wealth in the 1920s. By the 1980s, these had become necessities. Instead of displacing the subsistence economy with its basis in kin and exchange relations, the cash sector of the economy appears to have actually subsidized its continuing existence (cf. Carrier and Carrier 1989).

In recent years the Maisin have become more tolerant of the inequalities money enables. One now finds households that are visibly better off than others. Villagers have also become more accustomed to using money within the village, at a small market where women sell produce to each other, to pay youth to clear gardens, or for admission to events sponsored by church or sports groups. For all that, reciprocity remains central to the Maisin economy and moral system. There is no hunger in Maisin communities; the requirement to share, to support others, is too compelling. Maisin are keenly aware of the dangers money can bring, of the threat it represents to their ancestral way of life. They need money; there is no turning back. Yet, at least for the time being, the Maisin appear to have been more or less successful in balancing the opposed logic of gift and commodity systems of value. As we shall see in later chapters, however, there has been a price to pay—an often acute shame over their "poverty" and a burning desire to find a road to money that nearly led the people to sell off their ancestral birthright. That the commonsense morality of reciprocity remains so powerful despite the challenges of modernity reflects in no small part the continuing vitality of intimate family relationships in Maisin village society, to which we now turn.

Notes

1. Large crocodiles are periodically seen in the wide river that divides Uiaku and Ganjiga, usually at night. In 1986, a teenage girl was killed while washing laundry, and in 2000 a close friend of ours was severely mauled in a crocodile attack.

2. See Chapter 3 for an example of such a story.

3. Kahn (1986) describes a similar attitude towards taro and "famine" among the Wamirans in Milne Bay Province. Food is symbolically elaborated in many Melanesian societies, closely bound up in the construction of gender, notions of the spiritual world, and the politics of leadership (Meigs 1984; Schwimmer 1973; Young 1971).

4. In the course of conducting structured interviews with 69 school children to investigate prosocial reasoning (Tietjen 1986), Anne engaged in a small but very revealing experiment. One day, at the conclusion of each interview, she gave the child a *toea* (penny), telling them that they were free to use it to buy gum from the trade store. If they preferred, they could instead give the penny to the church women's organization, the Mothers' Union, by dropping it in a tin at the door of our house. Our house wasn't visible from where Anne was working. At the end of the day, we were amazed to find that all but one of the children had donated to the church group (Tietjen, personal communication).

5. The classic work on reciprocity is Marcel Mauss's *The Gift* (*Essai sur la don*), first published in French in 1925 and still well worth reading (Mauss 1990 [1925]). It would be hard to find any study of a Melanesian society that does not discuss reciprocity, but works from the Trobriand Islands to the east of Collingwood Bay have been especially influential (Malinowski 1922; Weiner 1988). Discussions of gift exchange have figured centrally in anthropological discussions of gender, personhood, religion, economic change, and many other subjects (Godelier 1999; Robbins 2004; Schieffelin 1976; Strathern 1988; Sykes 2005).

6. At that time, the kina was worth slightly more than a US dollar. Following a series of economic crises in Papua New Guinea in the 1990s, the kina declined to less than US$0.25, causing considerable economic hardship as most manufactured items are imported. The prices for locally produced items, like tapa, have gone up over the years, but nowhere near the pace of inflation.

7. Papua New Guinea is home to many rare and spectacular insects, including the Queen Alexandra butterfly; with nearly a foot-long wingspan, it is the largest bird-wing butterfly in the world and is found only in the primary rainforests of Oro Province. Since the late 1970s, hundreds of villages across the country have taken up insect farming and collecting for a growing international market in exotic insects.

CHAPTER 3

THE SOCIAL DESIGN

I brought my freshly beaten tapa back to George and Mary Rose Sevaru's house, where I was staying in 1986, and hung it on a shaded clothesline to dry. When night came, I took it down, folded it twice lengthwise, and placed it under my sleeping mat to flatten it. The next day, I hung it on the clothesline behind the house to thoroughly dry in direct sunshine. It was now ready to paint. I was delighted when Lottie Ororogo and Martha Maiyova agreed to help me.

I prepared by observing Lottie design a cloth. Lottie was a widow in her late 50s. Thin but strong, she had recently undertaken her end-of-mourning ceremony, several years after the death of her husband, and proudly displayed the shell necklaces and the bright red shells lining her earlobes given by her in-laws to mark her full return to society. Lottie was among the last links to several abandoned traditions. As a young woman, she had acquired a V-shaped scar across her chest, burned on during the mourning period to honour a close relative. She had also participated in a custom that used to take place while the men were absent from the villages during the annual grass hunt. Women who had undergone facial tattooing together—who thus formed a kind of age cohort—would gather in the bush to tattoo each others' thighs and buttocks, areas of their bodies otherwise revealed only to lovers and husbands. Lottie had learned much about designing tapa and facial tattoos from her older sister, Nita Keru, a skilled and inventive artist and marvellous story teller (see Figure 1.2). It was pleasant to sit in the cool of Lottie's verandah as she rapidly sketched out a stunning design.

Prior to designing the cloth, women trim the edges with a knife. Often larger cloths are cut into smaller pieces as these sell more easily in the artifact market. One begins designing a cloth by applying an outline with a black dye called *mii*. The main ingredients are charcoal, made from the dried husks of coconuts, and the leaves of a creeper called *wayangu*, which produces a milky

Figure 3.1 Lottie Ororogo designing her cloth, 1986. (Photo by J. Barker)

sap that turns pitch black when wet. The recipe involves cutting up a quantity of *wayangu* leaves into a bowl or coconut shell and then mixing in the charcoal and some water, resulting in a sooty black mash. Some people also add a type of clay found behind Sinapa village that they say improves the density of the dye. The *mii* can be used immediately or over a few days by adding water as the mash dries out. As they decompose in the pot, however, the *wayangu* leaves produce an unpleasant odour and attract flies.

Women usually design several pieces of tapa at one sitting. When I arrived at Martha's house in the late afternoon, the favoured time for designing tapa, I found her and Lottie already hard at work on their own cloths. Each of us had our own pot of *mii*. As we set to work, there was little talking. Women usually design their cloths alone. Drawing a pattern takes concentration, but most women find it a peaceful and relaxing activity.

I was ready for my lesson. I already knew that there would be little or no verbal instruction. Maisin girls learn to make tapa, as with other tasks, by watching and imitating their elders. I had seen tapa being designed dozens of times, but as I nervously picked up my brush, I spent a few moments studying my teachers at work.

The method of folding an *embobi* skirt results in four panels (the longer *koefi* loin cloth has eight). In the eastern Maisin villages, many women draw across the panels so that the entire tapa is covered by a single design. Most Uiaku women, however, prefer to frame the design within single panels, replicating it four times.[1] A few women at this time were experimenting with commercial brushes, but I wanted to use traditional instruments—white palm twigs of varying thicknesses, with ends shaven to reveal stiff bristles. Following the example of my teachers, I braced my back against a house post and stretched my legs out straight, a flat board across my lap and the dye bowl close to hand. Next, I folded my cloth over, leaving a single panel exposed on the smoother side that had been the inner surface of the bark strip. I took up my brush in the proper position between thumb and forefinger with the pinky extended to guide my hand over the cloth, dipped the end into my pot of *mii*, and placed brush to cloth to make my first bold stroke. What emerged was an indistinct grey smudge. I tried again, this time pushing the tip of my brush well into the black mash. This resulted in a satisfactorily black line but also little piles of soot that smeared my cloth when I tried to brush them off. Moving *mii* from pot to cloth requires a knowledgeable and delicate touch.

The Maisin make only a few standardized designs. Most of these are emblems (known as *kawo* or *evovi*) belonging to clans that possess the sole right to make and wear them. These can never be sold.[2] A few gifted tapa designers have also created stylized representations of animals or spirits. Nita Keru, for instance, painted beautiful abstract butterflies, one of which now graces my study. Such special designs remain the property of the artist. Most cloths, however, bear abstract paintings. Some tapa makers etch the design on the sand or occasionally on paper prior to drawing the outline. Most just keep it in their heads. Every cloth is unique, but the more prolific tapa makers develop personal styles.

Designing requires a good visual memory. In Uiaku, the women usually begin with a single panel. They etch out the design with *mii* in parallel lines, allowing space for the red dye (*dun*) to be applied later. Once the design of one panel is complete, they lay the cloth aside to work on another while it dries. When they return to the first cloth, skilled tapa makers only glance quickly at their previous execution before turning it over to repeat the design on another panel. All four panels of an *embobi* will be completed this way. In the case of the eight-panelled *koefi*, only the middle six panels receive designs, usually much simpler than those on a typical woman's skirt. The panels always match fairly closely, but there are little variations, the results of tricks of memory or slight differences in the size of the panels.

I had given my design some thought, making a preliminary sketch in my notebook. A small crowd gathered as I gingerly pushed the black *mii*, sooty centimetre by sooty centimetre, across the cloth. As the pattern began to emerge, despite the fits and starts, I started to relax a little. Not bad! Then I noticed that everyone had gone silent. I looked up to see the entire group, including Lottie and Martha, staring at my cloth. They were clearly puzzled. Martha ventured that I wasn't drawing the lines in a way that would contain the red dye (*dun*). I traced the edges of the parallel lines with the end of my brush and she reluctantly agreed that they *were* drawn correctly. Yet she and the others continued to worry, certain that I had made a mistake. No matter how "Maisin" it appeared to me, my design clearly offended the local aesthetic sense. The Maisin way of learning and associated vocabulary, however, did not allow for a very exact critique. The Maisin use only a few words to indicate design motifs—"circle," "dot," "line," and so forth. Tapa makers may praise a design or state that it is "wrong," but they cannot easily give instructions in how to make it "right." Like a young girl, I was learning to design tapa by imitating the experts. Yet I was not a child. Simple as my design was, it was still much more ambitious than the scrawled lines of a five- or six-year-old. Although I have never considered myself much of an artist, I had nonetheless internalized my own cultural aesthetic which, despite my good intentions, must have guided my hand across the cloth.

Once the basic design was completed on all four panels, I began the tedious task of placing little dots of *mii* regularly along the outer edges of the parallel lines. Adding the dots, known as *sufifi*, is always done and is another indication of an underlying aesthetic at work. When I finished, I placed my tapa on the sand to dry in the hot sun, close to the several pieces Lottie and Martha had decorated while I had struggled with my single cloth. Martha spread a mat in the shade and brought out refreshments. Lottie pulled a completed tapa from her string bag and laid it out for me to sit on. It was the beautiful piece I had watched her design a few days earlier. Following Maisin custom, once I sat on the cloth, it was mine.

The design on a tapa cloth bears a number of similarities to a society. The circumstance of making a tapa and the form the design takes are always somewhat unique. Yet there are social conventions that guide the creation of tapa and aesthetic judgements of the quality of particular designs. These conventions do not exist in written law codes or constitutions. They are passed between the generations and are learned so thoroughly that people do not need to reflect upon them. They form a type of common sense. The main job of a social anthropologist is to discover and explore these underlying rules and conventions. We can rely only partly on what people explicitly tell us about their social norms. We must also look for behavioural patterns as well as the ways that typical behaviours sometimes contradict what people think ought to happen. Life in apparently "simple" societies like those found in rural Papua New Guinea is amazingly complex. All the same, we find patterns in the ways that people deal with complexity, deeply held values and conventions that provide guidelines for living. The challenges and opportunities of life lead to both the reproduction and transformation of _____ ver time. Maisin society is not _____ nd new, conventional and in _____ etween ancestral frameworks a _____

Also like _____ elements that fit together to p _____ hree key facets of Maisin social organization: the socialization of children into gendered adults, the formation of kin-based groups and categories, and the creation of alliances between groups through marriage exchanges and life transition ceremonies. While much has changed in Maisin society over the past century, the conventions of social organization have proven amazingly resilient, providing one of the strongest links to the ancestral past.

MAKING SOCIAL PERSONS[3]

The Maisin love children. People often expressed pity that Anne and I were childless. This concern at one point gave rise to a rumour that, as rumours tend to do, swept through the village with preternatural speed. I was across the river working in Ganjiga when I heard "Annie's pregnant!" I rushed back home to inform my very surprised wife of the happy news! Of course, people were disappointed by the truth but much relieved upon my return in 1997 to learn that we had finally had a child. The Maisin consider it a very bad thing to be alone. Orphans, unmarried adults, and childless couples appear anomalous. Folk tales often feature orphans who are forced to leave their villages because they have no parents to feed them. By the same token, the Maisin fret that childless couples will be left with no one to care for them when they become t[...]alamity never happens [...]ers assure that the old ar[...]elderly couples are given[...]eft alone. Still, the conce[...]nd neighbours. The Mais[...] fear them, for it is well known that sorcerers prefer their own company.

[handwritten annotation: Maisin consider is very bad to be alone. A moral person for Maisin is one who interacts / exchanges with others.]

A moral person, for the Maisin, is one who interacts with others. As we saw in the previous chapter, the Maisin take exchange to be the paradigmatic interaction. Put most simply, the job of turning a child into a social person requires incorporating them into exchange networks and teaching them the values of reciprocity. Caregivers typically scold a child who grabs for food or refuses to share something with others with the phrase *saa tamatan ka*—"Not human!" Similarly, people speak of adults who act selfishly as being no better than dogs and pigs. To be human in this highly cooperative culture is to exchange.

In that sense, a newly born baby is not yet socially human.[4] Its conception results from the mingling of fluids in the womb, a balanced donation of blood from the mother and semen from the father. Since women are assumed to possess a large quantity of blood, Maisin say that pregnancy requires several acts of intercourse with the same man to bring the semen into balance. Too much semen, however, will harm the fetus. As Anne has documented, Maisin consider pregnant women and newborn children to be extremely vulnerable to harm and traditionally impose a wide variety of pro[...]es. "Pregnant women are[...]ry" and thus subjected[...]as covering their breas[...]tive (Tietjen 1985:124).[...]k, as its soul is not yet f[...]usually experienced female relatives and, unusual for Melanesia, the father—take precautions. During the birth and for a few days of confinement afterwards, the mother is surrounded by kin both to take care of her and to ward off spiritual attacks. The umbilical cord and placenta are wrapped in tapa and taken to the bush to be buried or placed high in a tree. If these are eaten by animals, Maisin say the spirit will not attach properly and the child will suffer from madness. The person who takes the package into the bush must return by the same route, acting as a guide to the child's spirit, which might otherwise

[handwritten annotation: newborns + pregnant women are closely monitored by kin. easily attacked by spirits - vulnerable]

become lost. About a week after the birth, if everything goes well, the mother places her baby comfortably on a pillow in a string bag and carries it to her garden. At each fork or crossroad in the path, she places a token to help the baby's spirit find its way home—crossed sticks representing spears for a boy and grass rings, symbolizing the straps used to carry bundles of firewood, for a girl. After spending some time in the garden, the mother calls out, "Come, we'll go home now!" She'll do this every time she goes to the garden until the baby begins to smile and recognize people, the sign that body and spirit are uniting (Tietjen 1985).

A baby remains in this nebulous state of not being firmly human for upwards of a year. If it dies during this period—a not uncommon tragedy in an area of endemic malaria and other tropical diseases—the parents bury the child quietly in the bush. During this time, the baby remains nameless. Its acquisi[...] [a name signals the parents' confidence that it] will survive. Anthropol[...]ing mistakes and being [...] [i]n the naming of babies. [...] We asked the baby's ol[...] For several days, we spoke of Amura, whose vaguely French-sounding name we thought matched her beauty. When Frieda got wind of this, she paid us a visit. "Who told you her name is Amura?" she demanded. "*Amura* means 'nothing'! They were telling you the baby doesn't have a name yet." A few weeks later, Frieda and Gideon decided to name their daughter "Ani Baka," after Anne. As we'll see later in this chapter, people who use reciprocal kinship terms are expected to have very close and supportive relationships. The same is true of namesakes, who call each other *nombi*.

A mother typically breastfeeds a new child for 18 months to two years. She provides the main source of care during this period, but increasingly over time other members of the household and extended family pitch in. The Maisin say that an infant possesses little *mon seramon*, the mental and physical dexterity necessary for survival. Unlike Western culture, the Maisin do not associate physical and personality traits with biological parentage. The provision of food and guidance not only allows children to mature but shapes their physical appearance. Maisin thus refer to an adopted child as someone who is "fed" by their foster parents and grows up to resemble them. This nurturing relationship is conceptualized as an exchange. During the time of dependence, a child must "respect" (*muan*) their caregivers by being obedient to their requests. The huge debt incurred during childhood is expected to be reciprocated later by caring for aging parents and senior relatives. The Maisin never let their grown children forget this debt.

[handwritten annotation: babies are not given names until approx. 1 year of age]

Childhood is a time of great freedom. From the moment they can walk, infants spend much of their days in the company of other children, freely roaming about the village and gardens under the watchful eye of older siblings or cousins, although rarely far from their households (Tietjen 2006). They play games, visit relatives who give them treats, and take long naps when it pleases them. The degree of liberty can be surprising for a Westerner. I have never gotten used [...] through the village, wh[...] nething that bothers the [...] old children when they [...] f themselves ("Not hum[...] ctivity, take pleasure in their antics, and soothe their wailing when they have a tumble. What they don't do much is instruct them. Young children learn adult tasks primarily by watching, mimicking, and pitching in. As they get older, they are given more responsibilities. By the time they are eight or nine, children typically take on a wide variety of daily chores ranging from sweeping plazas, washing dishes, scraping coconut for cooking, and tending their own garden plots (Tietjen 1989:38–39). Work and play together serve to reinforce the prime social value of interdependence (Tietjen 1985).

When they turn six or seven, children encounter a very different mode of interaction in the community school. There they receive authoritative instruction in the mysteries of letters and numbers from a teacher who does not provide gifts of food and advice in exchange for their obedience. Their behaviour in school is highly regimented. Those who break the rules, by skipping classes or mocking the teacher, are subject to discipline. Rather than an exchange relationship, the school runs on the singular authority of the teachers. School thus provides children with their first exposure to the more individualistic disciplinary orientations based upon the measurement of time, work, and money familiar to members of industrialized societies. Different as these are from village experience, few children seem to have trouble adjusting to the new expectations. However, these forms of authority do not transfer back into behavioural patterns in the village. This is likely because "Maisin children spend much of their time when not in school caring for their younger siblings," thus reinforcing "empathy, patience, and other qualities that are beneficial in forming and maintaining relationships with others" (Tietjen 2006:65).

Gender Roles

Young boys and girls spend a great deal of time in each other's company. Sisters and brothers tend to be especially close, an alliance that continues into adulthood. From a very early age, however, children are prodded into gendered roles.

73

Figure 3.2 Ani and Sivonne Ifoki, 1982. Older siblings spend much of their day caring for younger brothers and sisters. (Photo by A.M. Tietjen)

Walking through the village, one comes across little ~~gi~~ ing up debris around th~~e~~ in the river. Girls are i~~n~~ heir mothers by caring f~~or~~ f the myriad other tasks but by their mid-teens t~~hey~~ ing trips and helping with house repairs.

[handwritten annotation: gender Roles: girls: cook, make mats, etc. boys: hunt, fish, house repairs]

Many youths spend a considerable part of their adolescence away from the villages attending distant high schools. The boys and girls who remain behind live largely separate lives. Teenage boys enjoy considerably more freedom of action than girls. One frequently sees or hears them roaming in groups through the villages late at night. In some cases, a group of male friends will build their own house as an independent base of action.[5] In the past, dances provided the main opportunity for romantic liaisons. Young people would don decorations and gather on the beaches during full moons, dancing to the steady rhythm of drums until dawn. If a couple were attracted to each other they would arrange to meet later. Girls often took the initiative in organizing trysts in the bush or even in the girl's house, using a younger sibling as a go-between. Today there are probably more opportunities for young people to get together—at sports meets and Christian fellowship meetings, for example—but few that are not under the watchful eyes of parents. Most adults disapprove of premarital sex, an attitude almost certainly not held by their ancestors. Still, judging from the gossip and number of babies born to single mothers, it still goes on.[6]

The Maisin used to mark the transition to adulthood with rites of passage. The most elaborate of these, the *kisevi* ceremony for first-born children, still occasionally takes place. I describe it towards the end of this chapter. In the distant past, I'm told, clans also initiated adolescent boys in a ceremony in which elders would decorate them and then share a feast. Girls had their own distinctive rite of passage in which their faces were elaborately tattooed with graceful blue-black swirls and geometric designs, resembling tapa designs. Tattooing was once a widespread custom across the Pacific Islands, including in Papua New Guinea (Barton 1918; Gell 1993). Anne and I were fortunate enough to observe one of the last tattooings in the early 1980s just before the practice was abandoned (Barker and Tietjen 1990). Anne witnessed the painful operation. After tracing a design on the girl's face with black ink made partly from pot soot, the tattooist used a needle to break the skin and push the dye underneath, wiping away blood as she proceeded. After allowing scabs to form and fall off and the swelling to subside, the tattooist repeated the operation, upwards of ten times in all, over a period of a month to six weeks. Usually several girls were tattooed together, remaining secluded in the tattooist's house

during the op[...] ed in traditional finery, [...] een of their
skin and bet[...] layed their
new faces ar[...] ouncement
that they we[...] 3 and 5).

*[handwritten note: puberty ceremonies: girls get tattoos on their faces * strength + endurance for female adulthood]*

Puberty ceremonies serve a variety of purposes. The [...]doned male initiations reinforced clan identity and membership. The female rite of passage was different. It was organized by households for their daughters and was not accompanied by public celebrations, feasting, or ceremonial exchanges. The overt purpose was to make the girls attractive by replacing their "blank" faces with "beautiful" ones designed by the tattooist. The tattoo equally stood for the strength and endurance required of female adulthood. The custom lapsed, we were told, because during the 1970s and 1980s so many girls left the villages to attend high school and to marry. In the early 2000s, Anna-Karina Hermkens, a Dutch anthropologist working in Airara village, was told that the custom ended because young women feared the pain, with some telling her that tattoos "spoiled the face" (Hermkens 2013:57). This is regretted by those who continue to regard women's tattoos as not only a key custom but also a mark of women's beauty and strength. Some hope that some girls in the future will agree to be tattooed before the last artists die out. I've heard that a few girls have received tattoos elsewhere in Collingwood Bay in recent years.

It is certainly true that adult women need to be tough. They work extremely hard compared to most men. Around 1905, the Anglican lay missionary, Percy John Money, took a photograph he labelled "Man the Protector—Woman the Porter." It depicts a man with a spear flung over his shoulder walking ahead of a woman whose shoulders are sagging under the weight of a loaded string bag, with a child riding on top. This was Money's best-known photograph, reproduced in several books and a regional trade magazine, the *Pacific Islands Monthly*. Hardly a day has passed during my visits to Uiaku when I have not witnessed an identical scene. Walk to the beach at dusk and you are sure to see women returning from a hard day's work in the gardens, straining under heavy loads of food and firewood as they head home to make the evening meal.

When not tending gardens, bearing loads, or cooking, the women are engaged in many other tasks: repairing mats, beating tapa, mending clothes, making string bags, and so forth. Unlike men, who spend pleasant evenings and sometimes days visiting friends, women have few opportunities for socializing. Socializing in any case usually entails more work. Public ceremonies such as bride wealth exchanges or church festivals provide women with the best opportunities to mingle with kin and friends but always while preparing and cooking food. Men appear to have it pretty good. Consider another

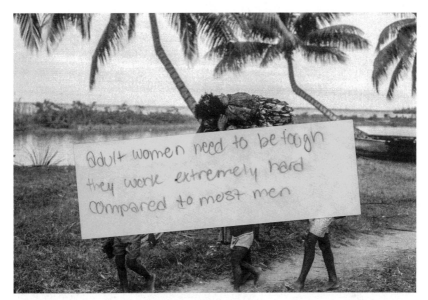

(handwritten note on image) Adult women need to be tough they work extremely hard compared to most men

Figure 3.3 Returning from the garden, 1982. Arthur, Clara, and Lincoln Sevaru accompany their mother, Mary Rose Sikana, as she returns from the garden bearing a heavy load of firewood and food. (Photo by A.M. Tietjen)

archetypical sce[...] peaks volumes. Senior [...] *Seniority of Males* [...] or of a covered shelter, c[...] under the shade of trees [...] inding whatever shade t[...] en the meeting ends, after several hours of conversation, young women bring refreshments. Climbing up to the platform at the end furthest from the men, they carry platters of tea and biscuits, crawling on their knees across the rough surface with eyes downcast, showing respect for the seniority of the males.

In Maisin thought, women and men exist in a complementary opposition (cf. Errington and Gewertz 1987; Lepowsky 1993). This is implied in conception beliefs, the idea that a child forms through the equal mixing of a woman's blood and a man's semen. Female and male are understood as essentially different but required to complete each other. This assumption underlies many other everyday assumptions. Maisin tend to associate females with soft perishable materials and men with hard and more durable products, that is, tapa cloth and mats as opposed to shell money and drums, each made only by one sex or the other (cf. Teilhet 1983). As in many Melanesian societies, the Maisin consider male and female essences to be dangerous to one another in certain circumstances. Thus, a man should not step over his pregnant wife nor a woman ever step over her husband for fear of causing sickness. Women face more restrictions then men. They should not bathe upstream from men, and it is thought that they will destroy the usefulness of hunting or fishing spears if they step over them. Compared to many Melanesian societies, however, the restrictions surrounding interactions between the sexes are fairly relaxed. Indeed, the expectation that husbands will assist in their children's births is extraordinary in a cultural region noted for male fears of female blood. By the same token, women do not go into seclusion when menstruating, although I am told their partners avoid sex during their periods.

Gender roles in all societies get reinforced in a variety of ways. Around evening fires, elders relate stories that endorse an idealized understanding of the complementary relationship of women and men by showing what happens when such a relationship is violated, as in the following tale:

A man cleared an area. He left the rubbish to dry and then set fire to it. He worked very hard indeed. He cleared a very large garden and soon it began producing food. But the man grew tired of this work and took to hanging around the village. His wife would go to the garden to harvest the taro. With nowhere to plant them, she had to leave the taro tops, which soon began to rot. She complained, "Husband, I cut off the taro tops but now they are rotting." Yet the husband paid no attention. He merely slept the nights through and spent the days visiting friends in the village. Eventually the wife finished the taro. She told her husband, but he paid no mind and kept hanging around the village day after day. Soon they were out of food.

One day, the wife called her children. "This afternoon, we will go to where some people have cut down sago palms. We will collect the ends of the logs and use whatever pith remains to make sago. Once we have eaten, we will feel awake and strong again. Then we can sleep well." So off they went. They spied the remains of a sago log that had been beaten for its pith. The mother said to her children, "Wait. I will look for a *yaau*" (a stick used to pry off the hard outer bark of the sago palm). As soon as she broke through the bush to the cut sago, she transformed herself into a grunting pig. The children also became pigs. Their mother called to them and they followed her into the bush. (Related by Frederick Bogara, 1 January 1982)

This story reveals a key difference between humans and pigs. Both take food from gardens, but only humans have the ability to make new gardens from old. The story portrays the husband and wife working completely separately. The husband makes the garden; his wife harvests it. Yet the garden cannot be reproduced without the aid of the man's digging stick to replant taro tops. The household soon consumes the entire taro crop and, with no means of reproducing it, faces starvation. The woman and her children are reduced to scrounging food from the debris left from making sago, which also attracts bush pigs. Hence, they become pigs themselves. The breakdown of the cooperative, procreative relationship between woman and man is thus equated in the story to the diminishing of the distinction between human and animal.

This ideal was often expressed to me in casual conversations as well as more formal interviews, but usually in an unintentionally revealing way. Maisin have a horror of being alone. The worst type of sorcery attack, described in Chapter 4, occurs to people foolish enough to walk home alone from their gardens, and many folk tales revolve around the figure of abandoned orphans—a situation virtually unthinkable in actual life. Similarly, Maisin often volunteered that men and women cannot survive without mutually contributing their labour. Yet this idea was always expressed, by women as much as men, as a scenario in which a man lacks a sister or a wife. "Who would bring his food and cook for him?" they plaintively asked.

The point [   ]ands more of women th[   ]en largely escape. This i[   ]ng people are expected [   ]d, in-laws, there is consic[   ]. The lives of newly mar[ried women are especially tough. They must meet the] unceasing demands of their husband's kin while submitting meekly to frequent tongue-lashings by their mothers-in-law. The tangible assets that Maisin women bring into a mar[   ]pass property to their ch[   ]which greatly increases t[   ]ition, women bring in m[   ]es from relatives in to[   ]hard run the risk of the[m returning to their own families, taking land rights] and, if bride wealth has not been paid, their children with them.[7] My village census revealed that it was not uncommon for a young woman to partner with a number of prospective husbands before settling down.

Maisin women have often told me that married life is "hard" (*wenna bejji*). Yet this was usually said less in protest than as an expression of cultural norms. As in all societies, individual experiences vary. Anne and I occasionally heard stories of husbands beating their wives, of adulterous scandals, and, rarely, of rapes. Yet the men who were known for "belting" their wives were gossiped about as "rubbish," and I heard of several incidents where a woman's brothers intervened to stop an abusive husband. Elderly Maisin insisted that women's lots had improved with Christianity. In the old days, they noted, a woman's head was shaved clean once she married; she could no longer make herself beautiful and join in dances, but now women are free to laugh, see their families regularly, go to high school, and find paying jobs elsewhere in Papua New Guinea. Yet these same elders often complained that young women today have too much freedom, that they don't work as hard as their parents did and "play too much" with boys. I've seen little evidence that this is more than nostalgia. Moreover, during her fieldwork in Airara in the 2000s Anna-Karina Hermkens (2013) recorded a disturbing number of incidents of young women being beaten by their husbands, suggesting that violence against women is on the increase. In Papua New Guinea as a whole, women experience elevated levels of violence, particularly in the urban areas where they are often separated from protective kin (Zimmer-Tamakoshi 1997).

We'll return in Chapter 6 to the question of how Maisin women's lives are changing. In summarizing this section, it's important to note that while women and men in Maisin society adhere to a set of behavioural expectations, they are not robots. Personalities differ, often considerably. The cultural system tends to favour meek women and assertive men, but the opposite also occurs and, within limits, is not considered improper. Many of my best informants on m___ ___ ___ ___men who, usually in th___ ___ ___ ___ freely and openly, whet___ ___ ___ ___ men monopolize talk ___ ___ ___ ___istening and often mak___ ___ ___ ___women have more latitude to speak their minds. The Maisin are especially respectful of elderly women, who are valued for the depth of their knowledge of traditions. Yet younger women can be assertive, especially when they feel that their husbands are not providing sufficient support for themselves and their children. Take the example of "Alice" (a pseudonym), the youngest of three wives in one of the five polygynous families living in Uiaku in the early 1980s. Spunky and funny, Alice was not afraid to bend gender rules on occasion. One day I heard women shrieking. I ran to the riverbank, thinking that someone had drowned or been attacked by a crocodile. Instead, I stood witness with a crowd of upset women as Alice waded ashore with her co-wives, each bearing a string of small fish for their supper. The rule is that only men can fish. The women shouting abuse were ashamed and furious at Alice. She calmly and defiantly faced down their fury. Her husband had been away in town for more than a month, she declared, and few of his clan brothers had helped out with providing meat to his large family, so the women had done it for themselves. This was a gutsy act in a culture where people feel public shaming keenly and fear retaliation from sorcerers for individualistic acts. Still, Alice had made her point.

Her husband's brothers should have been helping out more. They did so now, and the incident was not repeated.

Not surprisingly, Maisin men universally support the gender status quo. Yet so do most women. Middle-aged and senior women are able to exercise a considerable amount of authority over their daughters and even more over daughters-in-law. They are quick to criticize (usually loudly) any sign of laziness or immodesty on the part of younger women under their command. If you ask villagers why they should treat men and women so differently, you will certainly get their universal answer for this type of question: "It's our tradition. It came from the ancestors." The larger lesson here is that, for the Maisin, personhood is not given by nature; it is made in the context of social relationships. Men and women do different sorts of things that together make society possible. Yet, as persons, they also share common moral ideals. Good persons respect and follow the advice of their elders and, when they themselves become elders, care for those who are younger by providing the necessities of life an[d] r own generation generc he state of social amity 'eople learn these values in of social organizatio

mother, father & children families

ALL IN THE FAMILY: KINSHIP, DESCENT, AND MARRIAGE

Maisin families resemble those found in Western countries in many respects. With few exceptions, people spend most of their lives in households organized around a mother, a father, and their children. Yet, as in the case of most small-scale societies, the Maisin have a much more extended experience of family relations than most Westerners are used to. In part, this is the outcome of generations of intermarriage within and between Maisin villages. Everyone is related to everyone else, often in myriad ways. However, it is also a reflection of how culture shapes understandings of family. As an undergraduate student, I found the study of kinship both fascinating and daunting. All humans have families, but there exists a wide range of cultural variation. Understanding another people's ideas about families as they play out in real life presents a special challenge, I suspect, because to do so we must come to grips with some of our own most deeply held assumptions about human nature.

Most Westerners assume that the terms they use to refer to their relatives reflect biological realities. We have one mother and one father. We distinguish them from uncles and aunts, just as we distinguish our sisters and brothers from our cousins. Anthropologists call this a "descriptive" kinship terminology system, characterized by the use of different kin terms for members of the core "nuclear family" and everyone else. (It is also known as an "Inuit" or "Eskimo" system as it is typical of those societies as well as European ones.) Maisin kinship terminology, however, belongs to the much more common "classificatory" type, which does not reserve special words for nuclear family members. To the naïve English ear, it can sound like individual Maisin have innumerable mothers, fathers, and siblings.[8] Moreover, what you call someone often bears little relation to their biological relationship or relative age. Thus Maisin happily told me of marrying their "brother," "grandmother," or "grandchild." If you have spent your life assuming that families are biological units, it takes a bit of a leap to appreciate a system that applies only secondary importance to blood relationships. In dealing with a community in which kinship terms do not distinguish between close and distant relatives, you have to remind yourself that the Maisin word for, say, "mother" conveys a different sense than its closest English equivalent.

This does not present a problem for a child who grows up knowing nothing but the local kinship system. The Maisin employ a variation of the "Iroquois-Dravidian" kinship terminology, the most common type in the world. This kind of system makes distinctions on the basis of generation, seniority, and sex. Put most simply, you refer to members of generations relative to your own by separate sets of kin terms. Within those sets, you make further distinctions on the basis of relative age and sex. Thus, as a Maisin male, I refer to my biological father, his brothers, and all of the men he calls "brother" by the term *yabi*.[9] I refer to my mother, her sisters, and every woman she calls "sister" by the term *yo*. However, I refer to the opposite sex siblings of my father *or* mother by the term *yaya* (that is to say, my father's sister or mother's brother). Turning to the generation after me, my male children as well as the children of my brothers and those men I call "brother" are referred to as *teiti* (son) or *morobi* (daughter). I would refer to my sister's children, however, as *yaya*—that is, by the same term that they use for me. Relationships marked by the use of reciprocal terms tend to be especially warm and supportive. Grandparents, for instance, share a common term—*abu*—with their children's children. Those who call each other *abu*, or more often the familiar *bu-bu*, greatly enjoy each other's company.

Maisin kinship terms vary somewhat depending on whether one is referring to someone else or addressing them directly. The diagrams in Figure 3.4 set out reference terms. In such standard anthropological kinship diagrams, the triangles represent males, the circles indicate females, and the equal sign stands for a marriage. Each level represents a generation, moving from oldest at the top to youngest at the bottom. Younger siblings are positioned to the

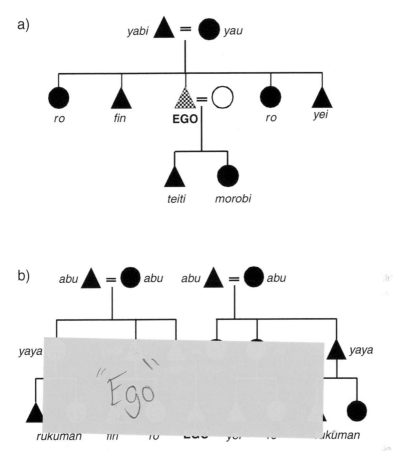

Figure 3.4 Maisin kinship terminology.[10] a) Maisin kinship reference terminology in the immediate (nuclear) family; b) Maisin kinship terminology in the extended family, indicating parallel and cross-cousins

left, older to the right. Maisin also have special terms for in-laws. Husbands and wives, for instance, are known as *fafi* and *sauki*.

Kinship terms are relative, dependent upon who is speaking. These diagrams assume that "Ego" is a male. If "Ego" were female, she would refer to her male siblings and parallel cousins as *ro* and her female siblings and parallel cousins as *fin* or *yei*.

Things get most interesting on one's own generational level. Again, assume that I am a male. I refer to my sister as *ro*. This is another reciprocal term: she also calls me *ro*. In contrast, I refer to my brothers by two different terms depending on their age relative to my own: as *yei* (older) or *fin* (younger). The term I use for siblings thus depends upon, first, their gender relative to my own and, second, their relative age if they are of the same sex as myself. Thus, if you are female, you refer to your brother as *ro* and older and younger sisters as *yei* and *fin* respectively. Things become slightly more complex when the categories get extended beyond immediate family to the people who, in English, we call cousins. The children of your father's brothers or mother's sisters are technically known as "parallel-cousins" while the children of your parent's opposite-sex siblings—that is, the children of those people you call *yaya*—are "cross-cousins." Cross-cousins share a reciprocal term, *rukaman*. Boys and girls often count *rukaman* among their closest friends. The relationship involves a great deal of joking and sexual banter during adolescence and beyond. In contrast, you address parallel-cousins using sibling terms, with one significant twist. The seniority of same-gender parallel-cousins is determined by the relation of their parent to your own, not by the actual age of the cousin. Thus, as a male, I refer to all of the male children of my father's older brother as *yei* and to all of the male children of his younger brother as *fin*, regardless of their actual ages. A female would do the same for the daughters of her father's male siblings and mother's female siblings. A cousin one refers to as *yei* might thus be considerably younger than oneself and vice versa.

It is a simple matter to incorporate newcomers into the system. Soon after Anne and I arrived in Uiaku, some of the older folk began to call us "daughter" and "son." We soon reciprocated. From there it was an easy matter to figure out what to call other people by following the lead of our kinspeople. In theory, the system has no limits. In their more enthusiastic moments, the Maisin talk about how conversion to Christianity made them *roisesinamme*, "brothers and sisters," to the entire world—a conceit that, given the expansive nature of their kinship system, is something more than a metaphor. All the same, biological desc[...] [...]ily relationships. One [...]ts as *taa besse*—literally [...] circle" for individuals. [...] defence if you are atta[...] needed (Lawrence 1984). The *taa besse* also marks the boundary for the incest taboo, the point at which sexual activities become permissible. Once they move to relatives beyond the *taa besse*, people usually cannot account for the kin terms they use with reference to actual shared ancestry; they instead take their cue from others. Thus if a man I call "father" (*yabi*) refers to another man as his "older brother" (*yei*), I know that I should also call that man *yabi* and refer to *his* male children as my "older brothers." Given the dense network of kin and marriage ties and the flexibility of the system, people often can come up with two or more possible kin terms for a particular person. Depending on circumstances, two distantly related women of the same age might thus refer to each other as older or younger sisters, as mother and daughter, or as cross-cousins. This is not a case of anything goes: the terms need to be plausible and both parties need to agree to them. The system, however, permits for a degree of negotiation unknown in European terminology systems.

Kin terms connote reciprocal expectations, although the strength of these vary with social distance. The *ro* relationship is ideally one of complementarity, for instance, while the *yei/fin* relationship denotes an asymmetrical relationship in which the senior partner takes care of the junior associate by offering good guidance, receiving "respect" and obedience in exchange. The *rukaman* cross-cousin relationship is idealized in Maisin folk tales as the model of symmetrical equivalence. Among close kin, the roles associated with the terms are more or less obligatory. The further one goes from close family, the more the terms provide a kind of template for idealized relationships that may or may not be enacted. Thus, when I first worked with Maisin, most of my male teachers—including several much younger than I—insisted on calling me *fin* ("younger brother"). And quite properly so, given the gift they were making of their superior knowledge. Yet when several of these same men approached me to make a gift towards the building of a new church, suddenly I was *yei* to their *fin*. And thus Maisin kinship terminology merges seamlessly into politics.

Descent Groups

The circle of kin that radiates outward from every individual is unique. This is because one's "kindred"—all those relatives traced through one's parents—are relative to a person's position in a family network and one's gender. Kinship terminology diagrams thus always specify an "ego" as a point of reference. All individuals draw upon their extended kin networks for various kinds of assistance, albeit to differing degrees. However, as in other small-scale societies, the Maisin also use principles of descent to organize themselves into more stable and well-defined social groups. Generally, they follow a unilineal rule of patrilineal descent, in which ancestry is traced through a series of male links. This is the most common pattern found in Papua New Guinea, although many of the societies to the east of the Maisin have matrilineal systems in which descent is traced through females. Regionally, one also finds several examples of cognatic descent systems, in which groups trace their descent from male and female ancestors.

The Maisin call descent groups "*iyon*," a word that they usually translate as "clan" and sometimes as "tribe." Such glosses, however, are misleading if we think of a clan or tribe as a distinct bounded group. *Iyon* is better translated as "division." The Maisin are born into a hierarchy of such divisions.

Depending on the circumstances, when people speak of their *iyon*, they may be referring to a group of households headed by brothers, to members of a village hamlet, or to one of several larger groups whose membership spans across the Maisin villages and beyond. It is usually clear from the context what level of grouping they mean.

It is useful here to make a distinction between a descent *group* and a descent *category* (Keesing 1975:29). A descent group is a going concern in which members actively associate with each other and hold common property and rights. Members of a descent category, on the other hand, tend to live apart and rarely if ever come together as a group. They possess less common property, and their association functions more as a shared identity. The line between group and category is fuzzy and shifting, but in practice every Maisin individual finds membership within a hierarchy of two or more lower-level *groups* and at least one higher-level *category*.

Maisin descent groups and categories are defined by reference to ever more distant founding ancestors. One can discern three levels. The smallest and most cohesive descent group is made up of males and their sisters (although not the children bo̶ _____ ____ ____ _____ from a male ancestor, typically a grandfa_____ _____ _____ _____ ce all the genealogical lir____ _____ _____ _____ Lineages have a physica____ _____ _____ _____ possible to their father'____ _____ _____ _____ ocal residence.[11] A man's wi̶f̶e̶ ̶r̶e̶m̶_____ _____ _____, but once bride wealth is paid, her children become members of the husband's lineage. Lineage members reside together within hamlets, forming cooperative working groups bound in generalized reciprocal relations. Those lineage members who have migrated to town also form part of this tightly knit group; migrants in paid employment send gifts of money and commodities first to their lineage members. Most tangible property passes down through the lineage. Fathers bequeath garden lands to their sons or, if they have no sons or the sons leave for the city, to the sons of their brothers. A man's fruiting trees, hunting spears, drums, magic, and other practical items usually pass down in the same lines.

Important as they are, lineages are not named, perhaps because they are impermanent. As generations succeed each other—as a fondly remembered grandfather becomes a great-grandfather, the memory of whose name gradually fades—older lineages break apart and new ones form. In contrast, "clans," which comprise the second level of descent group in Maisin society, do bear names and are thought of as permanent. They are conceived as all of the descendants of distant founding ancestors after whom they are named. Maisin clans include at least two lineages, but often several more and no doubt others that have become extinct and are forgotten. While a handful of elders may possess genealogical knowledge linking all present members back to the founding ancestor, most people simply accept the fact they belong to their fa... ... occupy their own haml... ...ages. A few of the large... ...any clans are further b... ...f the founder and rank...

land is passed down through small clans [handwritten annotation]

People often told me that land is passed down at the clan level, but a close study of actual patterns of inheritance showed that this is not true. Except in small clans (which operate much like lineages), clan mates tend to cooperate only on special occasions that involve feasting and formal exchanges with other clans rather than day to day. Yet clans form the keystone of an individual Maisin's identity. Migration narratives, whether fragmentary or elaborated, form part of a larger collection of symbolic properties that define clan identities. According to the histories related by elders, the ancestors emerged in possession of a number of emblems and ritual prerogatives and gained others en route to Collingwood Bay, the most distinctive of which are clan tapa designs known as *evovi*. A clan's estate may also include certain designs carved in wood or stone; names; special types of spatulas (used to spoon lime into one's mouth to chew with betelnut); forms of magic, songs, and ritual actions; and certain birds or plants to which the group shows "respect" by refusing to use or eat them.[13]

Collectively, clan properties are known as *kawo*—a much used and complex concept that in this context means something like "emblem." Some of these *kawo* may strike outsiders as rather esoteric. For instance, one clan claims the exclusive right to hold torches in both hands. I learned to be very careful around members of the Wofun clan after inadvertently acquiring a lovely tapa by praising its design; it turned out that one of their *kawo* obliges them to give away any object that is openly admired. In theory, the *kawo* belonging to each clan are distinctive. In practice, there is much overlapping that in turn gives rise to the occasional dispute over ownership. Still, the principle is clear: clan members share a common essence, which is confirmed in their histories and in the tangible presence of *kawo*. This common identity is further affirmed in the belief that sexual relations within a clan—even when the partners are not closely related—are incestuous. Clans are thus exogamous descent groups, that is, groups whose members must seek marriage partners from outside their membership.

Lineages and clans are descent *groups*. The highest and broadest level of association recognized by the Maisin, on the other hand, forms a *category*, as

Figure 3.5 Nigel Bairan and Priscilla Gaure wearing *kawo*, Ganjiga village, 1986. Note the *evovi* tapa design, the positioning of the large cowry shells, and the rooster plumes held in the teeth. These are all *kawo* emblems belonging to a branch of the Rerebin clan. (Photo by J. Barker)

members at this level do not share a common ancestor. The most significant of these associations are descendants of historic confederacies. After clans emerged from underground, according to the common accounts, they settled for a period along different stretches of the Musa River. Those who settled along the upper reaches are known as *Wo ari Kawo*. Clans settling along the middle section became known as *Mera ari Kawo*. (Some Maisin also speak of a third group, *Yun Fofo* ["water that is dirty"], that settled near the mouth of the river; others, however, group these clans with *Mera ari Kawo*.) The confederacies made their way separately by sea and over land to settle together at Gorofi, inland from Uiaku, before dispersing to their present sites after a series of conflicts.

According to Maisin elders, *Wo ari Kawo* and *Mera ari Kawo* engaged in competitive food exchanges in the old days. They were "food enemies" (*ruan rawa*) whose leaders garnered prestige in competitive feasts marked by days of dancing and feasting, culminating in a massive gift of raw food. The aim of the organizers was to create a spectacle and to build up the prestige of leaders by giving away more food than the opposing side could possibly match when their turn came. Leaders of the confederacies also sponsored even more spectacular inter-tribal feasts with non-Maisin villages in the region, to create war alliances or make peace after a period of hostilities (cf. Young 1971).

These functions have long lapsed, but oral traditions concerning Maisin origins and the old days of warfare and feasting continue to provide the basis for a key political and ritual distinction between two types of clans within the confederacies, known respectively as *Kawo* and *Sabu* (Barker 2005a).[14] The higher ranked *Kawo* clans have the right to host feasts and ceremonial dances in their hamlet plazas. In the past, they commanded the labour of their associated *Sabu* for food competitions and inter-tribal feasts. Members of the *Kawo* clans hold a number of prerogatives, which, like those for individual clans, are known as *kawo*. These include the right to wear rooster plumes in one's headdress when dancing, to speak first during public gatherings, to trim the edges of house thatch, and to erect a special ceremonial house during feasts. Because feasts provided the means by which the Maisin forged alliances, *Kawo* clans are also referred to as either "peace-makers" (*Sinan ari Kawo*) or as "owners of the drum" (*Ira ari Kawo*). *Sabu* clans lack special emblems but were considered to be leaders in warfare. They are thus also known as *Ganan ari Kawo* ("holders of the fighting spear"). *Wo* and *Mera* are alternatively known by the names of their two leading *Kawo* clans, Gafi-Simboro and Ume-Rerebin respectively. These paired clans are in turn thought of as older and younger brothers. Similarly, people speak of *Kawo* and *Sabu* clans as brothers, thus connoting an asymmetrical reciprocal relationship. Like younger brothers, *Sabu* are said to be impetuous and easy to anger. Their associated *Kawo* act as older brothers by "taking care" of them, tempering their anger with calming advice to which the *Sabu* should listen respectfully. The Maisin today often refer to the leading men of *Kawo* clans as "chiefs." Such men are respected and have influence; however, they are not chiefs in the usual sense of the term as they do not inherit an office and their effective authority is quite limited.

In sum, then, every Maisin is a member of a lineage and a high- or low-ranking clan within a confederacy. Each successive level encompasses a larger number of people and takes on distinct functions. Men inherit tangible property primarily from their fathers and fathers' brothers within lineages; they locate their houses in areas of the villages belonging to named clans from which they derive their strongest sense of identity; and as members of clans, they identify with historic confederacies with the rank of either *Kawo* or *Sabu*.

Variations on the Theme of Descent

The descent system, as I've described it so far, appears orderly. Indeed, at first this is the way things appeared to me. Less than a month after arriving in Uiaku, I sent one of my research supervisors a lengthy letter setting out the system. I was quite proud that I had been able to work it out so quickly from what a handful of people had told me about the proper duties of fathers, clan histories, and traditional leadership. People insisted that each clan possessed a separate history as well as distinct symbols and urged me to record these along with the genealogies that would trace their roots back to their founders. These oral histories, I was told, had not been previously recorded, as only clan members could tell them to each other. Since I wasn't myself a member of a clan, I could be a neutral, honest scribe. As I prepared for this great task, I imagined that as I compiled the clan histories and genealogies a massive epic would emerge, a sort of Maisin *Lord of the Rings*.

Alas, things didn't work out that way. A few elders told wonderfully rich clan histories, and I collected a great deal of information about such things as clan tapa designs and the duties of *Sabu* and *Kawo* leaders. However, most people only knew fragments of their histories and even less of genealogy; many of the clan emblems, I was told, had been forgotten. More troubling, I soon discovered that histories and claims to particular *kawo* often overlapped. Elders were adamant that they were giving me the unvarnished truth and warned me not to listen to members of other clans who were "stealing" their stories. It soon dawned on me that the main reason people had been eager for me to record the histories and genealogies was their hope that I would somehow certify their version as the true one, backing up their claims to have been the first to arrive in Collingwood Bay (and thus the true owners of the land). I had stepped into a political quagmire. It was then I realized that I could never publish the histories, although I have provided copies of the texts to clan members over the years.

I don't [...] me, although doubtless [...] had failed [...] constantly [...] of a clan a[...] of these th[...] groups by [...] However, [...] census re[...] member in [...] occupying [...] tion of on[...] househol[...] cial system is, the identity history—all to legitimate d purpose.[15] y first village a single male (the children), the popula- de up of four the course of generations, some clans have divided due to disputes or in search of better gardening lands, resulting in the present mix of concentrated and dispersed clans. The growing and shrinking of clans and the movement of members has no doubt gone on since time immemorial even if this reality is not acknowledged in oral traditions, which tend to refer to clans as if they were equal in size and formed coherent bodies.

To make matters even more complicated, many clans have internal divisions. Several are referred to alternately by their "big name" and by the names of paired sub-clans, ranked as older and younger, who are said to be the direct descendants of two ancestral brothers. For example, one can speak of the Wofun clan alternately as "Wondi-Joba." In some cases, sub-clans may possess different insignia, and in at least one case a single clan possesses both *Sabu* and *Kawo* branches. The more details I learned, the more I appreciated that the singular term "clan" was a matter of convenience—for me, not the Maisin, who referred to any and all social groups from lineages to entire countries as "*iyon*." Usually one can fairly easily identify exogamous descent groups that correspond to "clan" in the anthropological sense. Yet consider the case of "Rerebin." This name is claimed by groups in all Maisin villages. In Uiaku proper, it designates a descent group, but elsewhere it forms a descent category. Rerebin in the village of Ganjiga is made up of three large descent groups, each with its own distinct set of clan emblems and ancestral name. Most significantly (at least for an anthropologist), while the component groups are exogamous, there are no restrictions on marriages between them. This would seem to place Ganjiga Rerebin at a more general level than clan. However, members became very upset with me when I referred to the component groups by name. Not only was Rerebin their "real name," they told me, but those folks across the river in Uiaku had no right to use it. At the other extreme, the three surviving members of the Simboro clan all claimed to represent independent branches with their own emblems that had been introduced generations ago by non-Maisin women who had married into the society and brought their fathers' *kawo* with them.[16]

As the [...] ons and claims piled up, [...] hat the Maisin had been [...] bt to torment me! The [...] ly when a row breaks o[...] in that people are forgetting their ancestral rights and identities and that, as they do so, the boundari[...] re is probably some trut[...] vernment and mission, n[...] hose identities were like[...] ect more than a little no[...] orical charters for Maisin descent groups provide a general framework, but they also permit negotiations, political manoeuverings, and change. This is nothing new. The current descent system is one of many examples of culture providing for both continuity and change in the simultaneous process of replicating an ancestral pattern while adapting to the conditions and potentialities of the present.

Marriage and the Making of Alliances

A Maisin child is born into a household that reaches outwards through a hierarchy of descent groups and a radiating network of kindred. Together these provide security and a framework for action. A person's success in life depends on their ability to meet responsibilities to close kin and to create and maintain bonds with more distant relatives and strangers. The most important of these bonds is marriage. As in many cultures, the Maisin regard marriage not merely as a union between two individuals but as an alliance between households, extended families, and clans. This is not to say that love and affection are not involved. The rich oral traditions related by elders over the evening fires include many romantic stories of courtship. While the emotional bond between husband and wife varies as much here as in most places, I've been impressed by the stability of Maisin marriages once children appear and even more so by the evident affection most spouses show for each other. Yet, if you ask villagers why people marry, you inevitably receive very pragmatic answers: people need children to care for them in their old age and to replace them when they are gone, assuring the survival of their households and lineages; clans rely on marriages to recruit new members who learn the histories and take possession of the *kawo* emblems, thus allowing the clan to

[Handwritten annotations overlaid on text:]
Success in life = meet responsibilities to close kin + have bonds with relatives + strangers
marriage: an alliance between households, extended familys and clans.

reproduce itself through time; and the often complex exchanges triggered by marriage provide aspiring clan leaders with their best opportunity to show off their managerial abilities.

Clans are exogamous units: their members must seek mates from outside. Normally, the first moves are made by individuals and their immediate families. Old people insist that this was not always the case. As late as the 1950s, elders often tried to arrange marriages through a practice known as "sister exchange" in which two clans agreed to provide each other with wives. Such arrangements were made while the children were still very young. As they grew up, the matched couples were called "husband" and "wife," although they continued to live with their own people. By the time they became teenagers, they spent increasing amounts of time working in the gardens of their prospective in-laws, a practice anthropologists refer to as "bride service" or "groom service." Clan leaders liked these kinds of arrangements because they automatically brought the contracting groups into a balanced relationship: a wife for a wife, a husband for a husband. Even in the "good old days," however, the betrothed children often had their own ideas. If just one of the four betrothed persons died, refused to settle down with their assigned partner, or eloped with someone else, all of the careful diplomacy was for naught. Elopements could trigger violence, especially when one clan had already done its duty by providing a wife for the initial marriage. The eloping couple had to flee for their lives, leaving their clan mates to face the spears and war clubs of the aggrieved party.

While individual young people have a greater say than in the past, their parents and clan elders continue to influence their choices. They nudge their sons and daughters towards potential partners who have shown themselves to be hard workers in the gardens and who are deferential to their elders. They strongly encourage their children (particularly their daughters) to marry within their own villages, to assure that they will remain nearby to take care of their aging parents. The survey of households that I conducted in 1982 revealed a very high level of village endogamy; almost 75 per cent of marriages in Uiaku had occurred within the bounds of the village. Yet even at that time, an increasing number of Maisin were looking further afield to partners in other Maisin villages and, for the large number who had moved to the town, to non-Maisin mates. Ultimately, so long as the preferred spouse is not a member of the clan or a close blood relative, young people enjoy a considerable amount of freedom. Many people live for brief periods with a series of partners before settling down. Once a couple has children, however, they rarely divorce. The main exception is when a man is physically violent or when he takes a second or third wife.[17] Some women return to their brothers rather than tolerate an

Often no wedding ceremony, when 2 are seen eating break-fast together on a verandah they are called "husband" + "wife" *(handwritten annotation)*

unhapp[...] [...]aisin wives who, without kin nearby, may find themselves trapped.

The first public indication that a couple has decided to marry comes when they appear sitting and eating breakfast together on a verandah or house platform. From this point on, they are called "husband" and "wife" so long as they remain together. Often there is no further ceremony. On other occasions, for reasons of family pride or because they hope to make the union stick, parents and clan elders take matters in hand, temporarily separating the couple while they arrange for a wedding ceremony. A few devout families will approach the priest to arrange for a church wedding, but this is rare. Because of the strong strictures against divorce in the Anglican Church, most couples prefer to live without church approval until they are certain that the relationship will last, usually after the birth of several children.[18] At that point, they seek and receive a blessing from the priest and have their children baptized.

While uncommon, the rare wedding ceremony reveals much about Maisin assumptions concerning marriage. In the morning, the bride is richly adorned in traditional dress and decorations and then brought to her husband's hamlet accompanied by a boisterous crowd of kinfolk from both sides of her family. After the crowd settles down, she is led by two clan brothers, each gripping an arm, towards her husband and male in-laws, who sit passively on a house verandah. As she draws near, three or four middle-aged women belonging to the groom's side get down on their hands and knees in a line in front of the ladder leading up to the porch. The bride walks across their backs to smash a large clay cooking pot with her foot before climbing up to join her husband, symbolizing her break with her old family. Sometimes her kin will then present a gift of raw garden vegetables, tapa, cooking pots, mats, shell money, and cash. Clan elders from the groom's side loudly proclaim that they will soon provide the wife's people with large quantities of three types of items, such as bananas, taro, or tapa, to be delivered as separate gifts in the near future. Speeches, feasting, and much merriment follow before the crowd disperses. The next morning, the bride brings the ceremony to a conclusion. Still decorated and surrounded by a crowd of jovial female in-laws who urge her on, she sweeps litter from the grounds of her husband's hamlet from one end to the other.

The sweeping ritual signifies the new responsibilities of marriage. As in so many areas of Maisin life, these weigh especially heavily upon women. The new bride not only takes on the heaviest burden of work but moves from her family to live among comparative strangers. Some young brides find the prospect so frightening that they are accompanied by a younger sister or cousin who stays with them until they become accustomed to their new home. The young husband is by no means left off the hook. Both his own people and his in-laws watch his actions intently to see whether he treats his wife well and willingly takes on the duties of creating a new household, separate from his father's. In the early stages of a marriage, a couple comes under the authority of their respective in-laws. They are expected to make themselves available to work in their in-laws' gardens, to help with the full range of household tasks, and to provide regular supplies of food, tobacco, and betelnut. They should do this with the greatest deference, never complaining and certainly never criticizing their in-laws. Over time, as people get used to each other, the stress of the relationship eases. Yet even with the most sympathetic and caring in-laws, most people find the initial stage of marriage very trying, which may account in part for why so many early relationships break down.

I have personally experienced some of this. When they heard that Anne and I had married only a few months prior to leaving for Papua New Guinea, several of our Maisin friends came up with the idea of staging a traditional wedding in our honour. We were duly assigned fathers and mothers and "adopted" into different clans. The wedding never came off, but I quickly found out that my new "in-laws" meant to treat the arrangement as something more than fun and games. Every time I passed Anne's "father's" house, he called me over to sit with him and share any tobacco, rice, or betelnut I might be carrying. He was a lovely person, and I enjoyed our time together, but it wasn't long before I found myself avoiding his part of the village in order to preserve my dwindling supplies and to get on with my work. The arrangement complicated my research in an additional way. The Maisin show respect towards in-laws by never uttering their names. This taboo added some difficulties in compiling a village census and doing genealogies as there were certain names I couldn't say (the same, of course, was true for my informants). Although they take the business of dealing respectfully with in-laws very seriously, the Maisin also see humour in the situation. Young men are fond of a game in which they corner a new husband, spouting off insults about his father-in-law. If their victim so much as cracks a smile, his "insult" is immediately reported, forcing him to offer a gift to his aggrieved in-laws to set matters right. One elder summed up the relationship with in-laws as follows: "You can sit with them, tell stories, and make fun. But we respect them. We can't make fun of any in-law.... They can demand that you work for them. You should do this before they say too much. If you live in another place, they will send a message for you to help—say, to make a new garden.... You married their daughter so you must respect them. They must respect you because you are their daughter's husband."

The respect relationship between in-laws derives from a conception of marriage as an asymmetrical exchange between clans. When one of their sons marries, a clan incurs a significant debt to the wife's people who have gifted her labour and children to them. This debt is marked from the start by the custom of the parents of the young man sending a pot of cooked food to the new wife's people as a signal of their approval of the union (Tietjen 1985:133). Balancing [...] perspective of the clan [...] nequal relationship to c [...] mer times, sister exchang [...] natching the gift of a wor [...] trical exchange with a s [...] ovides another appealing strategy. If a couple has a large number of children, they often will foster one to a family on the husband's in-laws' side, either to a couple in the mother's clan with few or no children or to older people whose children have left home. The wife-takers are still expected to present the wife's people with periodic gifts of food and labour, but the gift of a child removes the need for a large bride wealth payment.

[handwritten annotation: gift of a child removes the need for a large bride wealth payment.]

Most people, however, put together a bride wealth gift (see Plate 4). A bride's family will urge her husband to give the bride wealth quickly, but usually a man waits until several children are born. The longer he waits, the greater the pressure. If his wife leaves him before bride wealth is presented, she has the right to take her children back to her natal clan. Further, a man's own reputation suffers, and he runs the risk of annoying his in-laws. They may just grumble, but if things go on too long they may decide to stage a *waafoti*, a shaming ceremony. One morning, the husband will wake up to find his in-laws sitting solemnly in front of his house. They will not leave until the man and his embarrassed clan mates pool their resources and pay a diminished bride wealth on the spot. As a further inducement, the Maisin believe that angered in-laws are quite capable of engaging a sorcerer to retaliate against a "selfish" son-in-law who fails to meet his obligations.

The Maisin call the ceremonial presentation of bride wealth *wii jobi* ("vagina payment"). It's a big event. A husband organizes his own *wii jobi* with the aid of more experienced senior kinsmen, his clan brothers, his wife, and more distant kin. In the past, the essential component in a *wii jobi* payment was *kerefun*, strings of polished white shell discs about a fathom long (1.6 metres).[19] Today a typical bride wealth presentation includes an abundance of tapa cloth, mats, clay pots, shell ornaments, garden produce, cooked pork, different types of store goods, and cash.[20] The organizer will assemble these things in his own village and then, accompanied by clan siblings, carry them to his in-laws' house to present them. The in-laws usually know well in advance that the *wii jobi* is coming and offer cooked food for their guests and later, after this is eaten, sit down with them to chew betelnut and smoke.[21]

The giving of a child in adoption or the payment of bride wealth changes the relationship between groups linked by a marriage. Up to this point, the husband's clan risks losing children produced by the marriage should it break up, since they will return with their mother to her own people. They are now *bona fide* members of their father's clan regardless of the fate of the marriage. It may appear from this that the father's people have purchased the wife and her children, but this doesn't reflect Maisin assumptions. These exchanges, they say, should bring the two groups into a balanced state, marked by amicable relations. In actuality, the presentation of a generous bride wealth payment in the context of a boisterous celebration marked by feasting and dancing to which both sides contribute does act to build confidence and a strong alliance. The important point, however, is that this is an alliance in which the *perception* of balance remains important. Perceptions are subjective. Even the closest of marital alliances experience flare-ups in which one side or the other feels that things are out of balance, that the other side is not meeting its obligations, that they are being taken advantage of. As we shall see in the next chapter, unhappy relationships in general not only make life unpleasant, they threaten life by tempting the wronged side to resort to sorcery. The Maisin thus have both positive and negative inducements to cultivate good relations with their in-laws well after the two groups have, in principle, achieved a state of balance.

RITES OF PASSAGE AS SOCIAL THEATRE

So far in this chapter, I've been describing kinship, descent, and marriage as sets of rules that guide social behaviour. This isn't the whole story. In order to reveal the underlying patterns of a society, anthropologists distill presumed rules and frameworks from far more complex lived realities. Yet Maisin are not given a rulebook or script early in life for how to live. Assumptions and expectations about kin and in-laws guide behaviour but do not determine it. People adjust their actions according to the circumstances of the moment and strategize as to what is in their best interests. This does not mean anything goes, for people also continually evaluate others' actions largely in terms of the frameworks we've examined in this chapter and will only tolerate a certain amount of licence. Yet rules are constantly tested, stretched, and adapted in the course of everyday life.

The anthropologist Victor Turner (1974) suggests that we should think about social life less as a set of normative rules than as a kind of improvisational theatre. In this social theatre, people shift between acting on the stage and observing from the audience. There are no set scripts, but instead there are generally accepted rules and scenarios upon which people innovate. The theatrical analogy is especially compelling as a way of approaching public ceremonials.

In Uiaku, thes[...] major life
transitions: rit[...] I want to
briefly examin[...] ion social
theatre: the ini[...] ceremony
following a dea[...]

First born children have high status.

First-born children (*membu*) enjoy an exalted status in Maisin society. The arrival of the *membu* marks the start of a new generation for the father's clan. As the first in a sibling set, the *membu* is expected to take on more responsibilities and to defer many of the freedoms and pleasures of adolescence until undergoing a special ceremony, the *kisevi*. By the same token, the *membu*'s younger siblings are expected to treat him or her with respect and deference. In *Kawo* clans, a male *membu* belonging to a senior lineage is often groomed to take leadership positions. The *membu* thus exemplifies the principle of seniority that underlies the structure of descent groups. At the same time, the appearance of the *membu* raises the stakes of the marriage contract, for until the bride wealth is presented the status of all the couple's children is uncertain. The birth of the *membu* thus increases pressure on the father's clan to meet their exchange obligations to the mother's people. At the same time, it triggers a parallel set of exchanges around the person of the *membu*. These begin with gifts of raw food quietly delivered to the mother's people around the time of the birth and for several years thereafter. It should climax with the *kisevi* in which the mother's brothers play a crucial role.

I say "should climax" because the *kisevi* rarely happens any more, sometimes because first-borns may be away attending high school during the critical period but mainly because the ceremony is very expensive to mount, requiring a large accumulation of garden produce, tapa cloth, shell money, cash, and other valuables as well as the coordination of many stakeholders. I haven't seen a full-scale *kisevi*, but I have extensive descriptions from participants, including *membu* themselves. The ceremony is organized by the two clans allied in marriage. The father's side invites the mother's relatives to initiate the first-born on a certain day. The morning after an evening of feasting and dancing, the *membu*'s maternal uncles bathe and decorate the *membu* in traditional finery. Paralleling the wedding ceremony, the *membu* walks across the backs of a row of crouched senior maternal kinswomen (although no pot is broken) and then sits silently on a mat covered with tapa with a maternal cousin on either side. Sometimes making short speeches, the uncles step forward to swing a shell necklace or tapa over the head of the *membu* before laying it over the initiate's neck or legs. These gifts typically include the prized *kawo* emblems of the mother's clans, giving the *membu* the right to use them in the future, although usually not to pass on to their own children. The first round ends when the *membu*'s mother swings a small clay pot over his or her head and then smashes it to the ground. The paternal kin now come forward, swinging their gifts of tapa, money, shell necklaces, and so forth over the head of the *membu* and placing them in a pile for later distribution to the mother's people.

By all accounts, the *kisevi* is very exciting. Hundreds of people attend, including non-Maisin guests from across Collingwood Bay. People get very excited as the piles of gifts mount on top of and beside the *membu* and will often rush back into their houses or to their canoes to find additional things to give away—so much so that the old people say, "After this *kisevi* they will cry for there is nothing left in their houses." The ceremony involves an impressive amount of management, especially on the part of the *membu*'s paternal family. The public performance is ostensibly between two clans, but no single clan possesses the resources to mount a *kisevi*. Organizers have to call upon their extended kin to make donations of food and gifts, to build shelters for guests, and to help with cooking and ceremonial dances. Veronica Kaivasi proudly told me how she and her husband, Simeon Wea, spent years organizing the *kisevi* for their daughter Damaris through extensive negotiations, fed by smaller exchanges, with their respective kindreds. As it turned out, many of the mother's people made significant contributions to the gifts that they later received back from the father's clan. I found a similar backstage flexibility on the part of the father's clan. Further extending the networks involved, the maternal uncles called upon many of their own classificatory "brothers" to place gifts upon Damaris, thus making a much more impressive presentation, even though they actually belonged to different clans. One couple related to both Veronica and Simeon decided to split the difference—the wife sat with the father's people while the husband participated on the mother's side.

Any large exchange involves similar backstage adjustments and compromises in which the organizers draw upon kinship links and exchange obligations to produce a certain public appearance. The formal purpose of a *kisevi* is to publicly demonstrate that the parties to a marriage have achieved a state of balance, as exemplified in the public exchange of gifts over the body of the *membu* to which they have a common claim. Because they are both actors and audience, the participants in a *kisevi* are fully aware of the social complexities even if they have differing perspectives on the details. The talk of clans conducting an exchange thus forms a kind of shorthand for what is in fact a much more entangled set of social interactions. Participants judge the success of a *kisevi* by the degree to which the organizers create the *appearance* of clans achieving a balance and the affirmation of the status of the firstborn. By this measure, Damaris's *kisevi* was a great success, raising the public stature of Simeon's clan.

In modern times, the *kisevi* has become optional. The *roi babasi* or "face cleaning" ceremony that ends a person's mourning for a close relative is a different matter (Barker 1985). When a person dies, his or her surviving spouse and parents go into mourning. Other close relatives may also choose to formally mourn the deceased by wearing dark clothes, allowing their hair and beards to grow, and by avoiding a certain food or activity. A spouse faces especially stringent requirements. At the moment of death, they are considered to become like infants, incapable of caring for themselves. They become the responsibility of their in-laws, the family of the deceased. The spouse initially goes into seclusion. Over succeeding days and weeks, the in-laws formally reintroduce the mourner into the world of the living one step at a time: they take them to the bush, thus giving them permission to relieve themselves; they give them cooked taro, sweet potatoes, bananas, and other foods, thus giving them permission to feed themselves; they take them to the garden area, thus giving them permission to resume work on their own gardens; and so forth. The in-laws usually lift restrictions within a few weeks. The bereaved then returns to his or her own people to remain in a state of semi-formal mourning for a period of months lasting into years during which they wear dark clothes and neither comb nor cut their hair and beards. The period of mourning is brought to a final conclusion with a public ceremony in which the mourners are "cleaned up" by the family of the deceased.

The *roi babasi* resembles a *kisevi* in some ways. Like the *membu*, the bereaved spouse is bathed, clothed, and decorated by his or her in-laws before being presented with gifts of clothing often including tapa and, in the case of women, practical implements like cooking pots and mats. Also like the *kisevi*, the *roi babasi* creates a new status for its subject. Once the ceremony is concluded, the surviving spouse no longer has obligations to their in-laws. They are free to remarry if they wish. There are also important differences. While a few families with larger resources may mount large ceremonies marked by feasting and traditional dancing, most are small affairs bringing together the immediate kin. The ceremony normally lasts just a few hours, ending with a small dinner for the guests.

Over the years, I have participated in many *roi babasi* ceremonies. All follow the general pattern outlined above. And all have been different, often significantly so. The pioneering anthropologist Bronislaw Malinowski (1954) argued that death tears apart the social fabric in small-scale societies, and so the function of mortuary ceremonies is to calm people's grief and fears by reasserting social connections. Most Maisin would be comfortable with that explanation: the *roi babasi* is meant to resolve the relationships between people connected

Figure 3.6 *Roi babasi* (face cleaning) ceremony, 2007. A recent widow, Mary Anne Tagore, has had her hair trimmed and been dressed in new tapa and decorations by her female in-laws, who present her with clothes and clay cooking pots to begin her new life. (Photo by A.M. Tietjen)

through the deceased, to express a state of balance and amity (*marawa-wawe*). Yet there is a big difference between what ought to be and what people do or have to contend with. Most Maisin in my experience look on the *roi babasi* not only as an obligation but also as an index of the state of social relationships. Hence, any particular *roi babasi* is open to several readings. If a person remains in mourning for a long time, for instance, people will often wonder whether the in-laws are holding up the ceremony because they are angry, perhaps feeling that the survivor had not cared as much as he or she should have for the deceased. If the in-laws are really angry, however, they are much more likely to rush the *roi babasi* in order to shame the surviving spouse and his or her kin. In one case, a widower was made to undergo the ceremony only three days after his young wife's death. His in-laws claimed that they felt, as Christians, that they should not allow the husband to suffer the privations of mourning, but few bought this argument, telling me that the husband had not taken care of his wife during her illness and so was being punished with a shamefully rapid and abbreviated ritual. Every *roi babasi* I've attended has provided abundant fodder for community gossip.

Customs and ceremonies like the ones examined here are "polyvocal" in that they speak on several registers at once. They draw on an ancestral past that gives them their authority and structure. Yet they are performed in the present by people who bring a diversity of agendas and perspectives to them. Each performance is familiar and different. They provide occasions for enjoyment, renewals of social ties, vicious gossip, quarrels, and the advancement or crushing of the political ambitions of their organizers. They demonstrate in the most dramatic fashion that culture must be lived and innovative to survive and thrive.

Uiaku is a small, intimate community. People's lives take place largely in the routines of gender-based subsistence activities and interactions with kin and in-laws, periodically broken by celebrations in which people affirm their identities and social relationships. Yet this is not their whole world. Maisin also contend with spiritual forces that reinforce and disrupt their best laid plans and hopes. Their lives are also shaped by institutions like the church and school, which became essential parts of village experience in the colonial period and connect them to wider regional and national systems based on utterly different principles than kinship and reciprocal exchange. In the next two chapters, then, we need to enlarge our picture of Maisin society by considering the wider realms of the spiritual world and the community.

Notes

1. In the 1980s, most *embobi* were composed of four panels. As tapa sales increased in the 1990s, women made more small pieces, cut to one or two panels, which were easier to sell.

2. Maisin today are emphatic that most cloths bear abstract designs (*amai kayan*— "just designs") and that tapas bearing clan designs may never be sold. Yet Percy John Money and Rudolf Pöch recorded design names for most of the tapas they collected before 1910 for the Australian Museum and the Museum of Ethnology in Vienna respectively. In 1982, Sister Helen Roberts and I showed photographs of the Australian Museum tapas to women in Wanigela and Uiaku. Most, but not all, were identified as clan designs, albeit several no longer made. This raises the intriguing possibility that named designs were more numerous and common in the past and that the strict prohibition on selling tapas with clan designs is in part a product of the commercialization of the cloth (cf. Hermkens 2013).

3. Any social system is immensely complicated and there is no single way to provide an overview. In what follows, I've focused on normative values and frameworks with periodic reminders that actual behaviour is always more innovative, variable and interesting than generally shared orientations and rules suggest. But there are further

decisions an analyst must make. As we've seen, reciprocal exchange is a key practice and value in Maisin society. This is true in all Melanesian cultures and anthropologists have emphasized their relativistic nature in contrast to more individualistic Western cultures. A movement known as the "new Melanesian ethnography" has experimented with ethnographic accounts organized upon Indigenous concepts and values, particularly reciprocity. Marilyn Strathern's groundbreaking *The Gender of the Gift* (1988) has been especially influential. In it, she argues that Melanesian persons are best understood as "dividuals" as opposed to the Western concept of the "in-dividual"; that is to say, as "partible" persons whose being is continually composed and decomposed in exchanges of things, ideas, and values with kinfolk. This is a powerful model not only for taking exchange seriously but in the way it dispenses with domains like the economy, social organization, religion, and so forth that do not exist in Indigenous conceptual systems and for the fluidity it suggests for gender. Strathern's approach has influenced the ways I think about Maisin experience, yet I don't use her framework here for a couple of reasons. First, there is a real danger that by focusing on the literal treatment of Maisin concepts like *marawa-wawe* one would exaggerate cultural "alterity" at the expense of recognizing commonalities, especially in the ways people actually live their lives. This makes the key object of ethnographic description, the translation of cultural experience into understandable terms, very challenging. Second, her theoretical language is exceedingly complex, even for specialists. I mention it here to remind readers that all ethnographic descriptions exist in tension between culturally relativist and generalist poles of analysis. Strathern is also criticized for ignoring social change, but several superb new works draw creativity on her insights to examine the changing experiences of Melanesians in the modern world, particularly Holly Wardlow's (2006) work on Huli "passenger women" and Alice Street's (2014) study of a Papua New Guinea hospital.

4. This is not to suggest that Maisin parents do not love or care for newborns. They do, and the death of a baby is experienced as a tragedy. Full *social* humanness, however, is recognized as a potential that emerges out of the child's developing social interactions; it is not a biological given.

5. In many other parts of Melanesia, boys underwent initiations at the onset of puberty and then lived apart from their mothers and sisters in special male cult houses (Godelier 1986; Herdt 1981; Tuzin 1980). In comparison, the relationship between adolescent girls and boys among the Maisin is quite relaxed, although according to elders this was less true in the past when adolescent boys were expected to live together in bachelor "clan houses" (*iyon va*).

6. Maisin had a more relaxed attitude towards premarital sex in the past, perhaps because of the belief that a boy and girl had to have sex repeatedly for pregnancy to occur (Barker 1986). Even today, a girl who has a baby prior to marriage is usually not harshly criticized. The baby is welcomed by her family and remains with them when she later marries.

7. This is not an option available to non-Maisin women who have married into the community. Far from their kin, most experience extreme loneliness, especially during the period they are learning the difficult Maisin language.

8. This was not immediately apparent to the earliest students of non-Western kinship systems. Lewis Henry Morgan (1877) introduced the distinction between "classificatory" and "descriptive" kinship systems, jumping to the bizarre conclusion that terminologies that grouped together fathers and mothers with their siblings were relics of an earlier period of "primitive promiscuity" in which children were ignorant of the true identity of their biological parents.

9. To add to the complexity, some terms differ depending on whether they are used to *refer* to someone or to *address* them directly. Thus, if I was talking to someone about my mother I would say "*au yo*" ("my mother"). If I wanted her attention, on the other hand, I would call out "*Yau!*"

10. This sketch includes only immediate family terms. Maisin kinship terminology also includes affinal (in-law) terms, plural forms, and honorific variants meant to convey one's respect towards the addressed relative.

11. This pattern has become complicated with the large-scale out-migration of younger Maisin to the urban areas since the 1960s. Still, when men retire from their jobs and return to the village, they usually establish themselves in their fathers' areas. In a few cases, however, a man may live for a time or permanently with his wife's people if his natal hamlet is overcrowded.

12. Fostered children become members of their adoptive father's clan, although they retain informal privileges in their birth father's clan as well.

13. The Maisin system of emblems bears some similarities to forms of totemism found in Aboriginal Australia where social groups are associated with particular natural species or objects.

14. I capitalize the types of clans to distinguish this use of *Kawo* from the more general sense of emblem (*kawo*).

15. The powerful idea that origin histories may form a type of social charter for their owners was first suggested by Bronislaw Malinowski (1954), based upon his study of the Trobriand Islanders.

16. There are further complexities. A number of resident clans claim to have foreign origins. Most are associated with different Maisin clans to whom their ancestors attached themselves as *Sabu* warriors in the past, either during the migrations into Collingwood Bay or later as migrants and refugees. One, however, is a fully fledged *Kawo* ally in the *Mera ari Kawo* confederacy. Sometimes I was told that the members of these clans were "not really Maisin," although their members have lived for generations in Uiaku and differ only in terms of distant ancestral origins. Another complexity is that lineages sometimes claim distinct *evovi* differentiating them from others in their clans. In one case, an expert tapa artist had created and bequeathed a number of named

tapa designs to her children, which they claimed as *evovi* that could only be made and worn by themselves (cf. Regius 1988:30).

17. In the early 1980s, five men living in Uiaku had two or three wives. Most Maisin frown on polygyny, in part because it contradicts Christian teachings but mostly because of the fights that often erupt between co-wives. Genealogies reveal a much higher level of polygyny in the past when leading men took on additional wives as a mark of prestige and to acquire additional labour for their feasting gardens.

18. Marriage is a sacrament in the Anglican Church. Couples who divorce after being married in the church or blessed by the priest are subject to church discipline: they are not allowed to receive sacramental wine and bread in communion services, and their children must await adulthood before they can be baptized. In the past, Anglican bishops sometimes took the extreme step of excommunicating divorced individuals who remarried, symbolically condemning their souls to eternal damnation. The practice of blessing established marriages is a face-saving compromise that allows the church to continue to proclaim marriage a sacrament while quietly allowing for divorce in the early years of a marriage when it most often occurs.

19. A "fathom" is a traditional measurement: the distance from one outstretched arm to the other.

20. Many parts of Papua New Guinea have experienced a massive inflation in bride wealth with the introduction of money. In places where people are known to have access to money, either through their own jobs or via relatives, the bride's people may demand exorbitant bride wealth payments, or, just as often, the husband's people use the occasion of the exchange as a public display of their wealth and influence. Bride wealth payments running in the tens of thousands of kina are not unusual. The money component of Maisin bride wealth is comparatively small, generally a few hundred kina. Still, this represents a large sum for most rural Maisin, and those with few working relatives to call upon often find they have to delay bride wealth payments to avoid a shamefully small prestation.

21. The hosts of feasts never eat with their guests. They keep some cooked food back to enjoy after their guests have left or retired for the night.

CHAPTER 4

THE SPIRITUAL REALM

I looked forward to finishing my cloth. Unlike the beating and designing stages, which tend to be solitary activities, applying the red dye known as *dun* is a social event. I had often passed groups of women chatting happily in the cool area under a house or tree, while they applied *dun* to their tapas from a shared pot. This looked like fun. I also assumed that applying the dye would not tax my meagre technical skills nearly as much as the hard labour of beating the bark or coaxing the sooty black *mii* into neat parallel lines.

First, we had to make the dye. Lottie and I gathered the materials. We walked along the beach until we came to a moderately tall tree the Maisin call *saman*. Lottie wielded the long knife she had brought to slice off a lengthy strip of bark, which she bundled into her string bag. We then strolled behind the village to gather leaves from a second tree known as *dun*. Unlike the wild *wayangu* creeper used in making the black dye, *saman* and *dun* trees are owned. One must seek permission to harvest them if they do not grow on one's own land.

We returned to the village and crossed the river to Martha's house. In the comfortable shade underneath, she and Lottie prepared the *dun*. Lottie used her knife to shred the inner bark from the *saman* bark. She then layered pieces of bark and leaves into a small steel pot. Once it was nearly full, she added water to the brim and placed the pot over a fire. We settled back to enjoy a snack and conversation while the pot boiled away for the next 90 minutes, with Lottie occasionally adding water. As the water heated up, the vegetation released a pinkish dye. The leaves and bark gradually combined as the water took on a satisfactorily bright blood-red hue. Martha brought out a collection of dried pandanus fruits whose tips had been crushed to expose the fibres. The *imongiti*, as these are known, come in a variety of sizes and make handy brushes. Martha dipped one into the bubbling pot of *dun* and tested it on a scrap of tapa. We were ready to begin.

There is an etiquette to sharing a *dun* pot. Once she has arranged herself and her tapa near the pot, the owner is often joined by women from neighbouring houses and relatives visiting from other parts of the village, each bearing a bundle of her own unfinished cloth. When they arrive, each woman takes up one of the host's tapas to work on. When the host feels that she has received sufficient help, she gives the others permission to turn to their own cloths. Usually a pot of *dun* is used up in an afternoon in this pleasant activity (see Plate 3).

We were joined by a few women, but only one brought her own cloths. Clearly I was to provide the entertainment for the day! I immediately broke with custom by reaching for my own cloth, unwilling to risk messing up Lottie's or Martha's creations, and tentatively dipped my pandanus brush into the dye. I found to my relief that applying the *dun* was much easier than working with the black *mii*, but it still required concentration and a steady hand. My first tentative strokes resulted in a blotchy pink stain. I was surprised by how quickly the cloth absorbed the dye. When one splotch seeped across the black line, I jerked my hand up. Bad idea! Spatters of red now festooned what was supposed to be a white area. So I stopped and paid closer attention to Martha's and Lottie's technique. They dipped their brushes into the hot liquid, flicked off the excess, and then applied it to a line, using a light hand and rapid forward brush stroke.

After a while, I got the hang of it, and my lines took on a satisfactory consistency, even if the colour was not as boldly red as my companions'. I was surprised by how quickly the work went. *Dun* dries rapidly. You don't need to wait long upon completing one panel before flipping the cloth to work on the next. We hung each piece on a clothesline as soon as it was finished, leaving the painted surface exposed to bake in the sun for a short time before turning the cloth inside out. When the women were satisfied that the cloths were thoroughly dry, they took them off the line. Much like a little kid bringing home his first shop project, I proudly showed my tapa to Mary Rose and George. I don't know if they really liked it, but they were very kind.

The vibrant red of the *dun* quickly fades in the bright Papua New Guinea sunshine, and the cloth itself is easily damaged by moisture, so cloths are stored in a dark corner of the house, usually inside a suitcase. Most tapa doesn't stay packed for long. While a few women regularly make cloth, most take up the demanding chore only when an opportunity arises to sell it or it is required for an exchange or dancing. Even so, George told me that it is best to hold a few well-designed large *embobi* back in the house for special occasions. When an important visitor arrives, for instance, one should show respect by spreading out a handsome tapa for them to sit upon. George and Mary Rose welcomed their children returning home from high school in this way.

Figure 4.1 Recently completed tapa drying on a clothesline. (Photo by J. Barker)

I was reminded of how Lottie had honoured me with her beautiful tapa earlier when I had been designing my own.

Tapa has many facets for the Maisin. In the past, it was primarily a utilitarian object. This is no longer the case, but even in earlier times tapa was much more than simply clothing. It was and still is a type of wealth. A villager would not think of sponsoring or participating in a major exchange without a good supply of cloth. Along with other types of wealth—cash, food, shell necklaces, and so forth—the public giving of tapa serves to demonstrate the giver's social status while affirming or creating social relationships upon which that status relies. As we saw in Chapter 2, tapa is also a commodity, something that can be converted into cash to be used to purchase goods from the trade store, pay school fees, or buy airplane fares to Port Moresby.

At a more subtle level, tapa speaks to religious and cosmological assumptions. It took me some time to understand this. Early in my research, I read an article stating that Maisin clan designs derive from mythological stories (Schwimmer 1979).[1] This turned out to be true in only a few cases. The Jorega clan, for instance, associates a fern-like design known as *sividi* with a marvellous tale set in the Musa swamp area during the origin times. There are a few instances of clan designs associated with specific events in the migration histories. Most, however, are simply emblems. A couple of my favourite tapa makers, Natalie Kitore and Nita Keru, drew fanciful images of animals, insects, spirits, and people. The vast majority of tapas worn and sold by Maisin, however, bear abstract designs.

My conclusion that Maisin regard tapa as a purely secular object unravelled in a curious way. On the day before I was to leave Uiaku at the end of two months of research focused upon tapa making and tattooing in 1986, I visited Agnes Sanangi and her sister Natalie Kitore to tie up a few loose ends. We were just running through the etiquette Maisin observe when sharing a pot of *dun* when Agnes added some new and surprising information. "In the old days," she said, a woman would announce to the household that she was about to apply the red dye. The night before, she and her husband refrained from sexual activity. The following morning, her husband and children left the house while she prepared the *dun* inside. She explained that if men were present or children were running around and making noise, the *dun* would dry out. Once the *dun* was ready, the tapa maker invited other women to join her in the privacy of the house. The *dun*, Agnes added, was "very strong," unlike the black *mii* dye, and thus had to be handled carefully and only by women. While listening, I thought of how when a newly tattooed girl first emerges from the tattooist's house she wears a special tapa known as *wamatuvi* that is dyed entirely red except for an unpainted fringe at the base. The Maisin thus seemed to associate the red dye with women, perhaps more specifically with women's blood. This association was subsequently confirmed by Anna-Karina Hermkens (2013). Several of her elderly informants told her that the red dye was called *tambuta* (an extremely bright or "ripe" blood red) during the time it was in the house.

These observations, so casually revealed, opened up a whole new dimension of tapa to me. They suggested that in the past the Maisin associated aspects of the making of tapa with the essence of femininity (cf. Hermkens 2013). Making tapa, especially the final stages, thus connected to a complex of practices and rituals involving food taboos, birthing, infant care practices, and gender etiquette (Tietjen 1985). Many of these practices had spiritual sanctions. Were a man to break the taboo on entering the house while the *dun* was present, I was told, he would become ill. Agnes told me that Maisin women stopped secluding themselves while using *dun* sometime around the end of World War II, although she was unable to tell me why.

Of course I asked Agnes and Natalie why they had not told me about this fascinating custom during our many sessions together. I already knew the answer: "You didn't ask." I have no reason to doubt their explanation. There was nothing secret about the older way of handling *dun*. Elderly men spoke as readily about it as did women once I knew to ask. The problem really lay with me. My job was to make sense of Maisin life. So I asked questions, sought explanations. Many of my informants were very happy to speak about aspects of spirituality. Indeed, they told me that my questions were quite stimulating. However, the Maisin experience the spiritual world much more than they rationalize it. They feel no need to pull together often contradictory bits of ritual practices, observances of taboos, or encounters with spiritual forces into a big picture. Much of an individual's knowledge of the spiritual rests upon tacit, unarticulated assumptions. Thus, if the intrinsic incompatibility of red *dun* and men is something that everyone just knows, there is no reason to expect that anyone would think to volunteer the information to an anthropologist.

There is no subject so fascinating or challenging to study as the religious dimensions of a culture. The contemporary religion of the Maisin is rather like one of their finished tapas. One sees, at first, the bold patterns of red bounded by black, the equivalent of the widely shared religious beliefs and practices we shall examine in this chapter: church services, ideas about the nature of spirits, sorcery and healing practices, and rituals to deal with the passage between life and death. The basic elements of a tapa design are quite limited. Yet, as you develop a greater knowledge and appreciation, you become aware that every tapa design combines those elements into a unique expression. In this chapter, I focus mostly on the general, shared aspects of Maisin religious experience. However, as we shall see, the Maisin's approach to the spiritual realm is highly innovative and creative. This, more than anything else, explains why 90 years after most people became Christians, their religious lives retain a strong Indigenous signature.

CHRISTIANITY

St. Thomas Church is the largest building in Uiaku, although it is easily overlooked by visitors. It sits at the very back of the mission station, behind wide grassy sports fields edged by neat croton-lined paths that run past the teachers' houses and classrooms. The church itself looks like a long shed, its roof a patchwork of corrugated iron sheets in various shades of rust. Closer in, one notices a space between the sloping roof and sago-rib walls to allow light and cooling breezes into the building. You enter at the far end facing the altar, making your way between two sets of small logs that form the pews. The altar sits on a raised platform of sand and gravel that takes up the front quarter of the church. The back wall and the altar are richly adorned with tapa cloth, but apart from this there are few decorations. The simple interior, however, is clean and attractive. Prior to each service, a few women from the Mothers' Union sweep the floor, rake the gravel, and place a few clay pots filled with flowers along the edge of the altar platform.

On a typical Sunday, perhaps one-third of the adults from Uiaku and Ganjiga show up for the 8 a.m. service. As people quietly shuffle in, they divide, the women moving to the left pews and men to the right, with school children of both sexes occupying the front rows on the right, under the watchful eye of a deacon or school teacher. The number of adolescents and unmarried young adults attending ebbs and flows. Most weeks there are few, but the ranks swell on occasions like sports meets and youth fellowship gatherings that bring visitors to the village. By the late 1990s, the singing of Victorian-era hymns in the old "church language" of Wedau had been replaced by lively contemporary gospel songs in English and Maisin, usually led by young people playing guitars and sometimes a battery-powered electronic keyboard.

The services follow a standardized format in simple English, based upon the Anglican *Book of Common Prayer*. Bible readings and prayers are also in English, as is the sermon when a Maisin-speaking priest or deacon is not available. Prior to the mid-1980s, Church authorities discouraged clergy from working in their own tribal groups. Neither of the two priests serving Uiaku during my first fieldwork could speak Maisin. They delivered their sermons in simple and, to my ears at least, fractured English with a Maisin deacon or church council member providing translation. The rest of the service is not translated for the benefit of those who cannot understand English (a majority in the early 1980s). Indeed, the liturgy allows for very limited participation from the congregation. The congregants sit passively through the readings and sermons, chanting brief ritual responses to the prayers and coming forward to receive communion in a never-changing rhythm that echoes Anglican services around the world. The sermon allows for more variation, but only lay readers, deacons, and priests licensed by the bishop are allowed to preach.[2] Most of them stick to a simple formula of reiterating the Bible lessons and urging their flocks to obey God and love their neighbours. They rarely refer to events or concerns in the local community.

I had come to Uiaku to study the impact of Christianity on Maisin culture and so became a regular member of the small band of congregants attending church in 1981–83. I had plenty of time, perched uncomfortably on my hard pew, to speculate on what Christianity meant to villagers. My early impression was: not very much. To be sure, there was a small minority who faithfully attended church, studied the Bible, and prefaced each meal with a grace. Still, most people did not bother, and there seemed to be few if any consequences for missing services or for failing to contribute money to help pay the priest's salary. People also got away with flouting key Church teachings, most notably about marriage. It seemed that their adherence to Christianity was quite superficial.

I was mistaken. Christianity has a profound presence in Maisin life. All but one adult in the village have been baptized, and all received instruction in the religion as children; community meetings commonly opened and closed with prayers, and speakers often urged their listeners to adhere to Christian teachings; and church festivals, particularly the patron saint's day, were major social events, involving nearly all villagers in the preparations and celebrations. As of 2000, Uiaku had produced eight priests, two of whom rose to prominent positions in the national Anglican Church. People from across the community took great pride in their identity as Christians, insisting that the appearance of missionaries on the Uiaku beach in 1890 had transformed life for the better by ending tribal warfare and ushering in peace. People told more intimate stories about how they had recovered from life-threatening illnesses after experiencing visions or dreams of Jesus, Mary, and other biblical figures or of how their faith in God had preserved them from a terrifying sorcery attack.

Even taking such attitudes into account, many observers would probably still assume that the Maisin were not "really Christians," pointing to spotty attendance at church services and common belief in such things as magic, spirits, and sorcery. Indeed, a small but growing minority of Maisin feel this way and have left the Anglican Church to join denominations like the Pentecostals and the Seventh-Day Adventists that insist upon a radical break with many traditional customs as a condition of being a Christian. Yet it does not follow that Maisin Anglicans are not Christians. From a nonsectarian point of view, it is clear that Christianity has assumed a bewildering variety of guises during its 2,000-year history and expansion across the globe. Ethnographers are not called upon to judge which if any of these versions is legitimate. As part of a holistic study of their culture and history, our job is to investigate what people mean when they identify as Christians (cf. Barker 1990a; Cannell 2006).

It is important to bear in mind that Christianity is not new for the Maisin. The village church was established long before the birth of the oldest living villager today.[3] The present generation does not regard Christianity as a foreign religion but as much a part of their identity as the origin stories of the clans. Yet the way Maisin understand Christianity differs significantly from the types of beliefs found among congregations in Western countries. It is largely the product of a "long conversation" between external church authorities and sacred texts, notably the Bible, and local cultural assumptions about the nature of spiritual powers.[4] This conversation has progressed in two overlapping registers. The first and most overt has to do with the official teachings and requirements of the Church. The Anglican Church of Papua New Guinea is a hierarchical organization, with authority flowing down from the bishop, through licensed priests, deacons, and lay-evangelists, to ordinary congregants. The Church exercises considerable control over the performance of services and teachings. Historically, there has been little space for local innovation, although this is now beginning to change with the encouragement of youth fellowship rallies and other largely lay-run initiatives. While conservative regarding its own practices and doctrines, the Church has historically been tolerant of local customs and beliefs. Unlike many Protestant missions operating in Papua during the colonial period, the Anglicans did not insist that converts separate themselves from their pagan neighbours and called for reform rather than abandonment of most Indigenous customs such as death rites and dancing (Wetherell 1977). If the congregants of St. Thomas Church don't insist on taking a larger role in church services, this is not because they are uninterested but because they accept a version of Christianity that accords the leading liturgical role to the clergy. If the Church has failed to reshape social practices to fit its doctrines, this is because its officials for the most part have seen little reason to do so.

Over the years, the Anglican Church has made some concessions to local culture (Barker 2014). The practice of blessing couples after a child or two has been born represents a compromise in which the Church recognizes marriage as a sacrament while allowing the Maisin a flexible means of dealing with the strict rules against divorce. Along with decorative tapa drapings, some local cultural colour in church services has been encouraged by Church authorities. Since the 1970s, parishes across Collingwood Bay have often celebrated patron saint days and Easter with feasting and traditional dancing (Gnecchi-Ruscone 1997; Hermkens 2007). During the 1980s, Deacon Russell Maikin translated the liturgy into Maisin and set it to traditional drummed chants to be performed by a choir in traditional dress during celebrations of Easter and the parish feast day honouring Saint Thomas (see Plate 7).

Still, the general picture at the level of official Anglican practices and doctrines is one of balanced separation: acceptance of the authority of the clergy in their own sphere of action on the part of villagers and tolerance of villagers' beliefs and actions in their daily life on the part of the clergy (Barker 1993). This is not the end of the story, however, because the long conversation has also carried on at a second register, in the course of people's life experiences. Drawing upon the thought of Max Weber, a great pioneer in the sociology of religion, Clifford Geertz (1973:100) has argued that, at its core, religion is a response to intractable crises of meaning that radically challenge our sense that the world is comprehensible, endurable, and ethical. When faced by a calamity (or opportunity, for that matter), most Maisin do not stop to sort out Christian doctrines from Indigenous beliefs. Instead, they draw on the

Figure 4.2 Celebrating Easter in St. Thomas Church, Uiaku, 1982. A chorus of men in traditional dress chants the liturgy in Maisin accompanied by drums. (Photo by A.M. Tietjen)

full compass of things they know or suspect, seeking confirmation from kin, neighbours, and clergy as they do so. The result is an ever-evolving popular religion made up of both local and imported ideas and practices.

The remainder of this chapter focuses mainly upon this second register: the religious beliefs and practices of everyday life in Uiaku. Our concern is to understand the ways that Maisin think about and experience spirituality, whatever the source of their ideas. That understanding, in turn, is dependent upon a conception of the nature of the cosmos and their place in it.

COSMOLOGY

John Wesley Vaso and Weston Nonisa had an extraordinary story to tell, and I wondered if I heard them correctly. Two weeks earlier, John Wesley's father, John Hunt Vaso, had failed to return from hunting bush pigs. A search party was sent out. Early in the morning of the second day, Weston came upon John Hunt stumbling up a garden path. He was accompanied by three figures that vanished into thin air within seconds of Weston's arrival. A few days later, I got the full story from John Hunt himself. The hunt had been promising at first. His dogs scared up a large boar, but every time he drew close to throw his spear, the animal escaped deeper into the bush. Eventually, he found himself in the deep forest, well beyond the garden zone. It was getting dark. The pig suddenly transformed into a large old man with dirty hair and a twisted beard. John Hunt knew at once that he had been lured by a *yawu kosaro*, an extremely dangerous bush spirit. The spirit grabbed him and in the ensuing struggle through the night and part of the next day attempted to kill him by dragging him across sharp sago thorns and then trying to drown him. On the point of collapse, John Hunt called the name of his deceased younger brother. He felt a tap on his shoulder. The *yawu kosaro* vanished to be replaced by his brother and two of his deceased aunts. His brother asked, "Why are you worried? If he wanted to kill you, he would have done so." Exhausted, John Hunt slept, protected by the ghosts. The next morning, they woke him up and led him to the garden path where the group encountered Weston.

Fantastic as the story sounded, no one doubted its truth. Every adult knew similar tales of encounters with ghosts, spirits, and other supernatural beings. Such encounters were infrequent, initiated by the spirits themselves, and could happen to anyone—including me! I was interested in interviewing healers who I had heard had the ability to see the reflections of spirits mirrored in water as they passed. One of the most powerful was a wizened blind woman living alone in Ganjiga, Marcella Adeva. When I first visited, I was unnerved by Adeva's milky blue eyes that seemed to see right through me. She abruptly cut off my questions and engaged in an animated argument with, as far as I could see, herself and then retreated to her windowless hut. A weird voice issued from inside, demanding to know who I was and why I was so interested in "mother." My research assistant explained that Adeva's two deceased daughters resided with her in the hut. They ordered me to leave. A few days later, I was invited back by the daughters and completed the interview. It was a freaky experience, but informative. Like ordinary villagers, I came to rely on healers for insights on spiritual matters. I found them remarkably engaging and open in sharing their knowledge and experiences. All considered themselves good Christians whose healing powers derived from God. Indeed, two of the most respected were senior members of the Mothers' Union.

Like most Melanesians, the Maisin assume that they share the physical world with a host of spiritual entities and forces. They are not, however, particularly superstitious in the sense of being credulous. Stories of encounters with the supernatural get weighed and assessed according to what people know of these forces; they question and sometimes reject claims that strike them as unrealistic. Nor do the Maisin live in a kind of communion with the spiritual world. Some people pray to the Christian god, and many more allow the priest to pray on their behalf, but only sorcerers and healers regularly appeal directly to spirits for help. People don't pay much attention to spirits except when they intervene directly in their lives, as when the *yawu kosaro* attacked John Hunt.

If the Maisin understandings of spirits strikes many of us as strange, it is because most people in industrialized societies work with different assumptions about the nature of the things—that is to say, with a different cosmology. Most Westerners, if they believe in God or gods at all, conceive of spiritual entities as residing far away, concerned and caring perhaps, but nonetheless leaving us to deal with our day-to-day affairs as best we can. The business of explaining spirituality is mostly left to specialists like theologians, religious ministers, or clairvoyants. It is possible in the West to get by without concerning oneself at all with spiritual matters or denying their existence entirely, and many people do. People thus share a general set of cosmological assumptions that makes it possible to define themselves as "very religious" or "not religious" at all. Such claims would make no sense to the Maisin because they work from cosmological assumptions that place living humans and supernatural forces within the same physical environment. The Maisin simply *know* that there are spiritual entities that periodically intrude directly in people's lives in the same way that we "know" that germs cause sickness. For most people most of the time, these are commonsensical assumptions that require no further explanation.

Maisin notions of the supernatural tend to be rather fluid and flexible. Apart from the clergy, who speak only about Christian entities, there are no Indigenous authorities to assure orthodoxy. A handful of healers claim knowledge about specific spirits, but most people share only a vague understanding of the spiritual world. Aside from responding to inquisitive anthropologists, people talk about the supernatural mostly in response to events that are believed to have spiritual causes. They draw upon oral traditions, general assumptions about the nature of the spiritual, and the state of social relations at the time to come up with plausible explanations. The more significant the event, the wider the range of speculation as to the spiritual causes.

Here is an example. In January 1983, the Vayova River overflowed its banks after weeks of heavy rains. A large portion of Ganjiga village was flooded. While no houses collapsed, several were seriously undermined. Nobody doubted that the disaster had a spiritual cause. Many people in Ganjiga suspected that sorcerers from the Uiaku side of the river had called on spirit familiars to cause the flood in retaliation for a long-standing feud. The Uiaku people, however, raised other possibilities: some Ganjiga people had annoyed other villagers by making gardens on disputed land, thus prompting a sorcery attack, or perhaps God had sent the flood to punish Ganjiga people for lax church attendance. During a long, contentious meeting to discuss the disaster, several people noted how one of the clans on the Uiaku side had traditionally possessed magic to cause flooding and so surely was involved. This was vigorously denied by the senior members of the clan, who protested that their ancestors had given up the magic when they became Christians. In the end, nothing was resolved but people worried about a retaliatory spiritual attack for some time.

The Maisin recognize that spirits and spiritual forces are powerful and usually invisible to living humans. Explanations cannot help but be variable because so much rests upon surmise. All the same, an examination of many explanations clearly reveals common underlying assumptions. These concern the nature of spiritual power, the types of entities that embody that power, and the relationship between living humans and the divine.

Spiritual entities share a trait of "strength" or "power," *anno wenna*. When applied to humans, the term describes physical strength: an adult may evince *anno wenna* but an infant does not. When applied to supernatural entities, the concept resembles the eastern Melanesian and Polynesian idea of *mana*. *Anno wenna* is not a substance; it is an attribute of entities that effect transformations (Keesing 1984). This potency is at once dangerous and creative. Humans must prepare themselves through certain rituals to build up their own "strength" before approaching spiritual entities if they wish to survive the encounter. Approached correctly, spiritual force effects the positive transformations necessary for survival: success in subsistence activities, for instance, and the maturation of children. Unfortunately, spiritual forces may also be manipulated to cause misfortunes as in the case of sorcery attacks or disasters like the Ganjiga flood. Humans have no choice but to try to manipulate spiritual forces, to draw upon and direct their transformative power. Yet humans ultimately cannot control the divine world. With the somewhat ambiguous exception of the Christian god, spiritual entities are intrinsically amoral. They can aid, harm, or ignore the living as they please.

The Maisin encounter a range of entities that manifest spiritual *anno wenna*. Some places, like gardens for instance, hold spiritual potency through their association with ancestors. The most common form, however, is magic. Individual Maisin use magic for a wide variety of applications: gardening, hunting, fishing, healing fevers, sexually attracting a mate, preventing pregnancy, and so forth. People are secretive about the magic they possess, but the forms I've seen or heard about all involve special leaves, barks, or odd-shaped rocks over which a simple incantation is chanted. Before using their magic, owners prepare themselves by avoiding sexual intercourse and eating foods deemed to be "hot." Those who fail to prepare or use magic improperly may be harmed and even killed by it. Whenever people come into contact with spiritual forces, they take on the quality of *anno wenna* themselves and

117

pose a risk for others. Hence, magical practitioners take precautions when their magic is active. They don't share food with others and keep their magic out of sight. Stepping over magically treated objects such as hunting spears will make a person sick.

The Maisin's environment is inhabited by a variety of spirits. The most commonly encountered are spirits of the recent or distant dead. As Christians, Maisin state that when a person dies, their spirit (*yawu* = "breath") eventually goes to Heaven. Yet people expect ghosts to linger around their homes for some time after death. One never sees them directly. They appear to their kin in dreams and visions, or to healers as reflections on the surface of water as they pass. The recently deceased retain their names and identities. They are known as *kaniniwa*, a word also used to denote "soul," "reflection," "shadow," and "picture." When a young person dies suddenly and unexpectedly, his or her ghost may hover around the village for days or even weeks. People do not venture into the gardens at such times. Women and children, whose "strength" is not as great as men's, are especially vulnerable to attack from the ghost, who may be angry over its untimely death or just lonely. The Maisin often attribute the deaths of babies to ghost attack. All the same, the recent dead can also be very helpful. They often appear in the dreams of their close relatives, showing good places to make gardens, to hunt, or to fish.[5] Some also act as spirit familiars for sorcerers and healers, as we shall see later in this chapter.

For the most part, however, the spirits that the Maisin believe inhabit the bush and garden areas are anonymous. *Waa*, as they are called, were once human, but their specific identities have been lost. Maisin know of them mainly through folktales. Ghosts in these stories sometimes appear as old people, ravenous for human flesh; in others, they trick the living by donning skins that make them appear as sexy young men and women. The stories are often gruesome, but in general the Maisin don't worry much about *waa* as they are not imagined to be very interested in the living and only attack when disturbed, as when people speak loudly or let their children run wild when first clearing a garden.

At a further remove from the villages, in the deep forest and in rivers flowing down from the heights of the mountain wall, dwell certain spirits that may never have been among the living. Very few hunters venture this far and thus rarely encounter them. John Hunt's *yawu kosaro* belonged to this group. A few elders I worked with claimed to know the names of some. I purchased a striking tapa cloth whose design featured a monstrous form, with spades in the place of its legs and arms. The woman who designed the cloth, herself a healer, came from the Aisore clan, which traditionally had the magic to call this spirit from its home in the mountains to cause flooding. Maisin more often encounter another form of bush spirit that inhabits the bodies of river eels. These eels, called *yun tamati*, "water men," attack women by invisibly entering their bodies through their vaginas and causing severe sickness marked by cold chills.

Prior to the arrival of the missionaries, the Maisin do not seem to have recognized any deities. However, everyone today knows of God, Jesus, and other Christian figures through church services and the Bible. Most villagers treat biblical figures as divine entities that continue to exist and influence the world. Angels or figures such as Jacob from the Old Testament or the Virgin Mary, sometimes visit in dreams, usually when people are seriously ill. Some friends told me that they had been visited by Jesus himself, although they were only able to look upon his feet, not his face. In general, people consider such interventions as benign, occurring at moments of personal crisis. They thus form an exception to the assumption that spirits are amoral. Yet there is some ambiguity on this point, especially in Maisin thinking about God. The Maisin accept church teaching that God is an omnipresent being. They credit him with the creation of everything and, as we'll see below, hold that faith in God and Jesus provides protection against sorcerers. Yet not everyone sees God as always benign or helpful. Like a lesser spirit, he can be capricious or moved to anger by slights. Many assume that God's interventions in the world must be on a scale with his greatness and power. Thus, people tend to attribute major natural disasters to God's anger. Elders who remembered the Mount Lamington volcanic explosion of 1951, which killed around 4,000 people in the central part of Oro Province, told me that it was God's revenge against the Orokaiva people of the area who had angered him by failing to keep their churches neat and clean.[6] Most people saw the typhoon of 1974, which levelled Tufi, as another instance of God's revenge against local failings, and similar rumours circulated after Ganjiga was flooded.

Magic, ghosts, spirits, and even God as Maisin think of them exist in intimate relationship with living people. They exert *anno wenna*, transformative strength, upon which the living depend for the fertility of their gardens and the renewal of society. Yet they are unlike people, who are constrained by the moral requirements of reciprocity. The transformative power of spirits reflects their amoral nature: the ability to act in self-willed ways without consequence to themselves. All the same, perhaps because they depend upon them for survival, people assume that spiritual forces respond to human entreaties and interactions, whether in the form of magic, prayers, healing rituals, or sorcery attacks. Thus, when something goes terribly wrong (just as when things go exceptionally well), there is a reflexive tendency to assume that the explanation for why spiritual forces have acted rests ultimately in human relations and actions, the moral domain. This brings us back to the incident that opened this section. John Hunt and everyone else I talked to about his encounter with the bush spirit was convinced that a sorcerer had set him up. I pressed John Hunt to describe the spirits he encountered, hoping to learn details about Maisin cosmology beyond the vague outlines most people supplied. I was disappointed. He only wanted to talk about why someone wished him dead. Unless he could deal with what he considered the real causes, he might well be attacked again. Discussion of local religion thus turns on an understanding of morality and its limits, a location occupied in the Maisin imagination by the terrifying yet familiar figure of the sorcerer.

MONA'S DEATH

Over the course of a week in October 1982, I overheard a growing chorus of concern about Mona. Mona was a middle-aged widow who had suffered from a debilitating illness for over a year. Her alarmed family had turned to every medical resource available to them: the government-sponsored village medical aid post, traditional medicines, and a prayer service led by the priest.[7] When the nurses at the small hospital in Wanigela failed to cure Mona, her working relatives put up the funds to transport her to hospitals in the city of Lae and then Popondetta to be examined and treated by doctors. The doctors decided they could do nothing for her and sent her home. This was the clearest evidence, as far as villagers were concerned, that Mona was suffering from "village sickness." Powerful as they were, it was well understood that Western medicines were impotent against sorcery (cf. Street 2014).

Soon after, under a gloriously bright full moon, I canoed across the river to Ganjiga where Mona was staying in the care of a clan brother. She was emaciated, nearly a skeleton, lying on a thin mattress on the verandah where the occasional breeze cooled her feverish body. A group of men sat nearby, speaking in low tones. They were keeping *gumema*, a vigil to protect her from further attacks by spirits or sorcerers, who are believed to take advantage of the weak. One elderly man was applying bush medicine to her legs, which were paralyzed. A few nights later, a larger group gathered for a spirit séance. Accompanied by a chorus of young girls, the healer Adeva chanted spirit songs through the night, occasionally pausing to spray red betelnut spittle over Mona's body. Adeva later told me that during her trance her spirit had left her body in search of Mona's soul, which had been stolen and hidden by a sorcerer. She had been successful in returning Mona's soul to her body, but could not stop the sorcerer if he chose to steal it back again.

As Mona continued to decline, I heard increasing talk about how sorcerers were getting out of control. People reflected upon several recent deaths. If Mona were to die, perhaps her angered relatives would retaliate with sorcery against those they felt responsible. Where would it all end? The village councillor declared it time to have a meeting. Nearly all adults from Uiaku, Ganjiga, and the nearby village of Yuayu attended. Several people spoke, including (unusually) two women, reviewing all of the reasons someone might have wanted to hurt Mona or her family. In the end, several people claimed that a Yuayu man had employed sorcery after being rejected as a suitor. He and his relatives denied this vigorously. As people reviewed past tensions and spats, the elders reminded everyone that the purpose of the meeting was not to accuse or punish the sorcerer but to bring the community together, to find an answer to the social tensions that led to "all of the ladies dying." One speaker after another stated, "We have not gathered here to blame anyone." The underlying message seemed to be that healing the poor woman's body depended upon healing the social breaches in the society. Russell Maikin, a church deacon, confirmed this at the end of the meeting. He first asked everyone to join him in a prayer for Mona's recovery. He then prompted the assembly to shout as one: "She will be well!" But Mona didn't recover and so the meetings continued. After the third gathering, she quietly passed away.

The reaction to Mona's illness was not typical. Early death is common in the area. People suffer from a wide range of serious diseases like malaria, dengue fever, dysentery, and tuberculosis. Accidents from machetes, wild boars, or falling trees are not uncommon. Western medical facilities are sparse at best. During the 1980s, the village aid post offered only a small range of medicines, often running out, until closing down entirely in the late 1990s after years of intermittent government funding. Most deaths occur among infants and the very old. Close relatives will sometimes attribute them to sorcery, but people usually accept such tragedies stoically. It is different when an adult, in the full vigour of life, suffers a serious accident or a life-threatening illness, and it is especially frightening when they die. Not only are such deaths tragic, they are dangerous to the living for they may touch off a sorcery feud that will threaten the survival of everyone. This is the dark side of reciprocity: An eye for an eye. Payback. Coming in the wake of several deaths of middle-aged women, Mona's sickness thus triggered panic. People needed to know the reasons behind the attacks before they spun out of control. Fortunately, no one else fell sick in the weeks following Mona's death, and talk of sorcery gradually faded away.

Sorcery and witchcraft beliefs are very common, and anthropologists have devoted much attention to them.[8] Variations are found across Melanesia and, indeed, much of the world. In centuries past in Europe and the American colonies, church and government officials put hundreds of mostly poor women to death on charges of witchcraft and accused many more of secretly practising the black arts. Yet concerns about sorcerers and witches have receded in the industrialized world, and for many its persistence elsewhere is perplexing. Dismissing sorcery beliefs as "superstition" fails to explain why people like the Maisin accept its existence. Consider this: The Maisin know about germs, readily use Western medicine when available, and understand that carelessness leads to accidents. Further, nobody admits to actually practising sorcery, although some people—mainly healers—claim to know a great deal about how it is done. People thus know about alternative explanations for misfortune, and they possess no direct evidence that sorcerers even exist. They also know that the Church officially frowns upon sorcery and that many Westerners are skeptical of its very existence. It is possible that some Maisin occasionally resort to trying sorcery.[9] However, from an empirical standpoint, sorcery exists as a *post facto* explanation rather than an actual practice: as an explanation after the fact. The Maisin don't require proof of the existence of sorcery any more than most of us do of germs; they know it exists in large part because it provides a satisfactory explanation of why misfortunes like serious illnesses happen.

THE MEANING OF SORCERY

As we shall see, Maisin have long wanted to rid themselves of sorcery. However, from their perspective it defies common sense to deny its reality. No one questions whether sorcerers exist, although people do argue over specific interpretations and accusations. In the case of serious mishaps, people reflexively wonder, "Why did this happen?" They may think awhile about the identity or methods employed by the sorcerer, but inevitably they focus upon the state of social relationships. This is because sorcerers are assumed to be most often motivated by moral breaches or to be hired by people who are retaliating for some wrong. Talk of sorcery, then, intrinsically connects two things: personal misfortunes and the state of social relationships.

Before turning to this connection, we need to examine the ways Maisin talk about sorcerers and the closely related person of the healer. Unlike healers, who may be male or female, sorcerers are always male. Sorcerers and healers derive their power by virtue of having one foot in the world of the living and one foot in the spiritual realm. Both are thought to make themselves "hot" by shunning "cooling" foods, avoiding sex, and refusing to share their food and possessions with others. They take on the traits of spirits. People are wary around healers but live with them and use their services. In contrast, they imagine sorcerers to be solitary, living at the margins of the community, avoiding contact. Like spirits, sorcerers are thought to be amoral and self-willed. Lacking reciprocal morality, they are prone to jealousy and selfishness and are quick to anger. They are greatly feared, yet there is also an element of tragedy in the Maisin image of sorcerers, for they are the victims as much as victors of their powers (cf. Stephen 1995). Maisin describe sorcerers as *dagari*, a complex concept that combines the characteristic of greediness with being physically crippled. Sorcerers exemplify individualism for the Maisin, which in this reciprocal society is generally not a desirable trait. Indeed, the sorcerer in many ways represents the antithesis of moral being for the Maisin: he is a figure of evil. Shrouded in secrecy, powerful and feared, he is at the same time lonely and vulnerable. Sorcerers must always be on guard against retaliation from others with similar or greater powers. Even if they are successful for a time, their engagement with spiritual forces slowly erodes their health and eventually kills them. Thus, the Maisin often picture the sorcerer as physically bent and twisted, a man both suffering and causing pain.

Maisin are troubled by four main types of sorcery and witchcraft. The most terrifying originate from outside. In the old days, Doriri warriors would raid the coastal villages from their homes in the mountainous country to the west of Collingwood Bay. Maisin today fear their modern-day descendants, known as Kosaro, who they believe come down from the mountains in packs during the dry season to ambush unwary villagers as they make their way to and from gardens. The Kosaro sing a siren-like song that mesmerizes their victims, leading them off the garden path and into the bush. They are struck down and cut open. The sorcerers gut them like pigs, replacing their innards with magical substances. They then close up the victims and send them on their way back to the village to drop dead a day or two later. Equally feared are the Yafuni, female flying witches from Milne Bay Province to the east, who leave the bodies of their hosts during the night to roam far up the coast (Kahn 1986; Malinowski 1922). Yafuni are said to be physically brutal, leaving wounds and bruises on their victims visible only to healers. Kosaro and Yafuni are suspected whenever a sudden death inexplicably occurs. When a young man died in the midst of a soccer game at Wanigela, for instance, everyone I spoke to was certain that Kosaro or Yafuni were to blame.

Kosaro and Yafuni attacks, while terrifying, are rare. The more common homegrown types of sorcery are practiced only by men and rarely kill their victims immediately. The older form is known as *wea* ("poison"). While exact techniques vary, they all involve the sorcerer surreptitiously collecting something from the victim—such as some hair, a piece of clothing, or sand from a footprint—and heating this up, mixed with magical potions, in a bamboo tube over a fire. This was a type of "sympathetic magic," operating according to a similar principle as voodoo dolls: as the tube got hot, the victim broke into a deadly fever. Maisin believe that a second type of sorcery has mostly supplanted *wea*. This is known as *yawu* ("spirit" or "breath"). A sorcerer practising *yawu* befriends a dead spirit, often that of a close relative. At the bidding of the sorcerer, the *yawu* familiar steals the soul of the victim, hiding it in the bush. Bereft of his or her soul, the victim gradually weakens and dies. This is what most Maisin thought had happened to Mona.

Because sorcerers operate in secrecy, their presence can only be surmised. Except in rare cases where an apparently healthy person suddenly drops dead—a clear indication of Kosaro or Yafuni attack—the idea that a sorcerer has been at work usually begins as a suspicion, carried in worried whispers by loved ones. The Maisin are far from credulous. When a person gets sick, people first treat them with bush medicines or, in more serious cases, take them to the small hospital near the Wanigela airstrip or the provincial hospital in Popondetta for Western-style biomedical care. The relatives watch closely. The failure of these resorts firms up suspicions that sorcery must be at work. This bring us back to the two main purposes served by sorcery beliefs: when more immediate alternatives fail, they provide an explanation for misfortune and, just as importantly, suggest a course of action. For while sorcerers are perfectly capable of operating from pure malice, sorcery attacks are thought to usually be triggered by some action of the victim or their close relatives that either directly offended the sorcerer or led aggrieved parties to hire one. Thus, as suspicions harden into certainty, people engaged by the victim's plight begin to speculate on why he or she was attacked.

When a person suffers a serious illness or accident, they and their closest relatives rack their memories for things they might have done that provoked retaliation. In the close confines of village society, the list of slights and petty jealousies are endless. A sorcerer may attack or be hired to do so because the victim or the victim's kin stole some food from a garden or failed to share a smoke, or he may act out of jealousy because the victim possessed more valued things than others or because they were particularly successful as gardeners or lovers. The Maisin refer to such provocations as *daa*, a word English speakers translate as "mistake." A "mistake" is not wrong in any absolute sense. All the same, "mistakes" share a common feature: they deny reciprocity in some way. This facet is more obvious in the case of theft or adultery, but it is in play as well in cases where the sorcerer reacts in jealousy against someone who has a better garden, more valuable shell ornaments, or merely more friends than others. Success as much as deliberate misdeed can upset the fine balance of reciprocal relationships and trigger retaliation from a sorcerer. It was for this reason, you will recall from Chapter 2, that a villager decided to turn the iron-roofed dwelling built for him by his son into a shed rather than risk provoking jealousy by moving in.

A tragic illness or accident, particularly in the case of young to middle-aged adults, triggers a process of recollection and reflection that spreads if the victim fails to respond to treatment. A remedy depends upon healing the social breach that provoked the attack. Yet there is no certain way to know. It's at this point that families approach healers. While many Maisin know of bush medicines and some healing magic, healers are elderly women and men who in many ways resemble sorcerers and thus hold an ambiguous reputation. Because they also deal directly with spiritual forces, they too must prepare their bodies to make themselves "hot" and be cautious in their interactions with others. They make use of *yawu* spirit familiars whom they send out to recover stolen souls, as Adeva was attempting during the séance held for Mona. Healers are feared for their sorcerer-like qualities, but necessary. In their desperation, families go to healers in hopes they will use their powers to identify the "mistakes" that triggered the attack. Armed with that knowledge, the family may confront or, more often, send a gift to the aggrieved party in the hopes that they will desist.

There is no guarantee that such resorts will work. Indeed, they may make things worse if the individuals who are given gifts to desist feel falsely accused. The final resorts are to ask the Anglican priest to pray to God for salvation and, as we've seen, to hold a community meeting in which people are enjoined to air any and all relevant tensions. The cure at all these levels remains the same: restoring social amity by overcoming a breached relationship. People do not seek to punish the sorcerer or the people who may have hired him while the victim lives. This was the thrust of Deacon Russell's attempt at the end of the first meeting addressing Mona's illness to get everyone to shout in unison, "She will be well!" The health of the sorcery victim was tied intrinsically to the health of social relations within the community.

Anthropologists have long been fascinated by sorcery and witchcraft and have developed a range of explanations for such beliefs. Sorcery can be seen as a negative sanction that functions to reinforce social norms. Many Maisin are comfortable with that type of explanation. While they don't like sorcerers, they credit them with keeping people in line. Children grow up not only knowing that sharing things is good but also that those who fail to reciprocate get attacked and killed. They also learn of the dangers of standing out too much from the crowd, by owning too many things or by showing off their accomplishments. Sorcery thus acts as a kind of social levelling mechanism. The functionalist explanation, however, is not sufficient, for, as we saw with Mona, sorcery is just as capable of disrupting social life as reinforcing it. Many anthropologists see sorcery as a form of symbolic violence, a projection of the struggles and tensions between social factions. At any one time, sorcery accusations provide a fairly good gauge of the points and levels of community conflict. It is not surprising, given the tensions we've explored in Maisin marriages, that in-laws are often suspected of resorting to sorcery against each other. Finally, as we've seen, sorcery beliefs provide people with a framework for understanding why tragedies happen and how they should respond to them. In the words of one of the most famous students of the phenomenon, "witchcraft helps explain unfortunate events" (Evans-Pritchard 1937).

Such theories help us understand the workings and logic of sorcery beliefs among the Maisin. Yet they leave out, I think, a deeper dimension. A consideration of sorcery leads us back to the way Maisin conceive of the cosmos and the human place within it. The trigger for a sorcery attack in almost all cases is a breach of morality, a denial of reciprocal balance. This is easy for us to grasp. The notion of sharing is by no means a foreign concept for Westerners. What I have found foreign and to this day extremely difficult to comprehend is that the Maisin do not rank the wrongs that provoke attacks. The reasons given for sorcery attacks leading to death have often struck me as amazingly trivial and petty. One man I got to know quite well, for instance, was widely believed to have employed sorcery to murder his own sister because she had not shared a cigarette with him. That sorcerers kill just as readily for trivial as for serious provocations reflects the assumption that they, like other spiritual forces, are amoral and capricious. Yet it is clear that the Maisin nearly always reserve some blame for the victim. It is they, after all, who provoked the attack in the first place, they who made the "mistake" and thus brought the wrath of the sorcery upon themselves. Maisin understandings of sorcery thus reveal a rather bleak assessment of the human condition. To live a good and long life, a person needs to meet his or her reciprocal obligations to kin without fail. Yet it is virtually impossible to do so. No wonder, then, that the Maisin look upon old people with respect verging on awe. Anyone who has reached old age, it can be assumed, has successfully navigated the difficult shoals of social relationships and the perils posed by spiritual forces. It is equally little wonder that from the time of the arrival of the first Anglican missionaries, Maisin have tried repeatedly to rid their communities of the scourge of sorcery.

ON RELIGIOUS CHANGE

In June 1983, one of Anne's clan mothers—a superb tapa artist and tattooist—asked me to record a dream. I soon realized that Naomi Vatava was sharing a remarkable experience. Her long-deceased husband had appeared to her to lead her back across the migration path their ancestors had taken to the origin place of Bedaide where the ancestors first emerged from under the earth. As Naomi related the emergence of each clan bearing its distinctive insignia and

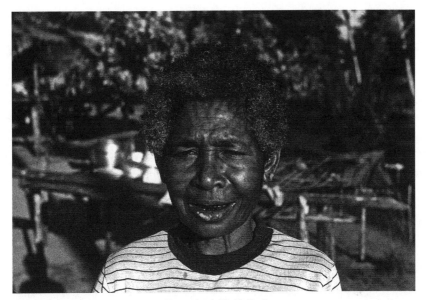

Figure 4.3 Naomi Vatava, 1982. (Photo by A.M. Tietjen)

rights, it felt like I was witnessing the event with her. The small crowd that had gathered fell into total silence as she reached the climax of the story:

> They called for the fourth clan to climb out. So those people got their things and began climbing. The people on top called out, "What are you bringing up?" They said, "If you people hit our children or do something wrong to us, we won't use our hands or sorcery (*wea*), but we will kill you with our eyes." So the people on top said, "Oh, we don't want them up here! Use the knife to cut the ladder off." When they cut the ladder, those people fell down and landed at the bottom. The wife asked, "What is that noise like thunder?" The husband said, "It is those people hitting the bottom. We don't want them to come up because if they do our community will be no good. So we cut the ladder." The people still in the cave called out, "All right. We all wanted to come out, so we worked on that ladder day and night. But you people don't want us up there and so you cut the ladder. We will live down here, but our language will be different from yours."

Having shown her this vision, her husband returned Naomi to the world of the living.

The phrase I translate above as "our community will be no good" in Maisin is *tauk ramara sii*—literally, "living eternally bad." It's a phrase I heard a lot during Mona's sickness and the aftermath of John Hunt's near-death experience

127

with the wild bush spirit. But it wasn't just fear of sorcerers or spirit attacks that prompted dark mutterings of *tauk ramara sii*. People said the same when the cooperative store closed for lack of funds; they said it when they failed to to build a new church; they said it when some of the school kids razzed their headmaster. They said it a lot. As I probed a bit further, I realized that *tauk ramara sii* was the negation of the key value of *marawa-wawe*. "Bad living" is a denial of reciprocal morality, a place in which people care only for themselves: where, as in Naomi's vision, people kill others simply by looking at them. It represents a breaking through of the unrestrained amorality associated with spirits into the moral world of the living. It is social death.

A preoccupation with the threat of uncontrollable sorcery likely preceded the arrival of the missionaries. When Percy John Money arrived in Uiaku in 1902 to build the first school and church, he was surprised to be approached by a group of men bearing wrapped bundles of objects, signalling to Money to take and destroy them in a fire. Money attributed the event to God reaching into the hearts of the unconverted Maisin. Yet Maisin repeatedly orchestrated purges of alleged sorcery materials over the following decades, requesting missionaries do the dangerous work of destroying magical substances. These must have been highly disruptive events since they entailed accusing individuals of sorcery. This in turn suggests that they were precipitated by crises, an impending sense of *tauk ramara sii*. In itself, the arrival of white men likely triggered such a crisis, not least the police killings of at least three Maisin men and the wounding of an unreported number at the beginning of 1900. In 1920, the district missionary supervised the destruction of "poison" lime pots in Uiaku, followed by a feast in which the alleged sorcerers were fed "cold" foods to end their power. This purge came in the wake of the worldwide influenza epidemic which killed many people in Collingwood Bay. A cult centred on a snake deity swept through the region during the same period, leading people to abandon their gardens to engage in weeks of all-night ritual dancing to heal their bodies and their communities.[10] Similar combinations of sorcery purges and healing cults occurred in the early 1930s and 1950s (Barker 1990b; 2001).

Looked at from the outside, the persistence of sorcery despite the century-long presence of Christianity and the periodic purges suggests that Maisin still largely adhere to "traditional" religion; that they are, as one anthropologist described a similar community in Milne Bay, "Sunday Christians, Monday sorcerers" (Kahn 1983). This is misleading. Maisin do not experience sorcery as a remnant of pre-Christian religion but as a living reality that adapts to its time. The purges of the past, I was told, focused on "poison" (*wea*) sorcery, leading to its demise and gradual replacement by the "spirit" (*yawu*) variety. I heard stories of how the dreaded Milne Bay "flying witches" (*yafuni*) relied on invisible spirit powerboats and cars to reach victims in distant places and of a secret market at Tufi where one could purchase newfangled sorcery techniques such as flashlights that killed merely by being pointed at their victims.

This last image, eerily echoing the climax of Naomi's story, suggests that while sorcery may be beaten back for a time, the threat of "bad living" forever looms on the horizon. It looms because, like sorcery attacks, *tauk ramara sii* tracks human failures, of people pursuing their own selfish interests rather than contributing to the welfare of the group. Putting aside the more exotic elements—the snake deities, spirit songs, trances, and the like—the healing cults of the past served to pull people together in the midst of crises that threatened to divide them. To borrow the terminology of the great French sociologist Émile Durkheim (1915), they were moments of "social efflorescence" in which people performed their society, healing as they experienced a communal wholeness. In anthropological parlance, the healing cults were "revitalization movements": responses to crises that drew upon and synthesized Indigenous and introduced elements in the effort to comprehend changes and forge a way forward (Wallace 1956).

Missionaries regarded the early snake and subsequent healing cults with suspicion, but they did not interfere. In one prominent case, the district missionary even praised the leader of a healing cult as an emissary of God and a sign of the inroads that the Christian faith was making on local religious understandings (Barker 1990b). It should be borne in mind that Christianity itself emerged out of a revitalization movement and that its 2,000-year history and long journey across the earth has been in no small part a story of merging and blending elements from many different cultures. In the Maisin case, this blending is masked by the conservatism of the Anglican Church, which in its basic ritual practices and institutional order has changed far less over the past century than the society the missionary arrived to transform.

By the 1990s, however, the stability of the local church was being challenged from without and within as new and generally more conservative theologically sects swept across Papua New Guinea (Barker 2012; Jorgensen 2005; Robbins et al. 2001). Maisin living in town encountered other branches of Christianity and brought them back home. Four families set up a Pentecostal chapel where they engaged in worship markedly more inclusive and livelier than the rigid Anglican mass. Several individuals, immediately identifiable by their gleaming white (non-betelnut-stained) teeth, began meeting beneath a house in Ganjiga on Saturdays for Seventh-Day Adventist services. Meanwhile, the young Anglican priest, himself a Maisin, initiated a youth fellowship group in Uiaku. This proved enormously popular, and soon chapters popped up across the parish in both Maisin and non-Maisin villages.

When I returned to study the anti-logging movement in March 1997, I found something of a religious revival going on (Barker 2003). The church services were better attended than a decade earlier, a large number of hymns had been translated into Maisin, and people were very excited about the arrival of two volunteers from the Summer Institute of Linguistics who were beginning the long process of translating the Bible into Maisin. For the first time, I saw people walking through the village carrying Bibles for personal study. During the weeks leading up to Easter, the youth held large rallies in each of the Maisin villages. Under palm leaf arches, richly festooned with flowers, young men and women joined in group dances and gospel singing, accompanied by guitars. The celebrations were followed by a meal and then hours of individual testimonials delivered by youth leaders, mainly males. Unlike the sermons given in church, the testimonials did not focus on biblical lessons but were highly personal accounts of the speakers' brushes with sin and their deliverance through faith in Jesus.

A few months before my arrival, there had been a purge of alleged sorcery objects. Members of the Melanesian Brotherhood, a religious order originating in the Solomon Islands, led a group of mostly young people to confront individuals thought to be hiding "old things": objects that could be used to compel spirits to attack others. As crowds gathered, owners reluctantly surrendered old ornaments, charms, and the like to the Brotherhood, who took them away to destroy. The owners I spoke with were still angry about the loss of their property and the implicit accusation that they were sorcerers, but the participants were still elated by the demonstration of God's protective power. I heard very little talk about sorcery per se, but several people declared that only faith in Jesus could save one from the sorcerer. This healing power was demonstrated at the youth fellowship meetings which climaxed with a laying on of hands for those experiencing illness. At the Easter service, I was startled when the heads of two adolescent girls slammed into the sand by my feet. They toppled backwards in turn as the priest laid his hands on their heads to bless them as they knelt at the altar rail. In the language of Christian charismatics, they had been "slain in the spirit," a form of religious ecstasy in which the Holy Spirit enters the body of the worshipper. Unfortunately, nobody had informed the congregation that in Pentecostal and charismatic churches fellow worshippers catch the slain so they don't harm themselves. The girls soon got up and returned to their pews without appearing to have suffered much harm. Their proud father told me afterwards that they had been sick for a long time, but now that the spirit of Jesus had entered their bodies they would be well.

It is perhaps not entirely coincidental that the religious revival occurred during a period of intense excitement as Maisin fought against the theft of

Figure 4.4 Christian youth fellowship gathering, 1997. (Photo by J. Barker)

their lands by developers (Chapter 6). Certainly the combination of sorcery purge and spiritual healing movement followed a familiar pattern. In addition, during this period young people were enthusiastically donning feathers and tapa to engage in traditional dances and resurrect dimly remembered customs. This was done primarily to fete visiting environmentalists and dignitaries, but there was no denying the enthusiasm with which people performed. I felt a bit like I had walked into the midst of a revitalization movement. Yet it was different from the earlier events as described by elders or recorded in mission archives. This time the healing "cult" occurred within the confines of orthodox Christianity, albeit a markedly more individualist form than the conservative Anglicanism most villagers were used to.

The shifting nature of Christian practice and discourse was unsettling for many elders. They recalled that in the past the village church provided a foundation of community unity. On big days like Easter, everyone pitched in to decorate the church, cook and share the feast, and contribute tapa and money to the mission. Young people respected and obeyed their elders, and so the hard work got done. They suspected the late night fellowship meetings were mainly an excuse to party and have sex. It is difficult to assess the reality of such claims or the long-term implications of an increasingly individualistic Christianity. However, the cultural reverberations are clear enough. The threat of things falling apart, of *tauk ramara sii*, always lurks on the horizon. It can be delayed by confronting sorcery directly. Yet, as one friend explained to me, it is not hard for a sorcerer to regain his power. The only lasting solution lies in the forging of unity in the community. And so it is to the challenges of building community that we must next turn.

Notes

1. Ziska Schwimmer's information on Maisin tapa was based on two quick visits to Uiaku in 1967 and 1975 (Erik Schwimmer, personal communication). While brief, the article's information on tapa making is mostly accurate and it includes a good translation of the myth associated with the *sividi* design, both owned by the Jorega clan.

2. Women are thus effectively barred from preaching in church services. During meetings of the Mothers' Union and youth fellowship group, however, some women offer prayers and short homilies.

3. Until recently, the Maisin did not keep track of their birth dates, making it very difficult to estimate precise ages. In 1982, I discovered that one of my oldest informants, Guy Kamanu, had been among the first Maisin baptized in 1911. Baptismal records indicated that Guy was a young adult at the time, so it is possible that he was born just before first contact with Europeans. While a font of information about the older culture, however, Guy had no personal recollection of Maisin life prior to the imposition of colonial rule.

4. Jean and John Comaroff (1991, 1997) use the phrase "the long conversation" in their magisterial study of the impact of Protestant missionaries on Tswana peoples in southern Africa during the nineteenth century. For other anthropological interpretations of Christian conversion, see Cannell (2006), Hefner (1993), and Robbins and Haynes (2014).

5. Dreams convey a critical source of truth and revelation in Melanesian cultures (Burridge 1960; Lohmann 2003).

6. Erik Schwimmer (1969) recorded similar explanations in the Orokaiva area 15 years after the disaster.

7. Limited Western health care has been available to the people of Collingwood Bay since around 1912, when a missionary nurse came to Wanigela. In the 1950s, the government established village-based aid posts run by medical orderlies with basic training in first aid and a limited range of supplies. Like most Melanesians, the Maisin make use of a wide range of medical options, including Indigenous cures, when they are sick or have an accident (Frankel and Lewis 1989).

8. Anthropologists generally reserve the terms "sorcery" and "witchcraft" for malicious forms of magic intended to harm people. In his classic work on the Azande people, Evans-Pritchard (1937) defines sorcerers as individuals who use materials to cause illness and witches as people bearing an inner substance that harms others. I follow

that usage here, but it should be appreciated that Maisin themselves don't make such distinctions, and a key technique I label "spirit sorcery" could just as easily be considered a type of witchcraft. The positive notion of witchcraft found in Western neo-pagan religions, notably Wiccan, is entirely alien to Maisin thought.

9.   The secrecy surrounding sorcery in Maisin culture is typical. However, there are a few places in Melanesia where sorcerers were public figures who enforced community morality, most notably the Mekeo people of the Central Province of Papua New Guinea (Stephen 1995).

10.   A healing cult focused on the figure of a python spirit known as Baigona was first reported in Miniafia-speaking villages on Cape Nelson in 1911. Over the succeeding decades, several religious movements promising healing and garden fertility spread across the Northern District, the best documented being the so-called Taro Cult of the 1920s (Williams 1928). Traces of these earlier movements, including stories of a spirit python, continued in Maisin healing practices in the early 1980s, collectively referred to as *sevaseva*. The "snake cult" of 1920, however, appears to have been the most intense of these collective movements. The endless nights of unceasing drumming threatened to drive the resident white priest mad, forcing him to flee Uiaku and depriving the Maisin of their own priest for the next 40 years (Barker 1987).

CHAPTER 5

COMMUNITY

Having completed my tapa, I packed it away and have rarely looked at it since. It was time to broaden my research. I was interested in everything to do with tapa: cultural heritage, local uses, and the implications of a growing market for the cloth as a form of "ethnic art." I had hoped to work with my favourite research assistant from 1981 to 1983—MacSherry Gegeyo— but he had since moved to Port Moresby. Community leaders nominated Roland Wawe, a cheerful 25-year-old bachelor who they felt had great leadership potential and would benefit from the experience. It was an inspired choice. I have had mixed success with my research assistants. Many find the work of conducting surveys, helping with translations, and other tasks boring after a while and stop coming. Roland, like MacSherry, had a keen curiosity about his culture. While at high school, he had started writing short plays depicting traditional activities and events. Towards the end of my stay, I joined an enthusiastic audience to watch the youth group perform one of Roland's works: a play about the elopement of two lovers and the subsequent battle between their enraged clans. Roland and I established a good working rapport right from the start. As the research progressed, Roland would often suggest topics that needed further attention and correct some of my more egregious mistakes.

Roland and I proceeded to conduct a systematic survey of households in Uiaku and Ganjiga focused upon tapa. I worked from a questionnaire of 12 standard questions. I asked women whether they grew any *wuwusi* trees in their gardens, who taught them how to make tapa, whether they worked with others when beating or dyeing the cloth, to whom they had recently given cloth, and whether they had sold any cloth recently. The survey progressed slowly, as we made time at each stop for chit-chat, betelnut, tea, and often a small meal. The survey often triggered extended conversations not only about tapa but about past lives and current concerns.

Figure 5.1 Roland Wawe, wearing a headdress he designed himself, with possum fur and bird of paradise plumes. (Photo by J. Barker)

At the conclusion of the survey, we paused to work out a list of the various ways tapa got used in the past and in the present. Old photographs suggest that from the 1920s the Maisin gradually replaced tapa as standard day-to-day clothing for adults with calico cloth purchased by plantation workers. Some Maisin women acquired sewing machines in the 1950s, and by the late 1960s, cheap shorts, t-shirts, blouses, and skirts had become the norm, with tapa worn mainly on ceremonial occasions. We had also learned of distinct types of tapa that used to be prepared for widows and widowers, to cover the heads of girls undergoing tattooing, and for other special occasions. Maisin also used to make large sheets of tapa to use as blankets during the cold nights of the dry season and as shawls to keep off the rain. In the past and to a lesser extent today, the Maisin traded tapa with neighbouring groups for cooking pots, pigs, and seagoing canoes. In the present, tapa remains an essential exchange item in formal prestations like bride wealth payments. On ceremonial occasions, Maisin wear tapa bearing the distinctive emblems marking clan and *Kawo* identities. Most tapa is made to be sold, but Roland demonstrated that even tough strips of old tapa are useful when one needs to tie up a bundle or lash sticks together to make a temporary shelter in the bush.

Armed with this basic catalogue, I began a second, more leisurely swing through the village, casually visiting households in the evenings and setting up longer interviews during the day. Things began in a promising way. People confirmed that tapa had a wide variety of uses and meanings. Among other things, I learned that most clans owned several named designs, not just the most prominent ones that I had seen people wearing on ceremonial occasions. This led me to systematically visit each named descent group to record the names of the designs they owned. Here I hit a roadblock. Often, all that people could remember were the names. Sometimes an elderly woman was able to trace a design on a blank strip of tapa or in the sand for me to photograph, but on other occasions people told me that while they had once possessed more tapa *evovi*, they had forgotten the patterns and even sometimes the names. Documenting the older uses also proved frustrating. Elders could provide descriptions of a variety of abandoned customs, but their information was often vague, and there were many contradictions.

Helpful as they were in filling out my survey, it was clear that people had other priorities with regards to tapa. Once my questions were answered, conversations quickly moved to money matters. The Maisin had exchanged tapa with outsiders for as long as anyone could remember. Towards the end of the colonial period, however, a market developed in Papua New Guinea for artifacts marketed to the (then) large number of expatriates working in the country and increasingly to tourists and overseas collectors of "primitive art."

Maisin tapa quickly found a niche, and by the early 1980s, apart from the rare sale of copra, had become the only local product people could reliably sell for cash or, in the case of the Anglican Church, for credit towards school fees and transportation costs for students heading back and forth to the high schools.

Times had changed from the days of the ancestors, people told me. Now you need cash to survive: to purchase basic necessities like clothing, medicines, and fish hooks; to pay ever-rising school fees and transportation costs for students fortunate enough to attend high schools; and for a few simple pleasures like tobacco or sugar. So villagers were relieved that a market had emerged for tapa. Success, however, brought new anxieties. Villagers were keenly aware that they had very little influence over the market. One could go to great expense covering the airplane ticket and the high freight costs to have a relative take a box of tapa to Port Moresby to sell, only to find that the shop owners were not interested. When they were, people had little choice but to accept the prices they set for the cloth. It wasn't long before the Maisin in town reported that the shops sold tapa for far higher prices than they paid the makers. Even Sister Helen Roberts in Wanigela, I was told by a few villagers, was making "millions" for the tapa she purchased on behalf of the Anglican Church.[1] It was unfair, but what could people do?

A second common complaint turned inward. Over and over again, I was told that tapa "belonged to all the Maisin people." Yet some women sold more and sometimes fetched higher prices, usually because they had relatives in town willing to sell on their behalf but also, in a few cases, because they produced cloths that outsiders considered especially fine and beautiful. Even women who I knew were doing better than others joined the chorus: all Maisin women should be able to sell the same amount of cloth for the same price. Anything short of this struck everyone as terribly unfair.

Reading through my notes on these interviews for this book, I am struck by their moralism. Frustrated as they might feel with the outsiders who set arbitrary prices and bought tapa if and when they chose, villagers directed their harshest criticisms at themselves. The problem, so I was told, is that people are too lazy to find purchasers for cloth, that they have allowed the quality of the cloth to slide, that those who have found success are too greedy to share their contacts with others, and that village leaders who should be working for everyone quietly make deals that benefit their own kin. Whatever success people enjoyed in selling tapa was countered by a keen sense of failure. "We are poor," people insisted. "Look at how dirty the village is. We have no shops, no good roads."

In previous chapters, we have seen how tapa provides a material reminder for the Maisin of the continuing importance of their ancestral culture.

Each piece of *wuwusi* a woman gathers from the garden, pounds into cloth, and decorates recapitulates basic and enduring aspects of life: the daily requirements of subsistence, the importance of kin, and the shadowy presence of spiritual forces and entities. Tapa, however, is also situated in the interface between the Maisin and the outside world. The focus of this chapter and the next shifts to this interface, to the ways the Maisin have adapted as their communities become increasingly integrated within wider regional and international political and economic orders. Compared to many places in the world, this process has, so far at least, progressed fairly smoothly for the Maisin. The people have not been deprived of their lands, sold off their resources for quick exploitation, or allowed their community to feel the scourge of alcohol abuse or gang violence. Yet, as my interviews concerning tapa reveal, the Maisin have often experienced this incorporation as a crisis of values requiring them to confront the very basis of their lives together as a community. This chapter, then, focuses on how the Maisin collectively manage the choices they face as members of a community. In particular, we look at two overlapping concerns—maintaining social order and making collective choices for action—concerns of law and politics respectively.

VILLAGER, CITIZEN, AND CHRISTIAN: THE CHANGING NATURE OF COMMUNITY

It's easy when visiting a village like Uiaku to see it as a world apart. Indeed, older ethnographies presented Melanesian village societies in this fashion, as timeless self-reproducing systems. Local Maisin do enjoy considerable autonomy in the ways they run their affairs, and to a considerable extent they draw upon age-old frameworks of exchange, kinship, and spirituality to do so. Yet, as we've seen, all domains of Maisin life have been deeply affected by the century-long presence of church and state and by the now-routine movements of people and goods between the villages and the rest of the country. What appears to foreign visitors as a "traditional" place would be barely recognizable to the Maisin's pre-contact ancestors. This is not only because of the presence of the mission station, intrusive sounds of radios and English words, or the transformed architecture of village houses. The very understanding of what a "village" is has been utterly transformed.

There is no equivalent in the Maisin language for the English word "community," yet it is clear that most people today think of their villages as communities, that is to say, as moral and political unities. This is a modern development (Barker 1996). People lived in villages long before the arrival of the Europeans, but they did not form communities. Instead they were aggregates of interacting clan-based hamlets allied with various "war" and "peace" leaders, the *Sabu* and *Kawo* of old. The Maisin clans were recent migrants into the area, and both oral and archival evidence strongly suggest that large villages like Uiaku were temporary arrangements for defence against enemy tribes. Abandoned village sites along the coast, marked by groves of tall coconuts, stand in mute testimony to the ease with which villages split up or were abandoned.

The work of both the mission and the government relied upon the existence of stable populations in permanent villages. The Administration appointed village constables, took censuses, and applied regulations, all of which assumed sedentary populations. The Anglicans also paid little heed to Indigenous forms of political organization and leadership. They built their churches and schools in the centre of existing villages to serve the whole population and in the process created, for the first time, village-wide institutions. Remaking villages into communities was a foundational project of the colonial era. They were the key units both for the regulation of local populations and for the incorporation of formerly autonomous local societies into the colonial system as a whole.

When Anne and I arrived in Uiaku in 1981, six years after Papua New Guinea had achieved independence, foreign missionaries and patrol officers were a quickly receding memory. Yet their efforts had left a deep and lasting imprint in the ways that the Maisin organized and perceived both their community and their place in the world. A few days after I arrived, Gideon Ifoki described how Uiaku was organized. The community, he told me, had three "sides" (*yovei*)—the village, the government, and the mission, each with distinct responsibilities, organizations, and leaders. Village activities included such things as making gardens, arranging work parties to build houses, and planning for major ceremonials, as directed by *Kawo* leaders and clan elders. Government activities focused on public works, such as the construction of medical aid posts, and undertaking economic initiatives for the benefit of the community. Two village councillors, who also represented Uiaku and Ganjiga at periodic meetings of a regional Local Level Government council[2] based at Tufi, provided leadership in the government sphere of interest with the help of committees made up of representatives from across their respective villages. Finally, mission activities included providing support for the priest and teachers and keeping the church and classrooms in good repair. The primary mission leaders were members of the church council, with representatives from across Uiaku and Ganjiga.

Gideon elaborated further. Village activities were organized as need demanded, but government and mission projects unfolded according to a schedule, with two days a week set aside for all members of the community to pitch in. Further, the government and mission "sides" encompassed several voluntary associations. The former included a youth club, which organized sports meets and dance parties for young people, and business associations. The mission side included the church council, the Mothers' Union, an elementary school Board of Management, and a Parents and Citizenship Association, which aided the school by purchasing badly needed supplies.[3]

It didn't take long to realize that Gideon's portrait of how the village worked was idealistic. Some of the organizations existed in name only, while membership in others waxed and waned. The distinctions between the categories of leaders and many of the activities often dissolved upon closer inspection. The "mission leaders" who organized church festivals, for instance, were at the same time "village leaders" who drew upon their kin networks to provide the needed food and labour. While there was always talk about the need for the village as a whole to undertake various projects, no person or organization possessed the authority on their own to plan or to order people to work. Everything depended upon people's willingness to participate. If they were unhappy with the organizers of some project or merely had more important things to attend to, they simply didn't show up. It was not uncommon for weeks to pass without any community work taking place.

Despite what appeared to me to be obvious contradictions, I found that many Maisin talked about the village in the same terms as Gideon. It was an accurate model of how most people thought things *ought* to work. This is by no means unimportant. In Uiaku, like most places, the heart of politics lies in the gap between what people think ought to be and what they actually experience. Keeping in mind that it is an idealization, we need to dwell a little longer on the three-sided picture of the village (see also Barker 2007).

Taken at face value, the model appears a direct legacy of the colonial period, a time when many Melanesians found themselves in a triangular relationship with missionaries and government officers (Burridge 1960). As the mission and government turned over their powers to Papua New Guineans during the late colonial period, some functions formerly exercised by European officials were passed on to local villagers. The modern village councillor, for instance, combines in his person some of the legal authority of the Native village constables and White patrol officers that preceded him. Yet more is at work here than simple substitution. The various offices and associations on the government and mission sides also reflect the growing integration of Maisin society into wider social, political, and economic networks. All have counterparts in hundreds of other villages where they were introduced as colonial authority expanded. Members of the Mothers' Union and delegates from the youth club regularly travel to the provincial capital for district meetings and social events. Provincial and national bodies set down rules of organization for their village counterparts and periodically provide small grants and training programs. In turn, the village committees, business associations, and school organizations take as their chief mandates the improvement of the village according to standards established on the outside: rationalized planning and sound fiscal management. For the Maisin, then, the former colonial triangle has expanded outwards from its local setting to bring them into a much wider set of relationships.

In speaking of the three sides of the village, then, the Maisin acknowledge their participation in these encompassing networks. They are not only villagers, they are also citizens of Papua New Guinea and members of the global Christian family. The community forms a nexus for these three networks and identities.

The three-sided model that Gideon and others described suggests that the village, government, and mission "sides" deal with different types of concerns. At a deeper level, however, the distinction implies discrete moral orientations that are somewhat in tension. Morality on the village-side is relational, defined in terms of reciprocal exchanges that ideally lead towards balance and amity. Citizens, on the other hand, are thought of as individuals who pursue their own self-interests within a free marketplace that determines their value according to absolute measures, the most basic being money. Their behaviour is ultimately constrained by a legal code that (in principle) applies equally to everyone. The mission-side presents yet another view of personal morality. While the Anglican Church promotes a strongly communitarian understanding of Christianity that contrasts with the individualism of citizenship, ultimately it too endorses a notion of individualism at odds with the exchange ethic. People should treat each other kindly and generously because, as children of God, their *personal* salvation depends upon it.

The idealized model suggests that the three sides with their distinctive concerns and moral orientations should exist in harmonious balance within the community. Yet rural Maisin do not participate equally in each of the three domains. The actual situation in Uiaku resembles less a triangle with three equal parts than a hierarchy of spheres. The village sphere is by far the most significant for the Maisin. The past century has introduced a new conception of community and an unheralded degree of specialized roles and forms of association. All the same, the degree of specialization is quite limited. People spend most of their time engaged in subsistence activities and meeting their obligations to kin and exchange partners. While they regard them as very important, villagers have only limited time left over for mission and government activities. Inevitably, the reciprocal values that are constantly reaffirmed in the village sphere tend to shape, although not determine, the ways people think about their roles as citizens and Christians.

This conclusion is corroborated by findings from a study Anne conducted on moral reasoning among Maisin men (Tietjen and Walker 1985). Drawing on a sample of 22 men including village, government, and religious leaders and non-leaders, she found that leaders in all three categories used more generalized and idealized forms of moral reasoning than non-leaders did. Her findings suggest that either leaders are selected for their ability to consider multiple perspectives or that "leadership itself and the role-taking experience it provides" are more important than education, age, or work experience outside the village in shaping moral attitudes (Tietjen and Walker 1985:988). Significantly, the interviews of leaders and non-leaders alike confirmed our ethnographic observations "that the issue of the relationship of the individual to the community is a moral issue of central importance to the collectivistically oriented Maisin" (Tietjen and Walker 1985:982). In contrast, the type of moral reasoning found in some domains of Western society—specifically the notion of individuals making moral choices based upon abstract universal moral principles—did not appear in the interviews.

In the final analysis, "community" for the Maisin is better understood as a project rather than as a place, one which has as its final goal the reconciliation of their identities as villagers, citizens, and Christians. The project reflects the changed conditions of Maisin existence since European contact, their incorporation into wider regional and international systems. That incorporation, however, is far from complete. To a degree unimaginable in industrialized countries, the Maisin remain largely self-sufficient, as much by necessity as choice. While people take their identities as citizens and Christians seriously, their assumptions about the nature of community continue to be informed primarily through their links with each other and thus largely in terms of reciprocity. Reciprocal values are especially central to the ways the Maisin talk about and deal with conflicts and social disruptions, that is to say, in the legal domain of community, to which we now turn.

THE LEGAL SYSTEM

The legal and political systems that exist in Uiaku today are hybrids of Western and Indigenous forms. Papua New Guinea is a modern democratic state with a constitution, an elected parliament, legal code, courts, and prisons. Every five years, the Maisin vote for a district and a provincial representative to the national parliament. Also, like other citizens, they are subject to the laws of the land. In principle, any adult villager who refuses to pay taxes or violently attacks another can be arrested and punished to the full extent of the law.

Practice, however, is another matter. From the earliest days of the colonial regime, it was recognized that Indigenous societies operated according to conceptions of justice that were often at odds with formal Western notions.[4] Few if any local people, for instance, considered it a crime to raid enemy villages, killing not just the men but anyone they happened across. Generally, the notion of committing a crime stopped at the boundaries of a person's kin and exchange networks. An additional complexity was that local societies often had very different notions among themselves of what types of behaviour constituted wrongdoing. Premarital sex, for instance, was perfectly permissible and even encouraged in some places and punishable by death in others. At the deepest level of difference, however, Western and Indigenous justice systems were and are oriented towards fundamentally different goals. Western law codes formally define offensive behaviours and punishments. If you are found guilty of a crime, you are (in principle) punished with a fine or imprisonment regardless of who you are or your relationship to the victim of your crime. Melanesians, in contrast, concern themselves with breaches in social relationships. An offence, real or perceived, will trigger retaliation, but not necessarily at the immediate offender, as a member of their kin may do. The community as a whole has a strong motivation to mollify those who have been wronged to stop a potential cycle of paybacks. Often the individual who caused the trouble in the first place—other than perhaps feeling shame—is left unpunished (Scaglion 2004).

As it expanded, the colonial regime put an end, at least temporarily, to most tribal warfare and established a legal system that in theory embraced all Papua New Guineans.[5] Practice was another matter. Government officers held authority to try cases, pass sentences, and arrest people who broke the law. But officers were thin on the ground; in a typical year, Uiaku might receive a couple of visits from the Resident Magistrate stationed at Tufi. The government relied heavily upon poorly trained and compensated village constables to enforce regulations and report crimes. Maisin elders recalled one village constable who became something of a tyrant, but generally—judging from patrol records and local memories—most did little more than show up when the government officer visited. In the early 1960s, with the establishment of a local government council for the Tufi sub-district, a local councillor took the place of the village constable. Patrols declined after this point, ending entirely in 1972, eroding the effective legal authority of councillors. The colonial regime had long made adjustments in recognition of cultural differences in the kinds of things Papua New Guineans considered crimes and their responses to them. For instance, the Papuan colonial regime wrote up legislation to deal with alleged sorcery and treated serious crimes like murder far more leniently than in Western countries. Local communities, however, were left to deal with most conflicts on their own, making use of long-standing practices such as compensation payments. Prior to Independence, the late colonial administration launched innovative experiments in developing a pluralistic legal system, setting up local courts in various parts of the country to deal with regular conflicts (such as theft or adultery) according to local understandings of justice.[6] These are now well established in many parts of the country, but not in Collingwood Bay. Here most conflicts and crimes continue to be dealt with locally, with only the most serious being reported to the tiny police detachment at Tufi. As we shall see, the threat of taking a case to Tufi remains potent in Uiaku but only as a last resort. On the rare occasions it happens, cases often languish for months before a travelling magistrate is available to hear them.

Considered broadly, a legal system is not limited to the ways people handle serious disruptions, conflicts, and crimes. It concerns the overall ways that people maintain social order, including in their daily routines. Such basic rules and expectations of proper behaviour are especially important in small-scale societies like the Maisin that effectively lack police and courts.

Like all people, Maisin maintain social order in their daily lives largely by adhering to shared norms and values. People experience enormous pressure to conform. From the time they can toddle, children are warmly praised for good behaviour such as sharing food and scolded when they misbehave. The nearly incessant gossip that forms a background buzz to village life provides an effective sanction most of the time. Except when they are in their gardens or the bush, the Maisin live their lives in full view of their neighbours. While people are very careful not to directly accuse someone of bad behaviour, which would in itself mark a breach of morality, gossip has a way of getting back to its subjects, forming a powerful check. Little rituals of etiquette also convey moral expectations. If you visit someone, you should bring with you a small gift of betelnut or tobacco; if you pass a group of seated elders, you should bow your head slightly as a token of respect; if you are standing in your canoe using a pole, you should place your feet in the hollowed centre of the log when passing near a village so as to not put yourself higher than others. Not to conform to these customs brings gossip, and gossip, in turn, causes one to feel shamed.

These kinds of sanctions are powerful because they form a kind of common sense, not open to critique. Consider another custom that I think of as the "falling down rule." One day I was standing at the riverbank when a young man poling a canoe lost his balance and flipped over. Because he had his feet positioned in the narrow slit of the hollowed-out log, he was trapped and in danger of drowning. Before I quite knew what was happening, the people around me flung themselves face down into the water. Only then did a few young men swim out to make a rescue. A few weeks later, the rescued man put on a lavish feast for those who had mimicked his fall. (Since I had not fallen, I was not included.) This all made perfect sense to everyone but me. When I asked my friends to explain the custom, I drew a blank. "It's just the correct thing to do," they told me, obviously puzzled by my simple-mindedness. From my perspective, the custom reflects the deeply held reciprocal reflex that runs through Maisin life. To Maisin, however, it's just the thing one does.

Maisin are very skilled at avoiding conflicts through the simple procedure of retiring to the privacy of a garden shelter or visiting a relative in town until tensions ease. Conflicts do periodically break out into the open, of course. Neighbours quarrel over ownership of a piece of land, couples get discovered in adulterous relationships, or villagers accuse others of stealing food from their gardens or houses. The Maisin repertory of wrongs includes much that Westerners would recognize as crimes in their own society because they cause damage to persons and property. A full listing of the triggers for conflicts, however, would include many actions that few outsiders would regard as crimes in any sense: neglecting to share one's food with sufficient generosity, making a show of one's material advantages, ordering others about, and so forth. At their heart, conflicts in Uiaku turn on a denial of reciprocity. Most conflicts get resolved quickly—the aggrieved parties talk out their differences; elders get involved and arrange for an exchange of food; or else one or the other disputant decides to back off, and the trouble gradually gets forgotten. Occasionally, however, the offence is simply too large to permit a ready solution, or the parties simply cannot let the matter rest and tempers continue to flare. The danger then is that the people who feel wronged may take matters into their own hands and retaliate, setting off a chain reaction of tit for tat that can threaten to turn a small dispute into a full-blown crisis, edging towards the kind of community breakdown we examined in Chapter 4.

Such a crisis threatened community peace towards the end of our first stint of fieldwork in 1983. One night, a boy from Ganjiga slipped into a house in Uiaku for a liaison with a girlfriend. Unfortunately for him, he went to the bed of the girl's mother, who raised the alarm. He was badly beaten by the girl's male relatives before escaping back across the river. A week later, an elder from the girl's clan, accompanied by his infant granddaughter, was sailing on his outrigger canoe past Ganjiga. One of the boy's uncles sped out in a motorized dinghy and cut the ropes holding the canoe together with a machete, causing it to capsize. Fortunately, the old man and little girl were rescued, but they could have easily drowned. In the aftermath, rumours spread that the young men on both sides of the river were pulling down spears and war clubs from the rafters of their houses in preparation for battle.

Lacking resident police or courts, the Maisin have two options when serious trouble breaks out: they can attempt to resolve the matter on their own or take it to an outside authority. Resolving a conflict internally requires the establishment of a new balance between aggrieved parties to end the cycle of escalating retaliation. Clan elders normally take the leading role. Immediately after the boy was beaten in the case related above, the village councillor from Ganjiga, who was also a senior member of a *Kawo* clan, visited the elders of the clans involved in an attempt to organize an exchange of food. Following the attack on the canoe, his efforts went into high gear to stave off another round of attacks. Another option would have been to convene a village meeting like that described in the previous chapter to deal with sorcery accusations. The aim of such meetings is to allow a full airing of tensions in the community in an effort to repair past wrongs and attain a new consensus. While the main players in a conflict are often subjected to public criticism, they are not punished. Indeed, to punish them would be counterproductive as it would likely be seen as a form of retaliation and thus escalate the conflict rather than resolve it.

People also appeal to extra-village authorities in response to major disputes. Elders remind villagers that, as Christians, people shouldn't fight; they should support one another and trust that God will see that justice is done. It is very difficult to tell how effective appeals to Christian values are. I suspect that on occasion they do give people a way to back down from further confrontations. Yet, when tempers run high, I doubt that people pay much heed. Appeals to the "law" are different because there is always a possibility that someone will brave the long voyage up to Tufi to involve the police and court in a local dispute. People admire the supposed efficiencies of the Western legal system. There is something very attractive in the neatness of clearly defined crimes and ready punishments as opposed to the seemingly endless back-and-forth of village practice. All the same, crossing the line from threatening to take a matter to court to actually doing so is fraught with risk. From the village perspective, involving the police and court may well be seen in itself as a form of retaliation, thus escalating a conflict rather than bringing it to a close.

This is basically what happened in the crisis between Uiaku and Ganjiga. Following the attack on the canoe, the Uiaku councillor sent up a request for the police to intervene. For once, the police boat had petrol, and so two policemen motored down to Ganjiga to make an arrest. People in Uiaku strongly supported the action. After all, the Ganjiga man had attempted murder. The Ganjiga councillor and his supporters saw matters differently. Having worked behind the scenes to reconcile the aggrieved parties, they felt betrayed. At the

Plate 1 Marua beach facing towards Airara village with the heavily forested Mount Suckling (Goropi) rising behind. The two women approaching are carrying clay pots filled with cooked food for a feast. (Photo by J. Barker)

Plate 2 Crossing the river from Ganjiga to Uiaku village. (Photo by J. Barker)

Plate 3 Applying the *dun* (red dye), Ganjiga village, 1982. Prisca Rairiga, in the centre of the photograph, received her tattoo a few months earlier. (Photo by A.M. Tietjen)

Plate 4 Part of a bride wealth gift. A live pig is trussed beneath the decorative tapa cloth. The bananas are a special gift, known as *tonton*. At the time of the marriage, the groom's male relatives promise to give three types of food to the bride's people—this was the third and final installment. The presentation is meant to impress viewers with the generosity of the groom's family. (Photo by J. Barker)

Plate 5 Iris Bogu. (Photo by A.M. Tietjen)

Plate 6 Rufus Yaga, the author's *toma* ("friend") and one of the finest Maisin dancers. His magnificent headdress is composed of bird of paradise, cockatoo, parrot, and rooster plumes, the latter denoting his membership in a *Kawo* clan. (Photo by A.M. Tietjen)

Plate 7 St. Thomas Day church procession, 2007. Fusing Christian worship with cultural heritage, the choir progresses into the church chanting the Anglican liturgy in the Maisin language to traditional drumming patterns. (Photo by A.M. Tietjen)

Plate 8 Maisin dancers greet the Stó:lō delegates, June 2000. Note the clan emblems (*evovi*) on the women's skirts. Women accompany the men's drumming by shaking dried bean pod rattles and branches. The arrival of outsiders supporting the anti-logging campaign triggered a revival of Maisin traditions. (Photo by J. Barker)

time Anne and I left the village, a few weeks later, tempers were still running high. Fortunately, clubs and spears remained stored away. The Ganjiga man who cut the canoe ropes paid a fine and returned to the village. A few weeks later, the long-planned food exchange took place and tensions eased.

Given distance and poor financing, the police and court at Tufi remain mostly theoretical sanctions for the Maisin. Still, my impression during my trips in the 1990s is that the Maisin have become more comfortable with the *ideal* of Western law. This shift in attitude is occurring as people return from working in the towns where reliance upon police and courts is much greater. It is also possible that the Maisin's success in fending off loggers in the National Court increased their regard for the system, at least as a means of dealing with outsiders (Chapter 6). I suspect, however, that the shift also reflects deeper anxieties. Many villagers worry that their communities, particularly young people, are less equal and less respectful of the values of reciprocity than in the past. One hears frequent complaints of petty theft and of fights breaking out between young men high on alcohol and locally grown marijuana. Young men who grew up in town, whose knowledge of Maisin and exchange connections are weak, are especially feared. The idea of throwing such miscreants in jail is appealing, even though it rarely happens.

On the basis of short visits, it is hard to gauge how real these concerns are. My impression is that Uiaku is by and large a peaceful and safe community. It has been spared the domestic violence and gang-related crime that have become enormous problems in Port Moresby and other urban areas. Yet people are anxious. They worry that outsiders wish to steal their resources while leaving them poor. They worry that the social problems in the towns will migrate to the villages. Their greatest concern is that the values that give order to their community are under siege. The good person is one who is generous, who willingly shares all she or he has in support of the community. Yet modern conditions make it increasingly easy for people to avoid reciprocal obligations, to act selfishly. Opting out of modernity is not an option. Villagers are keen to improve their material conditions with better schools, ready access to mass-manufactured commodities, and good medical facilities. How to achieve a better material life without forsaking the reciprocal values that provide security is perhaps the most urgent question the Maisin face today. It is at heart a moral question, one that is most vividly exemplified in the person and actions of community leaders.

LEADERS

The Maisin term for leader is *tamati bejji*, "big man." Maisin big men bear little obvious resemblance to their famous counterparts in the heavily populated New Guinea highlands. They do not own or manage huge pig herds, organize massive ceremonial exchanges, or boast of their achievements in swaggering orations. In fact, there is considerable diversity in the forms that leadership takes across Melanesia (Chowning 1979). Still, beneath that diversity one can detect some common principles. The key one is a pattern of political egalitarianism.

Maisin big men are like everyone else—only more so. When you walk through Uiaku, you see few if any signs of status. Some of the *Kawo* hamlets have large plazas and houses with trimmed thatch (a privilege enjoyed exclusively by ritually superior clans), but otherwise they look the same as their neighbours'. Most of the time, people go about the same subsistence tasks as everyone else. Apart from traditional ceremonial occasions when *Kawo* leaders dress in their finery, there is no clearly visible difference in rank between people. Leadership emerges when circumstances require or invite it; those circumstances, in turn, shape the nature of leadership and extent to which it actually gets exercised. There are endless gradations in which virtually any person, including women, may be considered "big" for a time. This became clear to me when I conducted a small and quite unsystematic experiment. I took a stroll along the entire length of Uiaku and Ganjiga, stopping to chat with every adult I encountered and asking them who they considered to be the "big people" of the village. Around a quarter of the 30 or so people I spoke with mentioned the village councillor and church deacon. That was the extent of any agreement. Most of my informants named people they turned to for advice, usually elders in their own clans. Several people nominated themselves. At the end of my stroll, none of the lists matched.

The term "political egalitarianism" is obviously relative. Clearly not all things are equal in Maisin society. Women are politically subordinated to men. Senior men and women likewise enjoy authority over their juniors. The most influential leaders emerge from a small subset of the society: middle-aged but still physically vigorous men. Further, belonging to a senior lineage within a *Kawo* clan allows a well-organized and connected man to stage large ceremonies within his own hamlet and thus demonstrate his managerial ability. Finally, men who have been to high school and worked for a time in professional careers are favoured for positions as "government" and "mission" leaders. The Maisin political system is thus egalitarian not in an absolute sense but in comparison to more hierarchical systems such as chieftainships or states, which possess formal offices that define leaders' powers and authority.

To a limited extent, Uiaku today has a hybrid system. While clan leaders more or less define their roles depending on circumstances and their own abilities, the village councillor occupies an official position with formal responsibilities as established by acts of the Papua New Guinea parliament. Yet the degree of actual specialization is in practice very limited. Village councillors are part-time volunteers. They receive no salary or other support that might give them an independent platform for action. Their effectiveness depends largely upon people's willingness to listen to them. Their connection to the "law" and the regional political system gives those who want to use it a bully pulpit from which to urge villagers to follow certain courses of action. But few councillors bother. Those who try quickly find that people only follow them to the extent that they wish to. They cannot compel obedience. The same is true for leaders working within village or mission spheres of action. The political process in Uiaku relies largely upon consensus. Leaders, whatever their position within the community, are best regarded as managers of consensus rather than as authorities.

The influence that Maisin big men enjoy derives from their reputations among their fellow villagers. People are willing to listen to big men and follow their lead because they have proven themselves exceptionally capable of doing the same things as everyone else. They are better gardeners or hunters, more generous in sharing food or pitching in when a new house needs to be constructed, and consistent in offering sound advice in planning for major events like a bride wealth payment. This is not to say that men who are exceptionally skilled automatically become leaders. I know of several superb gardeners, for instance, who are content merely to meet their obligations to their kin and otherwise remain out of the limelight. The people who become big men are partially thrust into their roles, but they also include ambitious individuals who take pride in their achievements. Just as reputation can lift up a big man, it can as easily take him down. There are always rivals waiting in the wings to move in if a big man's powers flag or if he slips up and annoys his followers.

While people recognize that being a village, government, or mission leader requires different skills, they expect their leaders to be "good men" who meet their exchange obligations, readily helping out their equals and giving sound advice and other aid to their juniors. They also expect leaders to be "strong" men who manage situations well so they work to everyone's benefit. Big men thus exemplify a dynamic that lies at the very heart of reciprocal morality (Burridge 1975; Read 1959). To be "good" requires that a person be selfless. Big men are generous to a fault. They are usually among the first to bring food to a feast or to pitch in on a community project. They offer sage advice for those who seek it, and they consult respectfully with other leading men before advocating a position at a village meeting. But such generosity isn't entirely selfless. As they give gifts of their produce, labour, and wisdom, big men build up a network of people reciprocally obligated to them. In turn, these are debts that can be called in when occasions require as, for example, in the organization of a bride wealth prestation.

Ordinary villagers admire and, indeed, are grateful for big men's willingness to assume the challenges and risks associated with making major decisions and pulling people along. At the same time, it worries them. To do what they do, big men must be "strong" (*wenna*). By this, Maisin mean that leaders assume roles in which they stand apart from the group to make decisions. As Anne's study suggests, leaders demonstrate an ability to consider different perspectives (Tietjen and Walker 1985). In brief, they act at critical moments as autonomous individuals, standing apart from the group. The non-reciprocal element in the big man's make-up puts him in the same category as sorcerers or spirits, entities that operate largely outside the moral constraints of community. Big men assume an oversized presence in ceremonial exchanges and other public occasions in part to put these concerns to rest. Still, the more influential a big man becomes, the more intense the scrutiny of his activities and the accompanying belittling gossip. People become concerned that he is using his position to benefit himself and his close relatives or that he is becoming a "big head" who makes decisions without consulting others. There may even be suspicion, especially in the case of older men, that they are resorting to sorcery to eliminate their rivals. Ironically, even hosting an especially generous ceremony may backfire if people feel that the manager is acting overly proud. The political system thus possesses an internal logic that limits the amount of power any individual can accrue. Many factors come into play, but gossip is the greatest leveller.

Modern circumstances make this contradiction between goodness and strength, reciprocity and individuality, especially acute. Since the time of the founding of the Christian cooperatives in the late 1940s, the chief political goal of Maisin leaders has been to improve the material conditions of village life. Three generations of leaders have now worked to get government grants and other forms of aid to build permanent classrooms, restock medicines in the health aid post, and obtain other social services. They have initiated a succession of local economic projects ranging from the planting of cash crops like cocoa to the establishment of tapa cloth cooperatives to bring money into the community. Because such projects require some knowledge of government bureaucracy, business organization, and financial management, villagers have increasingly supported leaders with high school education, who have worked for a time in professional capacities prior to returning to the village. Yet people are well aware of the ease with which money can be siphoned off by those in leadership positions and how projects can be manipulated to benefit leaders' families over everyone else. It is universally assumed by villagers that national politicians are corrupt, and they fret about whether their own leaders can resist temptation. This predicament exemplifies a persistent tension in contemporary village politics between the reciprocal morality of everyday life and the more individualistic ethic associated with money and "development."

THE POLITICS OF CONSENSUS

Politics, so the old saying goes, is the "art of the possible."[7] In Uiaku, political possibilities are constrained by the ways power is aligned inside and outside the community, by accepted decision-making procedures, and by what people perceive as the pressing issues of the day. In this section, we will consider the first two of these factors, saving the last for the conclusion of the chapter.

The Maisin participate in two political domains: the national electoral system and the village. Every five years villagers vote for a regional and a provincial representative to the national parliament who since 1995 also form a provincial assembly with members from districts elsewhere in Oro Province. The Maisin villages are also represented by three councillors on Cape Nelson Local Level Government (LLG) based in Tufi. While village schools and the small hospital at Wanigela remain under the formal control of the Anglican Church, the national government is responsible for most of the funding and for setting standards. In principle, the government also provides policing and funds various infrastructural and economic development programs. However, the police rarely venture far from Tufi, and funding for most other programs has steadily declined since Independence in 1975. This is a source of great frustration for the Maisin. A common complaint is that as soon as the election cycle is over, members of parliament forget the people who voted for them, preferring to enjoy the easy life of Port Moresby rather than work to improve the living conditions of their poorer rural brothers and sisters. The LLG is also regarded as largely irrelevant, despite the direct involvement of the village councillors and occasional small development grant.

The larger political system thus touches lightly upon Uiaku. In theory, a council made up of the Uiaku and Ganjiga LLG councillors and a small committee representing different parts of the community forms a kind of village government. In practice, however, such councils have virtually no authority and often do not effectively exist. Whatever influence village councillors enjoy tends to come from their leadership reputation in the community. Actual political power in the village is shared mostly between adult married men, although women and younger men are not without influence. They make their opinions known behind the scenes and resist decisions if they feel they are unreasonable or unfair, but they have no formal vote or means of setting political agendas.

The political process in Uiaku turns on the creation of consensus, especially among senior men. Sometimes agreement comes quickly; a course of action seems so obvious or urgent that people have little difficulty arriving at a decision. Most of the time, however, consensus building takes time and much talk. It is not a process that encourages snap decisions. Even once a decision has been reached, a consensus can easily be undermined if one or another of the parties involved changes their minds or new circumstances arise. Finding and maintaining a consensus, then, can be agonizingly slow and, once found, can disappear overnight. The Maisin are well aware of this. Over the years, I have often heard people express envy for what they perceive as the efficiency of decision-making among Europeans where lines of authority tend to be clearly established. Yet among themselves, the Maisin strongly resent any suggestion that an individual has the right to make decisions affecting others without their consent. If someone becomes a bit too pushy, others are likely to respond with the put-down "You are not the boss of me!" (always delivered in English). Even as they complain about the effort required to build and maintain consensus, people also recognize that the system possesses certain advantages. This recognition is partly pragmatic: courses of action backed by strong public approval are far more likely to be achieved than those imposed from above. There is also a near mystical faith that consensus in itself brings both social and material benefits. In the Maisin view, consensus represents a state of being, the elusive condition of social amity, a potent expression of *marawa-wawe*.

There is no clear line between the personal and the political in Maisin society. Most decisions beyond the level of the household require negotiations. Big events like bride wealth or end-of-mourning ceremonies often involve years of careful coordination between clan elders. It is in such ordinary circumstances that aspiring big men first demonstrate their ability to manage the delicate process of finding and maintaining consensus. Leaders draw upon the same skills and networks when addressing political matters at the community level, such as decisions on whether to build a new classroom or where to locate a public building, such as an aid post. However, there are crucial differences between the ways Maisin handle "village-side" affairs between the clans and those that concern the community as a whole. This is partly a matter of scale. With rare exceptions, such as initiation ceremonies for first-borns, "village-side" activities involve far fewer people than community-level affairs. More significantly, there is a shift in the way that consensus is perceived. The most significant commitments are no longer to one's own clan or kin. Indeed, clan loyalty is an obstacle. Political action at the community level depends on forging a consensus that appeals to sources of identity that transcend personal kin and exchange networks.

The means by which leaders attempt to forge consensus vary greatly according to the circumstances, the goal, and the people involved. In general, however, consensus building moves through two phases or, if a matter is especially contentious, back and forth between them. The first phase is one of semi-private negotiations between the parties most involved. These usually occur in the evening after people have finished their suppers and the village is quiet. Although the conversations are private, there is no secrecy about who is visiting whom, and usually people have a pretty good idea why. The aim of these discussions is to reach common positions before moving to a second public phase. If the matter under consideration is fairly routine—like planning a bride wealth ceremony—then the leaders of the groups involved will simply announce the decision to their clans. More contentious matters, however, require the convening of a village meeting to which all of the public is invited. Village meetings may also be called by village councillors or the church council to discuss community-level projects and concerns.

In general, village assemblies are not occasions for making decisions. That should happen well before people start gathering. Instead, they are forums in which positions get refined with the aim of publicly affirming agreement. They are, in short, moments of social theatre in which consensus is not so much made as *seen* to be made. The main protagonists are the senior men who usually do all of the talking. They occupy a central place in view of other villagers, usually on the raised platform of a shelter. Younger married men sit close by or lean against the side of the platform, sometimes quietly conferring with one of the "big people" on top. Elderly men sit a bit further out on the ground but close enough to hear the conversation and to volunteer an opinion if asked or if they feel the need. Further out again, women, young men, and children find whatever shade they can beneath nearby trees and strain to hear the discussion. A good turnout is considered critically important, even if most people do not speak. The more witnesses there are, the firmer the demonstration that there really is consensus.

Village meetings proceed at a leisurely pace. People slowly drift in around the appointed starting time, chew betelnut, smoke, and engage in casual conversation. At some point, one of the leaders will gauge that enough people have assembled and begin to talk. While there are occasional dramatic moments leading to bursts of energetic back-and-forth debate, most of the talk takes the form of speeches, often quite lengthy. I find these quite fascinating. Often as not, the speaker does not directly address the matter at hand but instead contextualizes it in terms of local history and the condition of social relations in the village. (We'll look at an example in the next section.) Often a speaker will preface his remarks by urging everyone on the platform to speak up in turn. The surrounding audience nods or murmurs when moved by a speaker's oratory or agreeing with his opinions. The talk proceeds at a gradual pace as speaker succeeds speaker. There is a great deal of repetition, but this is good because it demonstrates consensus. If all goes well, by the late afternoon all of the "big people" will have spoken, and the meeting will end with sugared tea and a small meal.

Although all of the men on the platform should and usually do speak, their words are by no means equally influential. People listen most closely to those men they consider to be especially "big." For their part, big men are masters of consensus politics. They have their own opinions and agendas, to be sure, but they are careful not to appear to be imposing these on others. They cultivate their relationships with other villagers, spending many of their evenings sitting on friends' verandahs quietly discussing the problems of the day. By the time an issue gets to a village meeting, big men are careful not to dominate the talk. They instead rely on their associates not just to back them up but to speak for a position as if it were their own, thus contributing to the appearance of agreement between equals.

The political process of consensus building is inherently fragile. It is often difficult to reach agreement and even harder to keep people on board once they do. Yet, for all the challenges, Maisin leaders have a remarkable ability to orchestrate consensus when the stakes are high enough. To do so requires them to appeal to all aspects of people's identities, as villagers, citizens, and Christians. This became quite apparent to me while observing meetings during the early 1980s.

A VILLAGE MEETING

On 28 June 1983, the Uiaku councillor called a meeting to discuss the floundering operation of the village store, the last remaining legacy of the cooperative movement that had started more than 40 years earlier. Although little more than a hut on high posts, the cooperative store was one of the few buildings in the area built almost entirely of imported materials, including expensive finished wood flooring and iron sheeting for the walls and roof. As a sign of their modernity, it gave the Maisin enormous pride, but it was also a constant cause for concern. The store was supposed to earn a profit that could be used for other local projects; however, no matter how high the managers jacked up prices for supplies of rice, matches, kerosene, and other basic goods, the store steadily lost money and much of the time remained closed. The Uiaku councillor was a middle-aged man who had worked for some years in the cooperative development office of the former colonial government. When he took an early retirement to return to the village and care for his aging parents, he took a personal interest in the store and had made its success one of his top priorities.

Figure 5.2 A village meeting, Uiaku, 1983. The councillor is making a point using the large blackboard propped up by the palm tree behind him. The senior men of the village are sitting on the shelter platform to his left. (Photo by J. Barker)

The meeting took place in the midst of the festering conflict between Uiaku and Ganjiga described in the previous section. The Ganjiga councillor had played a key role in organizing a food exchange to end the crisis. When the Uiaku councillor called in the police to arrest the Ganjiga man who had attempted to drown the Uiaku elder, the Ganjiga councillor and his followers took personal offence. The conflict between the councillors spilled over into the management of the cooperative store, to which both men had keys. Checking the books one day, the Uiaku councillor was alarmed to find that Ganjiga customers were receiving a dangerous amount of credit. To prevent further depletion of the stock, he changed the lock and called for a meeting. It occurred the next day in a cleared area in front of the store. Most Ganjiga people, including the councillor, stayed away.

During the 18 months I had lived in Uiaku, I had heard a great deal of talk about the cooperative store and its troubles. There was intense criticism of the young men who sold the goods, of the councillors who managed the business, and of the villagers who depended upon the store for basic necessities. Yet complaints rarely stopped there. Villagers had an emotional investment in that small steel shack which in a way embodied a shared history. People spoke nostalgically of earlier days when people worked closely together, church services were well-attended, and everyone pitched in to make formal exchanges exciting and successful. The store for many was an index of community. Like the body of a loved one, its health reflected the state of social relationships. It was an outward sign of inward divisions, of rivalries, gossip, greed, and other weaknesses. In short, discussions of the cooperative store followed the well-worn path of sorcery talk. Meetings to discuss the store often in turn involved a similar pattern of accusations and confessions, an airing of troubles to allow a healing of social relations. At one meeting I attended, a leader made the connection directly, stating "The cooperative is sick!" He attributed this to incessant gossiping and sniping in village life, which weakened the store.[8]

The meeting of 28 June reflected these concerns. Speaker after speaker denounced the social divisions they saw undermining the store's success. While some of the talk became heated, as we'll see below, the "big people" worked hardest at finding a point of consensus not just to defuse the tensions or plan future actions but more basically to restore the condition of social amity that the Maisin assume is a necessary condition for prosperity. The politics of consensus, as reflected in their speeches, relied on a strategy of blending the three orientations to community discussed earlier in this chapter by appealing to listeners as fellow villagers, citizens, and Christians.

Near the beginning of this meeting, a man who had served as the first store manager in 1965 reminded villagers of the history of the cooperative society:

> Our traditions say we must listen to what elders say and do it. Do it! Do it! The ancestors who came here worked together and made Uiaku's name good. Yet these young ones have not left it in good shape. The ancestors brought their *kawo* [i.e., traditional rights and privileges]. They were strong and fought a lot. When the missionaries came, they gave their *kawo* to God. They gave everything. That was a sign that they retain the traditions. The young ones are growing and we need to teach them what our ancestors did. If you elders had died and we spoilt [the cooperative], it would only be our fault. I am unhappy that you have to see what is happening.... Use your *mon seramon* [good sense]! God told us that things will happen. The strong wind will blow. The famine will come. If the flood must come to spoil the village, it will. If the fight comes, it will. We will argue and stay apart from each other. We know these things happen. So when someone does something bad, don't talk about it. We are Christians, so we shouldn't gossip. When we do bad things, we must go straight to that person and make *marawa-wawe* [i.e., amends re-establishing good relations].
>
> Teach the young ones to speak Maisin properly so they won't get confused when they make speeches. Don't let them spoil this building you started. My fathers, you made this building for us. We have intelligence and education, so must look

after it. Now it is not only the *Kawo* [leaders of the high-ranking clans] who talk. The spear *Sabu* [leaders of the low-ranking clans] may talk. You went to the big schools, so you may talk. All the *Kawo* must help each other and work together. I shouldn't say this, but I'm sad so I am reminding you. We should not forget these things. So my talk is finished.

The speech contained numerous allusions with which the audience was familiar. The opening themes of the ancestors giving and keeping their *kawo* reminded the audience of the origins of the cooperative movement in the building of the first iron-roofed church in Uiaku in the late 1950s (Chapter 1). When Bishop George Ambo arrived to consecrate the church, he found it surrounded on three sides by a sacred enclosure made up of criss-crossed branches called an *oraa*. The fence was composed of types of trees individually owned as *evovi* by the *Kawo* clans. The clans thus gave their "traditions to God." When the bishop blessed the church, he likewise blessed the conjoined clan emblems and thus the "traditions were retained." In this way, the clans fused their newly found Christian unity with the enduring traditions of clan identity (Barker 1993).

The speaker now addressed the old men sitting nearby, expressing regret that young people are forgetting their sacrificial act, which happened at the same time as these elders shared their money to found the cooperative. The speaker next asserted that God will send disasters to test the people, with a clear allusion to the flood that had recently damaged Ganjiga. As Christians, the people must resist the urge to quarrel; they must make peace with each other. The main thrust of his speech came at the end. Uiaku has changed. Young people no longer understand the meaning behind Maisin words. Christianity and education have so opened things that even lower-ranked *Sabu* members can speak in public gatherings. Yet it remains key for all the *Kawo* (here meaning both *Kawo* and *Sabu* ranked clans) to work together.

Other men echoed these sentiments and built upon them. The Uiaku councillor then stood up, pointing out that he was not a *Kawo* man but *Sabu* and thus in the old days would not have been allowed to talk. However, he said, "I have been elected as councillor, so I look after this place. We are all like that; when we have responsibility for the church or government-sides, we must do our work." Turning to the problem at hand, he said:

GC [the Ganjiga councillor] says that I went over him. How? Ganjiga people did not tell me what to do. The trouble was in my Ward so I wrote the note and sent it to [the police].... If this problem goes on all will be spoiled. If we solve it, all will be well. GC says I went over him. I have that right on the Government-side, so he

157

shouldn't complain. I don't like how my mother's brother[9] has responded to this. We are adults. We are no longer small boys! We mustn't act like that when we are men and spoil things. We must only do good. That's why I put a lock.... As a man representing the government I have the right to do it! I am the only one. Don't talk about my children or my wives.[10] I am the councillor and you should come straight to me.

In this speech, the councillor claimed a governmental authority. Mission and government leaders should work towards village cooperation and unity; to do so they must make independent decisions for the good of the village. It is inappropriate to gossip about their families, as one might about a traditional village leader, because they act on behalf of the national government and its laws. If people want to complain about how government-side leaders are doing their job, they should confront them directly.

The Uiaku councillor, however, did not intend to claim that government rules trump traditional values. He went on in his speech to argue that GC had failed in his role as a village-side leader by waiting too long to act when feelings began to heat up over the tryst between the Ganjiga boy and Uiaku girl:

GC was here when that happened. He is *Kawo*, so he should have taken his string bag across [i.e., gone to Uiaku with gifts and sat down in a friendly manner with the aggrieved parents].... What was he doing? He was there when it happened. He is a *Kawo* man and a councillor. If he had solved this problem, these rumours would not go around. It is spoilt because one person is playing. When you split up you will fight with spears again, and it is one person's fault.

In other words, as a high-ranking *Kawo* leader, GC had the responsibility and authority to keep order among his people. Because he did not act quickly enough, the conflict spread. By implication, the Uiaku councillor said that he had no choice but to call in the police because villagers themselves could no longer contain the violence.

These and the other speeches made that day did not resolve differences over the store, which remained closed. All the same, they reflected a wider consensus that the community needed to unite if there was to be any hope of material advancement. At a deeper level, they reflected a common understanding that unity draws upon all three facets of contemporary identity: village traditions, the Christian love of God, and the rule of law. Leaders worked hard to merge the three orientations but leaned, often subtly, towards one side or another. Their work then, as today, has been to build consensus within the evolving values and meanings of community. It is not easy.

THE MORAL POLITICS OF "DEVELOPMENT"

I was often struck by the passion with which the Maisin discussed the cooperative store. There was no denying that the store was in trouble. In the early 1980s, it was the only local source for basic goods such as rice, sugar, tea, matches, and kerosene upon which villagers had become dependent. People griped but tolerated the high prices set by the managers to cover transport costs. They appreciated the convenience of the store and felt pride that it was owned by the entire community. They even put up stoically with extended and frequent closings when storemen failed to show up for work or the stocks ran low. Such inconveniences were frustrating, but what was truly intolerable was that the store always lost money. Periodically, people would invest funds raised through copra or tapa sales or a small government grant to restock the shelves. Villagers crushed through the door on the opening day, hopeful that this time for sure the store would fill its central mandate: providing profits that would be invested in other local businesses. People regarded the store as their best shot at generating money locally to pay school fees, purchase medicines, and, most generally, create a more comfortable and secure material existence. Each time the store closed, its finances in disarray, there was a tangible sense of disappointment verging on despair.

I spent many hours listening to people gripe about the store and other community economic ventures that had also started with high hopes before floundering and failing. The tone of these conversations and speeches was often emotional and moralistic. While villagers castigated working relatives and politicians for failing to support community projects, they saved their harshest criticisms for themselves. The projects failed because people gossiped too much, because the young people no longer respected their elders, because members of clans thought only of themselves instead of pitching in to help the community as a whole. Left unmentioned was the fact that the lack of ready access to markets made it next to impossible for any local economic venture to succeed and that the mass exodus of young people to the towns made it impossible for households to devote as much time and labour to community ventures as in the past. My friends readily agreed that these were important factors when I brought them up—and then they returned to what was for them the salient point: the community was to blame for the failures.

Similar attitudes have been reported from across rural Papua New Guinea, including areas that have enjoyed considerably more success with cash cropping or which have economically benefited from the presence of factories, mines, and other projects (e.g., Errington and Gewertz 2004). Villagers often feel intense shame concerning their "poverty," as reflected in their continued reliance on subsistence agriculture, residence in bush houses without modern conveniences like electricity, and limited access to cash and the many things that cash buys. The sense of shame is powerfully mixed with a complex attitude of admiration, envy, and resentment towards Europeans and fellow citizens who have had the opportunity to embrace a European lifestyle.[11] Villagers attribute Europeans' economic successes to their supposed superior virtues of organization, self-discipline, hard work, and advanced technical skills (Bashkow 2006; Smith 1994). At the same time, Europeans as imagined by Papua New Guineans evoke disturbing feelings because they appear to operate individually, without regard to kinfolk, and they refuse to share their good fortune without any apparent consequences. These are traits, as we have seen, of sorcerers.

In North America, people tend to think of politics as a pragmatic business. At best, it is a process by which contending interests debate, modify, and commit to various policies; at worse, it is a contest played out by factions and individuals pursuing their own self-interests. This is also true in Maisin society, but as an outside observer one can't help but notice the powerful ways that deeply held moral assumptions condition political discussions. The intense shame many Maisin felt about their standard of living in the 1980s was shaped by their assumptions about reciprocal virtues. When villagers told me that they were "poor" and that the village was "dirty" and "backwards," they were referring not only to a lack of material development—important as this was to them—but also moral integrity. As we've seen, the Maisin equate moral uprightness with the pursuit of balanced exchange. The key concept of *marawa-wawe* entails an idealized state in which people transcend their obligations to each other by achieving a perfect state of balance that is at once material, moral, and spiritual. Despite their best efforts, however, the people were not materially the equals of Europeans (as they imagined Europeans to be) and thus were morally inferior as well. In an ideal world, the rich Europeans and elite Papua New Guineans in the towns would be obliged to share their wealth, to bring the relationship into equivalence. This did not happen, and people worried that the problem lay within themselves (cf. Burridge 1960).

Politics in Uiaku in the 1980s revolved around the conundrums of development. In the meetings I attended, most of the focus was directed at the failings of the community. The moral tone of the speeches, endlessly stressing the need for mutual support, resonated powerfully with speeches I heard at meetings dealing with sorcery accusations: much in the way that social amity produced good health, Maisin supposed that unity provided the essential foundation for prosperity. Political efforts, however, were also directed outwards. Village councillors spent weeks at a time in the provincial capital of Popondetta petitioning politicians and bureaucrats to release funds to support local development projects. Despite promises made by politicians around election time, government support for development projects usually failed to materialize, and many people were convinced that the government intended to leave them mired in poverty. I got my first sense of the desperation many Maisin felt about their poverty a month or so after I began my fieldwork when a delegation visited one evening to encourage me to entice my supposed circle of American businessmen to "develop" the Maisin lands. I disappointed them. Soon after, however, a representative of a logging company arrived to pitch a scheme to replace the rainforest behind the villages with a massive oil palm plantation. The villagers were ecstatic. Development was about to arrive, and integrity would at last be restored.

Notes

1. Sister Helen lived in a modest house at the mission station by the Wanigela airstrip. When I told her about the rumours, she laughed. She'd heard it all before. It was clear from her meticulous records, which she kindly allowed me to copy, that she was barely breaking even. When she died in the early 1990s, Wanigela ceased to be an outlet for tapa.

2. Local Government Councils were introduced by the Australian colonial government beginning in the 1950s to provide a degree of self-governance to local communities and to encourage village-level economic development. The Maisin received a few small grants from the Council during the 1980s for water tanks to supply village medical aid posts in Uiaku and Airara. In the mid-1990s, Papua New Guinea reformed its system of provincial and local government, replacing the latter with Local Level Government bodies with expanded responsibilities and authority. Like its predecessor, the Cape Nelson LLG appears to have little presence at the village level (May 2004).

3. Since the early 1970s, the national government has formally controlled local schooling in Papua New Guinea, setting the core curriculum while training teachers and paying their salaries. As of 2000, approximately 40 per cent of the schools were at least partially funded and controlled by churches and missions as were two universities (Gibbs 2005). In the two Maisin schools, children receive religious instruction once a week from the parish priest or a local catechist.

4. The word "formal" needs to be stressed here, as there is abundant evidence, despite the efforts to create international legal accords such as the Geneva Conventions, that members of modern nation-states often find it difficult to consider those they regard as enemies as moral beings to be accorded the same rights and considerations as fellow members of their own communities.

5. Given the thinness of the police force on the ground, it is doubtful that warfare was completely brought under control, and many acts of violence within communities certainly went undetected and unpunished. There is also evidence of police committing

their own crimes, sometimes with the knowledge of patrol officers (Kituai 1998). Since Independence, Papua New Guinea has struggled with a resumption of tribal fighting in much of the Highlands, increasingly with imported and homemade guns, and gang violence in the towns and along the road systems (Dinnen 2001; Gordon and Meggitt 1985).

6. Richard Scaglion, one of the architects of the country's pluralistic legal system, observes that "Papua New Guinea has been one of the more progressive of the Pacific nations in pursuing law reform" (2004:95). Efforts have included detailed research on legal proceedings in local communities, much of it carried out by anthropologists, and the introduction of new legislation and legal forms that recognize customary law, the most successful of which have been village courts.

7. The quote is attributed to the famed nineteenth-century German Chancellor Otto von Bismarck. Bismarck also once remarked, "Politics is not an exact science" (*Oxford Dictionary of Quotations*, 3rd ed., 1979).

8. This same man confided that he also suspected the young unmarried men who worked as storekeepers were sleeping around too much, thus weakening not only their bodies but also the virility of the store. This was not an explanation, however, that I heard from anyone else.

9. The Ganjiga councillor was a classificatory mother's brother to the speaker.

10. The Uiaku councillor had two wives, the Ganjiga councillor had three. The allusion here is to sorcerers, who were known to thrive upon rumour-mongering and gossip.

11. It is important to stress that most Papua New Guineans have had very limited experience of Europeans and other foreigners. Throughout the colonial period, the only European the Maisin saw with any regularity was the priest stationed at Wanigela when he visited the villages for a few hours once a month to celebrate the Communion service. Individual experiences vary. A handful of Maisin hold jobs that bring them into regular contact with foreigners. Rural Maisin's notions about Europeans have been built from their historical experiences, from mostly fleeting personal observations of foreigners in the towns and villages, and from what they hear from other Papua New Guineans. Europeans stand in sharp contrast to local peoples not only because of their light skins but also because they appear so wealthy and powerful, yet never seem to work very hard. They thus present a challenging puzzle that has long preoccupied rural Papua New Guineans (e.g., Burridge 1960). Their notions about Europeans are best understood as constructions built partially from experience and partially from Indigenous assumptions about human nature. As Ira Bashkow notes of the Orokaiva who live in the central part of Oro Province, "[they] project onto their whitemen, from their own evaluative viewpoint, their most pressing moral concerns" (2006:9). This is a kind of Indigenous anthropology, the equivalent of centuries of Western constructions of "primitive" peoples held up as the moral opposite of European "civilization" (Lutz and Collins 1993; Pagden 1982). In the end, both types of projections tell us at least as much about their authors as the people they aim to depict.

CHAPTER 6

CULTURE CHANGE: TAPA AND THE RAINFOREST

Early in 1995, I received a letter from our old friend Franklin Seri, then the Uiaku councillor. After updating me on recent births and deaths, Franklin mentioned he would be visiting Berkeley, California, in a few months as part of a delegation of four Maisin men to promote tapa cloth.

Needless to say, I was electrified. I hadn't been back to Papua New Guinea for eight years and had heard nothing about a visit to the United States in the infrequent letters I had received from villagers. Franklin's letter gave few clues as to what this visit was about, but he did mention that it had been organized by Lafcadio Cortesi of Greenpeace International. I quickly found Lafcadio's phone number through directory assistance. He was delighted that I had called! He had heard many good things about Anne and me from the Maisin and very much wanted us to be part of the current project he was coordinating. That project was to mount a major exhibition of Maisin tapa cloth at the Berkeley Art Museum in collaboration with Larry Rinder, the Curator for Contemporary Art.

The exhibition was intended to be highly innovative in several ways. First, it would showcase tapa as an art form on par with the Western creations that more typically lined gallery walls. Second, the tapa display would be tied to the theme of preserving the rainforest of Papua New Guinea from commercial exploitation, with the Maisin presented as Indigenous stewards of their ancestral lands. Finally, the exhibition would make use of modern multimedia facilities to tell the story of the Maisin in the most vivid way possible and to reach a wide "virtual" audience—a daring idea before the advent of social media. A special website was prepared, full of colourful photographs and detailed articles concerning the Maisin and tapa. Nick Bowness, another close friend of Lafcadio's, prepared a computer kiosk featuring a "virtual village" that allowed visitors to tour parts of Uiaku and to learn about the process of making tapa.

I agreed to write a commentary on Maisin culture for the website and to give a public lecture at the opening of the exhibition. In April, Anne, Jess, and I travelled to Berkeley. We were delighted to be reunited with Franklin. The other Maisin greeted us as family. Literally. John Ferguson Kasona had been one of the children Anne observed back in 1981–83. He and Ronald Ross Kania were members of the Jogun clan and thus Anne's "brothers." The senior member of the group, Sylvester Moi, belonged to a junior lineage of my adopted clan, Gafi, and was thus my younger brother (although older than me; see Chapter 3).

The opening was impressive. A large number of people came—artists and environmental activists, owners of local galleries, among others. The Papua New Guinea ambassador flew in from New York, praising the exhibition and declaring his country's dedication to conserving its rich cultural heritage and natural environment. The delegation, garbed in shells, feathers, and tapa, performed traditional dances and spoke about the importance of tapa and conserving the rainforest. The highlight was the tapa itself, beautifully displayed around the walls of a large room. The individual cloths were lovely, but our eyes were drawn to a spectacular piece, composed of 16 individual large *embobi* surrounded by a patterned fringe, occupying an entire wall. I had never seen anything like it. It had been specially commissioned for the exhibition as a material representation of the solidarity of the Maisin people.

This was not the first time Maisin tapa had been displayed in a Western museum nor even that a Maisin had travelled overseas to promote the cloth. In the two decades following first contact, government officers, missionaries, and scientists deposited significant collections of Collingwood Bay tapa and other artifacts in museums scattered across Australia and Europe (Barker 2001; Bonshek 1989; Hermkens 2013). In 1985, the Papua New Guinea government sent Franklin to represent the country's artistic traditions at a cultural festival in Scotland. The following year, Anne and I mounted a small exhibition on Maisin tapa at the Burke Museum at the University of Washington. The Berkeley show, however, was a watershed moment. Maisin tapa cloth was given a new significance by being associated with the hot topic of conserving the world's rapidly diminishing tropical rainforests.

In 1997, I returned for a six-week stay in Uiaku following my 10-year absence. The village looked much the same. Yet I saw immediately that the population was considerably larger and younger. Some families had returned from the towns to raise their children in the safer environment of the village, but most of the increase was due to the fact that fewer children now got into high school, and even those who did often couldn't find jobs and so returned home. The place also looked a little wealthier. People wore better clothes than

Figure 6.1 Sylvester Moi and Franklin Seri in front of the big tapa, Berkeley Art Museum, 1995. The rooster plumes in Sylvester's headdress and the cut of his loin cloth indicate that his clan belongs to the higher *Kawo* rank. Franklin's clan is *Sabu*, but at the time he was village councillor for Uiaku. (Photo by A.M. Tietjen)

before, and many households possessed new steel cookware, plates, and utensils. The casual daily exchange of food, betelnut, and tobacco was accompanied by a twice-weekly market at which villagers paid each other small amounts of cash for garden produce. And I heard more English and *Tok Pisin* (neo-Melanesian pidgin English) than in earlier years, although people of all ages preferred to converse in Maisin.

I was struck by the near constant coming and going of foreign visitors. At that time, Uiaku was not particularly remote by Papua New Guinea standards. The Wanigela airstrip was operating, making it fairly easy to reach Uiaku within a half-day of leaving Port Moresby. In the past, however, few outsiders had any reason to go there. In the two years we lived in the village during the 1980s, we saw only a handful of Europeans, several our guests and none who stayed longer than a few days. In April 1997, Uiaku was a destination. Each week brought new visitors. Village leaders spent much of their time arranging and attending meetings, while households found a welcome source of income by putting up the visitors. Indeed, hoping to cash in on this unexpected boom, one family was building a commodious guesthouse. This proved a sound investment, at least in the short term. Over the next few years, the Maisin hosted a steady stream of consultants working on land and conservation issues, activists providing workshops on small-scale economic development, and museum curators and researchers interested in tapa cloth. In 1998, the Uiaku mission station became home for a Peace Corps couple who spent the next two years helping Maisin market their tapa, and two Summer Institute of Linguistics volunteers who came to help translate the Bible into the Maisin language.[1] Within a 12-month period in 1999–2000, three foreign film crews arrived to shoot news pieces and documentaries for the Australian Broadcasting Corporation, the Canadian Broadcasting Corporation, and CNN. Meanwhile, delegations of Maisin visited Australia, the United States, Japan, and Canada to promote tapa and conservation.

The cause of all this activity was a choice made by the Maisin leaders in the early 1990s to prohibit commercial logging on their ancestral lands. The first part of this chapter explores the reasons why they made this decision and the larger political context that made it so significant for outsiders. The second part deals with how the campaign against loggers and the inrush of outside organizations and activists impacted the Maisin community during the closing years of the twentieth century.

RESOURCE DEVELOPMENT IN PAPUA NEW GUINEA

The choice Maisin were forced to make provides a particularly dramatic instance of a local response to two related developments colliding across

Papua New Guinea, the Solomon Islands, and Vanuatu in the late 1980s and early 1990s: a frenzy of clear-cut logging in some areas that, according to the critics, could entirely deplete the commercially viable rainforests within a few decades; and the almost instantaneous appearance of a wide array of local, national, and international non-governmental organizations (NGOs) in vigorous opposition.

I use the word "choice" in describing the actions of local people in these developments to draw attention to their importance as historical actors. It needs to be acknowledged, however, that in similar circumstances elsewhere, such as the Canadian north or Indonesia, Indigenous people have often been allowed little choice. Decisions on the fate of their lands have been made by powerful outsiders—national governments, commercial companies, or hordes of invading settlers. The Melanesian situation is different in that most people— even those in the towns—retain legal ownership to customary lands. Papua New Guinea has been described as a "nation of landowners" (Filer 1998a). Some 97 per cent of the land belongs to local corporate kin groups, like the Maisin clans. As a consequence, the local populations of Papua New Guinea enjoy an influence over the fate of their lands that can scarcely be imagined by most Indigenous peoples elsewhere.

Behind the clean simplicity of people making a choice over lands they own, however, lie many complexities. Between the mid-1980s and early 1990s, the Maisin leaders forged a consensus that industrial logging of their lands would do more harm than good and organized their people in opposition. This is accurate enough, but it tells us nothing of the people's motivations or under-standing. Nor does it tell us why they had to make the choice in the first place or the struggles they had to get powerful outside interests and the majority of their own people to respect it. To understand the choice and its implica-tions, we need to first consider the wider contexts in which hundreds of local communities in the Melanesian world are struggling with similar decisions.

Let's begin with the rainforest. Much of the lowland region of Papua New Guinea is covered by a dense carpet of trees, which provide a home for an astonishing diversity of species; there are at least 9,000 types of plants and 780 types of birds, including the spectacular birds of paradise that provide the country with its national symbol, along with untold varieties of insects (Pratt and Beehler 2015). Flying over the mountainous terrain, much of the country appears as virgin forest, untouched by humans. Population density in the heavily forested lowlands is, in fact, quite light compared to neighbouring Asian countries. Still, humans have been settled in New Guinea for at least 50,000 years and have had a profound impact upon the environment. This is most visible in the densely populated highlands regions, where intensive cultivation resulted in the replacement of most of the forest cover by grasslands long before the colonial period. Elsewhere, villages like Uiaku are surrounded by broad areas of secondary jungle where people make their gardens. More remote forests are less touched but periodically visited by hunters.

Tropical rainforests are biologically diverse. For centuries, forest products have circulated widely as commodities: rubber from the Amazon, bird of paradise plumes from New Guinea (for a time widely sought in the West for women's hats), medicines, and building materials. The very diversity of the forests, however, discouraged large-scale industrial logging. As Anna Tsing (2005:14) notes for Borneo, the big logging companies "prefer forests in which one valuable [tree] species predominates." Although the Australians recognized the commercial potential of logging in Papua New Guinea as early as the 1930s, most logging operations prior to Independence were small in scale. The situation changed dramatically over the next two decades. The trigger, according to most analysts, was the movement of powerful Japanese general trading companies, the *sogo shosha*, into the international timber market. The companies provided loans and trading contracts to Southeast Asian countries to secure large quantities of cheaply produced logs, most of which were used to produce plywood in Japan. This stimulated the emergence of logging companies with a strong inducement to maximize the rate at which trees were felled and the valuable logs extracted from rainforests in Malaysia and Indonesia. The rapid growth of the new market and the equally rapid depletion of the more accessible rainforests in Southeast Asia led the companies to seek out fresh areas to exploit in the Pacific Islands and Latin America. The giant Malaysian company Rimbunan Hijau moved into Papua New Guinea, becoming the dominant player in the forestry sector in the 1980s.

The new international market for logs encouraged a perception of tropical forests that ignored their biological diversity. Non-commercial trees, plants, animals, birds, and even humans tended to be viewed as, at best, obstacles and, at worst, waste. Inevitably, this encouraged a frightening degree of environmental damage as giant bulldozers cut roads along ecologically sensitive streams and giant trees were hauled out by chains, flattening everything in their path. The jumble of broken trees, gouged earth, and eroded roadbeds left behind by the loggers inhibited the recovery of the forest and, in many cases, the conversion of the land to agricultural use. The immediate commercial returns, however, were spectacular. The volume of logs exported from Papua New Guinea rose from less than 500,000 cubic metres per year in 1978 to a peak of 3 million cubic metres in 1994 with an estimated market value of around US$410 million (Filer 1998a:49). These numbers underestimate the actual rate of the cut, as there is evidence of substantial illegal smuggling of logs during this period. It is generally believed that the situation was even more out of control in the neighbouring Solomon Islands. Alarmed, some environmentalists warned that were this rate of cut to continue, the rainforests of Melanesia would disappear within a decade. This was an exaggeration, but there is little doubt that much of the logging was (and continues to be) unregulated, very damaging to the environment, and unsustainable.

From the outside, the near instantaneous appearance of a massive logging industry in Papua New Guinea looks like a textbook example of globalization, the embrace of even the most remote areas of the world within a single economic system. However, it is important to bear in mind that global trends and connections always take shape within localities. These localities, in turn, exert their own influences. In the case of Papua New Guinea, these influences kick in at two levels: the government and local landowners.

In principle, the government is the more powerful of the two. It establishes national policies guiding development strategies, reviews projects and issues permits, creates the regulatory and enforcement frameworks within which companies operate, and collects taxes and redistributes royalties to landowners. Since 1975, Papua New Guinea has relied primarily upon the exploitation of its abundant natural resources in its development strategy. Papua New Guinea is home to some of the largest open-pit gold and copper mines in the world, and these have provided it with the lion's share of national revenue. National planners have also encouraged large-scale development of oil and gas reserves, fisheries, oil palm plantations, and timber. The Parliament has enacted many regulations meant to assure that taxes and royalties generated by the projects flow back into government coffers, that Papua New Guinea citizens rather than foreigners receive job training and employment whenever feasible, and that the environment is protected. Unfortunately, the government has a limited ability to monitor companies and enforce regulations once projects receive approval. The revenues generated by the projects have yet to be balanced against often substantial environmental damage, underpayment of royalties, and theft of resources, especially in the fisheries and timber sectors (Kirsch 2006; Zimmer-Tamakoshi 1998).

As noted earlier, resource development in Papua New Guinea is additionally complicated by the fact that almost all land is communally owned. Projects legally require the approval of landowners before they can proceed, through a device known as "lease-leaseback" arrangements. A number of variations have developed since the late 1970s, but the basic procedure is for a landowner group to give or sell a long-term lease (usually 99 years) of a parcel of land to a middle party—either a government agency or PNG-based company—which in turn leases back the land to private companies for commercial development.

It is a setup that lends itself readily to confusion, conflict, and abuse. Building consensus, as we've already seen, is difficult in places like Uiaku. This is especially so when the stakes are high, as they always are with land, encouraging the resurrection of old arguments over ownership (and likely the invention of new ones). Local leaders come under tremendous pressure to find "development" for their communities, yet they face constant scrutiny from fellow villagers who suspect they will cut deals that benefit their own kin at the expense of everyone else. These suspicions are grounded in the reciprocal ethos we've been examining in this book. But they are also realistic, for there are strong enticements for leaders and others to shortcut consensus building. Eager to get on with a project, entrepreneurs and resource companies are often quick to sign contracts with individuals having dubious claims to represent landowners. Gifts of money, alcohol, and prostitutes, along with promises of rich returns, help grease the wheels.

Even when landowners reach consensus, projects are often challenged by disgruntled villagers once underway (Filer 1998b). Lease-leaseback schemes place landowners in the position of rentiers rather than partners. Some people get jobs and training, but for landowners most benefits come in the form of royalty payments and investments by companies in local infrastructure such as roads and medical aid posts. In principle, benefits also come back via the taxes collected by the national government and used to pay for such things as teachers' salaries. These arrangements, however, tend to be seen through a cultural lens of reciprocal obligation. Landowners view royalty payments as compensation not just for damage done to their lands but for the profits they would have received had they developed and sold the resource themselves. This situation inevitably generates conflict. Some of this is turned inwards, with villagers suspecting some families of benefiting more than others. But it often turns outwards as well, with suspicions aired that the land was "stolen" in nefarious schemes launched by alienated members of the community and corrupt politicians or, just as often, that the company is lying about its profits and thus stealing from the community.

Few Papua New Guineans accept that once they lease their lands, they surrender all control. In the early years of independence, the government and resource companies learned a hard lesson when a simmering dispute between villagers situated near the giant Panguna copper mine on Bougainville Island blew up into a disastrous rebellion that took a decade to settle (Dorney 2000). The ability of rural villagers to sabotage and close the mine—at the time, one of the largest in the world—and then fend off the national army chastened the government and resource companies. Companies seeking to start up new mining projects elsewhere in Papua New Guinea not only increased their royalty payments to landowners but promised significant investments in roads, schools, medical facilities, local development initiatives, and other services to win and maintain support—in effect, taking over government services even as they were declining elsewhere in the country. At the same time, despite promises, national government transfers to much of the rest of the country have been at best uneven, but often in sharp decline. This has resulted in a very uneven pattern of economic development, with booms occurring near mining and petroleum projects and deterioration almost everywhere else (Jorgensen 2006).

Mining and petroleum ventures have generated massive profits and equally massive environmental and social problems in Papua New Guinea. They have received a lot of attention, not least from anthropologists familiar with the regions in which they operate (Golub 2014; Jacka 2015). Far less is known about the operations of the logging industry. In part this is due to a relative lack of transparency. Lease-leaseback schemes generate a vast array of entities, many of them existing in name only as fronts for bigger Asian players. The lack of information is equally due to the fact that, compared to mining, logging requires little upfront investment and the resource is quickly removed in the form of raw logs which are then exported. The promoters of logging projects usually promise to convert the cleared lands into commercial plantations, yet this involves further foreign investment and often doesn't happen.

Even as talk about logging in Collingwood Bay was heating up in the early 1980s, the lustre was wearing off logging projects elsewhere in the country. A small but vocal group of conservationists, some of them in the government, were expressing alarm over some of the operations, but the main opposition came from disillusioned landowners who had signed on as partners. They complained of undelivered royalties, crumbling infrastructure, damaged gardens, and mysterious barges removing logs in the dead of night. The national government had its own complaints about companies that avoided paying taxes by underestimating the value of the logs they exported or even declaring losses. Politicians joined the chorus of criticisms, demanding the government enforce its own laws. Unfortunately, the government simply did not possess the means (nor, too often, the will) to do so. There were increasing incidents of local people blocking or sabotaging logging operations and demanding compensation for the damaged environment.

In 1989 Judge Thomas Barnett, an Australian member of the Papua New Guinea judiciary, released a detailed report on the logging industry. He then promptly left the country, fearing for his life. Conducted over two years and resulting in 20 volumes of findings, the inquiry painstakingly documented a "forest industry out of control." This was the direct result, in Barnett's view, of

Figure 6.2 The "big tree." The deep forest (*taima*) lies beyond the zone of secondary bush where Maisin make their gardens. Massive *ficus* trees are common. (Photo by J. Barker)

collusion between foreign investors and corrupt officials and politicians out to make a quick return by exporting commercially valuable raw logs as quickly as possible. He recommended the government cut back on timber harvesting, promote local processing of logs to retain more of the value, and adopt a new national policy aimed at curtailing corruption and building an environmentally sensitive and sustainable industry (Filer 1998a:92–97).

The Barnett inquiry unleashed a fierce debate within Papua New Guinea over the future of industrial logging. The government made substantive changes in its forestry policies, mostly voluntary but to some extent under the forceful prodding of its main financial donors, particularly the World Bank. A rapidly growing number of local and international environmental NGOs took it upon themselves to work with the government to create effective conservation programs while also serving as watchdogs against abuses. At the same time, the larger logging companies formed a national lobbying group, started a national newspaper, and vigorously promoted an image of themselves as good corporate citizens. The basic problems, however, did not disappear. Logging companies still faced the challenge of getting legal access to the forests at the cheapest possible price. The government still lacked the ability to monitor their operations, let alone enforce its new and improved laws in the field. It was a situation that invited dodgy backroom deal-making between companies and the government to give the appearance of meeting requirements without incurring the cost.

THE MAISIN'S CHOICE

The enormous profits to be made on the world market from Papua New Guinea's rich natural resources, the complexities of getting legal access to them, and the lax controls over companies once they begin operation all but guarantee abuses: bribes to pliant politicians, bureaucrats, and village leaders to encourage approval or to look the other way when a company fails to meet its promises, among others. It is tempting to see rural folk like the Maisin as innocent victims whose powerful desire to improve their material conditions is exploited by unscrupulous national politicians and foreign entrepreneurs. There is truth to this. Rural villagers often have only a dim understanding of how companies work or of the environmental and other effects of a mine or logging project and get taken in by often-inflated promises made by promoters. Yet Papua New Guineans all have very strong attachments to their lands. Even when they are desperate for development, they insist on exercising control over how it will proceed.

I was a witness to this in May 1982. From the time we arrived six months earlier, Anne and I had heard rumours that a major logging operation was scheduled to commence within 18 months. Once the land was cleared, the forest would be replaced with groves of oil palms, similar to a massive industrial plantation of the trees near the provincial capital of Popondetta (Newton 1982). On 18 May, villagers from several Maisin villages gathered in Uiaku to hear two officials employed by the national and provincial forestry departments outline the proposed project. The national officer did most of the talking. He told how he had been approached by a lawyer for a Philippine company who had heard of the desperate economic straits of the area and wanted to help. Good news was on the way! All the people had to do was form a local company in partnership with the Philippine company to sublet the land, and they would bring in the workers, clear away the trees, and set up the plantation. "It will not cost you a penny," he concluded. "And profits will come to the government, the company, and the people." The Uiaku village councillor spoke next, his voice cracking with emotion as he described his efforts over the years to convince the provincial government to promote logging in the area. At last it was going to happen! The meeting had the feel of a religious revival with people emotionally murmuring their agreement, sometimes repeating the phrases of the officers and councillor as they delivered the good news. Salvation—"development"—was at last coming!

One person asked whether any logging would take place in the gardening zone around the villages. After being assured that logs would only be removed from the deep forest, discussion shifted to the two topics most on peoples' minds. They were outraged that 75 per cent of the royalties would go to the provincial and national governments. A number of men spoke eloquently of how their ancestors had conquered the land. They didn't see why the governments should receive more in royalties than the owners. The second issue had to do with the ownership of the lands and whether the clans owning specific areas of forests or the Maisin as a whole would be compensated. An elder spoke up: "When the Australian government came, they asked questions about the land. They asked whether we would separate into clans or look after it as one Maisin land. People said, 'All Maisin fought for this land so we could have the land as Maisin. Whatever happens in future, we will use it as one land for all Maisin.'" There was general agreement that the royalties must be equally distributed among the villagers, but the overall share going to the people remained a sticking point.

Over the next few days, I visited friends and asked them about the project. Given the certain disruptions, including the appearance of a large expatriate workforce, was it really worth the risk? People assured me that it was. The village was mired in "poverty" with no products of interest to the outside world. Logging presented the one and probably only chance of "development" that would bring decent houses, access to medicine, and schooling for the children. I pushed a little harder. What if the loggers damage gardens, scare away the game, or pollute the rivers and reefs? "We will stop them," people said confidently. "We'll make them leave." Some people had relatives in town who had expressed similar concerns. These city folk, I was told, did not have the true interest of their rural kin in mind.

The project was blocked by officials in the Forestry Department who reprimanded the officer for his extracurricular activities. During his visit to Uiaku for St. Thomas Day in December 1982, Archbishop David Hand warned about the bad record of logging operations elsewhere in the country and the values of conservation. Meanwhile, some Maisin in the towns urged caution. This outraged village leaders, who protested to me that the Church "had done nothing" to help the villagers and that those in the town had "forgotten" their kinfolk and now wanted to deny them any hope for prosperity. Yet by 1994 at the latest, the consensus had swung to oppose industrial logging. The shift in opinion may have been partially due to the types of scandals revealed by the Barnett inquiry, but the main precipitating factor was more direct. Rumours had been circulating for some time that a group of men who had left Collingwood Bay as children to live in the cities had secretly signed an agreement with a logging company giving it access to the Maisin rainforest. Sometime in the early 1990s, a photocopy of the document showed up, followed by the revelation that Collingwood Bay had been listed by the government as a priority area for logging. People were outraged. Meetings were held in the villages denouncing the scheme, and village leaders were given permission to run full-page ads in the *Post-Courier* newspaper declaring Collingwood Bay the property of the local landowners. In 1996, the scenario was replayed when another secret contract appeared, this time bearing the signature of the then provincial premier, approving a bizarre scheme to clear-cut the rainforest and replace it with plantations of an experimental sap-producing palm for a new health drink. The proposal promised millions of US dollars each year to the landowners who would set up family farms alongside 50,000 Philippine migrant farmers. The contract was said to have gotten as far as the Prime Minister's Office and was awaiting final approval when it was leaked. Again, there were meetings and full-page ads placed in the press. The government denied any involvement.

The biggest challenge came in 1998 when a "Keroro Development Corporation" secured recognition from the national government as a "Representative Landowner Body." (It later was revealed that many if not most of the men listed as partners had never been approached for permission.) In its supposed capacity as a landowner association, Keroro invited the government to remove the land from customary ownership and then lease back 38,000 hectares of prime forest land to itself and a partner company, Deegold (PNG), for 50 years. The partners contracted with a Malaysian firm to clear-cut the forest with plans to develop an oil palm plantation later. Word leaked out in June 1999 just as bulldozers and other heavy equipment were being prepared to be shipped by barge to Collingwood Bay. The Maisin immediately sent a delegation to Port Moresby and managed to get the leases suspended. A complicated and expensive legal battle followed in the National Court with suits and countersuits between the landowners, Deegold, and the government. In 2002, the National Court ruled that the government had acted illegally, cancelled all leases, and forbade the companies involved from entering Maisin territory without the prior written approval of the people (Barker 2004a).

There was much talk in Uiaku about the looming court battle during my visit in June 2000. People kept returning to a point that I had also heard during the 1982 meeting when everyone was eager for logging to commence: "Our ancestors conquered this land." The move by Deegold, Keroro, and the unnamed logging company amounted to "theft." The consensus to oppose logging, then, rested on the same core principle that motivated the earlier consensus to allow it. Maisin own the land. It is their right to decide how it should be used, nobody else's. They are unified on that.

TO: LOGGING, AGROFORESTRY & MINING COMPANIES...
F.I.A., PNG Forest Authority, PNG Dept. Mining & Petroleum....
Cut this out and save for your future reference!

We Maisin leaders are tired of being the LAST ones to be asked to 'okay' projects proposed for our land. If you want to do *anything* on our land, FIRST get the approval of Maisin traditional leaders who live in the villages. State your business and speak in front of all the Maisin villagers. No dealmaking in Waigani, Popondetta, Asia or Australia. *Come to Collingwood Bay.* If that is not your style, then go 'help' people somewhere else in PNG. **WARNING:** The Maisin people don't want ANY projects where you buy our timber or minerals with no downstream processing. If that is what is on your mind, go someplace else.

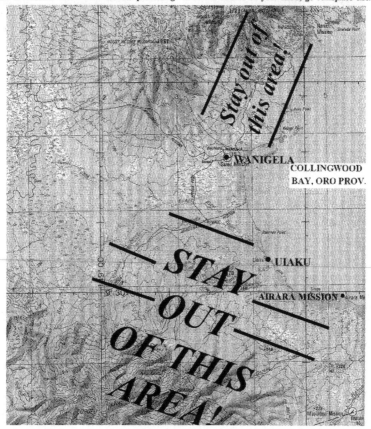

Figure 6.3 An anti-logging newspaper ad, 1996. Sponsored in part by Greenpeace International, this ad took up a full page of the *Post-Courier* following the Maisin's discovery that the government was on the verge of approving a logging concession on their lands. (Reproduced with permission of MICAD)

This is, however, by no means the whole story. Despite the united front Maisin leaders showed to the outside world, the consensus was fragile, as we shall see later in this chapter. Before that, however, we must return to the second widespread development of this period: the almost instantaneous appearance of local, national, and international NGOs arrayed in vigorous opposition to industrial logging that would have an extraordinary impact upon the Maisin.

THE PARTNERS

News of the Maisin's victory in the National Court in 2002 was disseminated around the globe within hours. Congratulations poured in from friends far and wide. To the outside world, this was a David versus Goliath story, an instance of a small and vulnerable Indigenous group taking on a powerful modern company, which had all of the advantages of lawyers and friends in high places, and winning. And so it was. Yet it was not their victory alone. We know of David's battle against the giant because the tale is recounted in the Bible. To the extent that the outside world knows about the Maisin, it is through their alliance with various, mostly Western-based organizations that have publicized their story. While the Maisin deserve the most credit for their victory, their wide circle of allies also played a critical role.

Environmentalists concerned with conserving the remaining rainforests of Southeast Asia form the core of these alliances. They make up the largest part of a burgeoning group of NGOs that grew in tandem with the expansion of industrial mining and logging in Papua New Guinea in the post-Independence period. Colin Filer (1998a:264) estimates that as of 1996 somewhere between 100 and 150 NGOs were operating in the country, a third to a half concerned with forest policy. The numbers have grown since then. NGOs range from organizations with a global reach, such as Greenpeace and the World Wildlife Fund, to village-based associations. They are mostly staffed by Papua New Guineans, but receive (or hope to receive) much of their funding from international environmental organizations, foreign government aid agencies, and national and international church groups and development organizations, as well as individual donors. The largest employ expatriates in senior staff positions and as consultants.

Environmental activists often portray themselves as opponents of "globalization," which they identify with the activities of multinational corporations and neoliberal capitalism. Yet the enormous expansion of environmental NGOs in the late twentieth century must also be understood as a facet of globalization. NGOs work within a global network that depends upon modern means of mass communication, forms of bureaucratic organization, and investments by supporters. They rationalize their efforts in terms of values presumed to be globally shared: the human rights of local peoples, the need to preserve pristine environments for the benefit of all humankind, and so forth. These are worthy aims, but they require international coordination in the manner (if on a vastly smaller scale) of the international companies that transfer logs from Papua New Guinea to Japan and Korea. The companies and the NGOs differ markedly in their visions of what is in the best interests of the world's population—unfettered development driven by capital markets seeking new sources of profit, or regulation with the aim of restoring a sustainable balance between the earth's environment and the needs of its human and nonhuman inhabitants.

In 1993, Lafcadio Cortesi, then an activist with Greenpeace International, came to Uiaku on the recommendation of a friend who had visited Tufi and fallen under the spell of Collingwood Bay. For some time, Greenpeace had been expanding from its earlier role as a radical environmental protest organization to promote "green" development projects, especially among Indigenous peoples. Cortesi saw that Maisin tapa cloth was exactly the sort of thing Greenpeace would be interested in supporting. His offer to help create an overseas market for tapa was eagerly accepted by the Maisin. A few months later, in 1994, villagers discovered that the National Forest Board had placed Collingwood Bay among priority areas for logging without first consulting them. Maisin leaders organized meetings and compiled a petition in protest. Cortesi facilitated these efforts, putting the leaders in touch with a lawyer in Port Moresby and with national journalists who could report the story from the Maisin point of view. He also helped to secure funds to place full-page advertisements in the national newspaper, the *Post-Courier*, to protest the project, actions that would be repeated in 1996 and 2000 in response to renewed threats.

The Maisin, via Cortesi, put out a call for help. The response was astonishing. Within a year, the Maisin went from a situation of political isolation to partnership with a bewildering array of outside organizations and individuals. The help offered and accepted by the people worked in three overlapping directions: publicizing the Maisin's situation to the outside world, securing legal protection of the rainforest, and enhancing the local economy and governance.

Although many of these interventions required a great deal of consultation and planning, the Maisin's sudden and unexpected engagement with anti-logging forces was anything but preplanned and only loosely coordinated, more or less on the fly. There was something of a chain reaction as a project with one group led to involvement with another. Larry Rinder, the curator of the successful 1995 tapa exhibition at the Berkeley Art Museum, for instance, helped develop a project with the Fabric Workshop, an independent museum in Philadelphia. Three Maisin women spent several weeks at the Workshop, creating innovative tapa designs on various types of media for a major exhibition. Fabric Workshop staff, in turn, visited the Maisin villages twice to confer on the project and to film in the communities. A second Maisin delegation travelled to Philadelphia for the grand opening. John Wesley Vaso, who once enjoyed a short stint as an announcer on the Papua New Guinea radio service before returning to Uiaku, was interviewed on the *Fresh Air* show on National Public Radio in the United States. During this time, one of the Maisin women visiting Philadelphia expressed regrets that there had been no opportunity to meet Indigenous people in North America. This planted the seed for another project, in which I played a leading role: an exchange between the Maisin and the Stó:lō First Nation of British Columbia. In June 2000, a delegation of five members of the Stó:lō Nation visited the Maisin villages to discuss issues of mutual concern, and the next year seven Maisin came to Canada. These exchanges were the subject of two documentaries, aired on the CBC's flagship science program *The Nature of Things*, hosted by David Suzuki.[2] Maisin delegations also visited New Zealand, Australia, and Japan.

Meanwhile, back in Papua New Guinea, steps were being taken to enhance legal protection of Maisin lands. Representatives of the Individual and Community Rights Forum (ICRF), a national NGO, held a workshop to inform landowners of their legal rights under Papua New Guinea law. Papua New Guinea officially protects only a tiny portion of its territory in the form of national parks, wildlife management areas, and wildlife sanctuaries. This is not so much the result of a lack of interest or determination as the fact that most of land remains under customary tenure. The same factors that make it difficult to alienate land for commercial development militates against putting it aside to be protected. Once they learned that having their lands declared a Wildlife Management Area would involve ceding some control to the government, most Maisin lost interest. By the early 1990s, however, the national government developed new policies that would recognize and protect conservation areas from uncontrolled logging. These policies were backed by the commitment of funds by outsider donors to identify areas for conservation and by the government's signing, in 1993, of the International Convention on Biological Diversity. These conditions, in turn, gave the environmental NGO community more influence and encouraged the emergence of new organizations focused around specific areas and projects. One of these organizations, Conservation Melanesia, made Collingwood Bay its first project and for the decade or so of its existence remained almost exclusively concerned with the Maisin. In 1996, Conservation Melanesia coordinated an inventory of the marine and forest resources of all the Maisin villages, including the Cape Nelson outlier of Uwe,

179

and provided educational workshops on conservation values. The organization eventually took on the challenging work of coordinating legal actions to stop the logging companies, eventually enlisting the aid of Australian lawyers. For these efforts, Lester Seri—the Maisin director of Conservation Melanesia and a trained biologist—was awarded the J. Paul Getty Wildlife Conservation Prize by the World Wildlife Fund in 2003.

This brings us to a third set of interventions intended to enhance the local economy and system of governance. In 1995, the leaders of the petition drive against the first logging proposal drafted a "Maisin Declaration" in support of their ancestral lands that was widely broadcast by Greenpeace in brochures and on the Internet (reproduced in full at the end of this chapter). While acknowledging the sustaining values of the forest for the community, the Declaration stated clearly:

> ... we do not only wish to live as our ancestors did. We seek to maintain our heritage but also to improve our lives and the lives of our future generations. We therefore require better opportunities for education, health and transportation, to name a few. The Government has failed to adequately assist us in developing these opportunities. We require money, information, training and technical support to develop them ourselves.

The various NGOs and other partners, under this scenario, would fill the breach left by the steady decline in government services. Workshops were held in the villages to provide basic training in small-scale development in areas such as insect farming and eco-tourism, but almost all the effort focused on the expansion of a market for tapa cloth. Delegates on the overseas trips spent part of their time meeting with "ethnic arts" dealers and shopowners, hoping to establish business partnerships. Several environmental NGOs began marketing tapa on their websites, accompanied with colourful pictures of the villagers and brief descriptions of the "Maisin story." Cortesi also worked closely with village leaders to start up a tapa cloth cooperative, described in the next section.

These various projects all required official approval from the community. This posed an immediate problem. Although the Maisin had come together to resist the illegal sale of their forest, they possessed no overarching form of governance. A solution came, ironically enough, via policy initiatives occurring at the national level. In the early 1990s, the Department of Environment and Conservation secured US$5 million to begin experiments with locally based "integrated conservation and development" (ICAD) projects (Filer 1998a:246). Several of these were set up around the country (e.g., West 2006), but a number of other communities, including the Maisin, independently adopted the model for themselves. In 1996, the Maisin Integrated Conservation and Development association, MICAD (pronounced "My-Cad"), came into existence with formal representation from all the Maisin villages. In principle, MICAD coordinated the work of the various partners, such as Conservation Melanesia and Greenpeace. Its leaders, however, had greater ambitions for it, seeing it as a kind of Maisin government that would give each of the villages a political voice in future developments and provide a range of services. One of the first orders of business after its formation was MICAD's decision that profits from the tapa business and hospitality charges to visitors would go towards the purchase of medicines for community aid posts. We'll look more closely at MICAD later in this chapter.

Cortesi's efforts and the establishment of Conservation Melanesia and MICAD provided a certain degree of coherence to these developments. Yet there was never a master plan. The various groups and individuals who became involved with the Maisin, mostly for short periods of time, had few if any organizational links with each other. They are autonomous, with their own goals, funding sources, and requirements. Thus, the Maisin in the 1990s became a focus for a loose and shifting coalition of sympathetic outsiders whose notions of how to help sometimes clashed. Greenpeace's policies during the 1990s had moved from purely confrontational tactics to encouraging small-scale sustainable local economic development, a goal that required wary cooperation with the Papua New Guinea government and occasionally traditional adversaries like the World Bank. During this same period, the Maisin were visited by more radical activists who urged a return to "traditional" values and rejection of most forms of modern economic development. The most influential of this group was the remarkable Sister Yasuko Shimizu, a member of the Mercendarian Missionaries of Berriz in Tokyo and founder of her own NGO dedicated to ending destructive logging in Melanesia. Forceful and energetic, this diminutive nun attracted a great deal of interest whenever she visited the area, sometimes with Japanese biologists in tow, lecturing the people on the need to preserve their ancient culture and to reject grants and aid from the outside, which might make them too dependent. Ironically, Sister Yasuko is also an ardent feminist who did not hesitate to protest the subservence of women in Maisin society. Equally ironically, despite her opposition to outsiders helping Indigenous people materially, in 1997 she provided the Maisin with a well-received gift—a satellite telephone which, during its three years of operation, provided a fairly reliable means of communication with the outside world.

It is impossible to say with any precision just why the Maisin attracted so much attention. Many factors were at work: the initiative taken by resourceful activists, the receptiveness of the Maisin to their new partners, the emergence of a political space in Papua New Guinea for NGOs like Conservation Melanesia, and sheer happenstance. While not everything, timing is important. The Maisin were the beneficiaries of the explosion of NGOs in Papua New Guinea, many of which were searching for worthy projects. More generally, the Maisin also benefited from other well-publicized campaigns occurring in the 1980s and early 1990s in which international environmental activists had teamed up with Indigenous peoples like the Haida of British Columbia, the Kayapo of Brazil, and the Penan of Malaysia to block industrial logging and mining projects (Brosius 2003; Turner 1993). While on a much smaller scale, the Maisin rejection of commercial logging fit neatly into a scenario of a plucky Indigenous people defending their lands, to which NGOs could respond quickly with money, advice, and international publicity.

The unusual political clout of NGOs in Papua New Guinea is also an important factor. Although politicians and civil servants often react angrily to the complaints of activists or simply ignore them, the NGOs are mostly tolerated and periodically encouraged. Part of the reason for this is that the organizations have strong support in the rural communities where most people live. However, it is also the case that many politicians share at least some of the concerns raised by the NGOs about deforestation. In addition, the NGOs fulfill some important needs. Despite its rich endowment of natural resources, Papua New Guinea is greatly dependent upon foreign aid, particularly from Australia and the World Bank, which have long insisted on more sustainable forestry practices. This has encouraged the government to bring in experts from some of the NGOs to help develop policies and to carry out projects. Finally, the NGOs have come to occupy a small but significant niche in the country as years of economic shortfalls made worse by mismanagement and widespread corruption have contributed to a weakening of state-provided services in most rural areas. In the late 1990s, for instance, Conservation Melanesia became a major conduit for mail and medical supplies to Maisin villages, years after local government services had completely broken down. Some politicians praise resident NGOs as examples of "self-reliance." For their part, NGOs echo the dissatisfactions of their local supporters with the failures of social services and a perceived lack of interest or will on the part of politicians to respond to their needs.

A final important factor attracting the NGOs to the Maisin has to do with their funding requirements. NGOs are voluntary organizations that rely upon donors to cover salaries and other expenses. Typically a great deal of fundraising is required, along with project proposals and reports on progress. Collingwood Bay was by no means the largest or most significant project undertaken by environmental NGOs in Papua New Guinea during the 1990s

(Filer 1997). Yet, it may have been one of the most visited. The core attraction, of course, was the David and Goliath story of fighting off loggers along with the presence of what could easily be portrayed as a suitable, sustainable economic alternative: tapa cloth. There were also other practical advantages. The setting of the Maisin villages makes for vibrant publicity materials—"unspoiled" thatched huts surrounded by lush tropical jungles backed by dramatic mountains, the tapa cloth itself, and the women with their "exotic" facial tattoos. Such images speak compellingly of a world that would soon be lost without outside help. What the images don't convey is equally important. Collingwood Bay was within a relatively easy half-day's journey from Port Moresby. It was cheap to stay there, there was no danger from crime as in the cities or tribal warfare as in the Highlands, and many people spoke fluent English. It was simply much easier to visit, consult, and initiate projects with the Maisin than in many other places in the country, and as more groups did so, something of a snowball effect took place.

None of the groups coming to the aid of the Maisin sought to change the community in significant ways. While their familiarity with the culture was not very deep, they liked the people and admired what they perceived as a "traditional" way of life. Their purpose was to help the Maisin sustain that way of life by providing them with the tools to protect their lands and to develop sustainable alternatives to logging, particularly the development of a market for tapa cloth. Yet such a sudden and large influx of outsiders with ideas, projects, money, and powerful outside connections was bound to have a major impact on a small, formerly remote community. Much of this impact revolved around the various functions and meanings of tapa.

TAPA, WOMEN, AND IDENTITY

From the start, it was clear that tapa would figure centrally in the effort to foster integrated conservation and development. The decision to block logging did nothing to alleviate the practical difficulties of starting businesses in the Collingwood Bay region. The lack of regular shipping along the coast and absence of good harbours had defeated innumerable earlier attempts to develop copra, cocoa, and other cash crops. There was at first much talk about possibilities such as insect farming or eco-tourism, but the main hope rested with tapa. After all, the Maisin had long enjoyed a small but fairly steady market for the cloth in Papua New Guinea.

Tapa had additional attractions for the Maisin's partners and sponsors. All the work that has been carried out in Collingwood Bay depends upon the financial support of donors in distant countries whose knowledge of Papua New Guinea is minimal. In appealing to them for funds, the partners have

183

to sell an attractive picture of the people and the cause. The cause, of course, was rainforest conservation, a global campaign that got its start in the highly publicized efforts to save the great Amazon forest in the 1980s. This generated a new political model of collaboration between environmentalists and Indigenous peoples that was quickly transferred to other parts of the globe. Thus, Indigenous "rights became entangled with conservation initiatives" (Tsing 2005:159). Tapa was ideal for this purpose. It was a sustainable product with a low environmental impact; it was easy to ship out of the villages to both national and international markets; and it was an iconic form of Oceanic art, a symbol of the continuing viability of an Indigenous culture. Purchasers of tapa could feel that they were supporting not only rainforest conservation and the rights of Indigenous people but also, more directly, the advancement of the economic position of women who, in general, have fared worse under globalization than men in the developing world.

Early in their relationship with the Maisin, Greenpeace initiated a "Painting a Sustainable Future" campaign to foster the development of a stable market for tapa. Village leaders formed a new economic cooperative with a governing council made up of two representatives (one male, one female) from each village. Villagers agreed that individuals should be free to sell their tapa directly to artifact shops if they wished. Still, the hope was that the cooperative would capture most of the trade and, on that basis, be able to secure better prices for the producers and generate a steady profit to pay overhead and invest in new projects. Maisin Tapa Enterprises was not an entirely new idea; the Maisin had created a similar cooperative, Haus Tapa, in 1982. It had floundered, most people thought, because the young men running it had mishandled the funds. Greenpeace organized a workshop on financial management for the staff of the new endeavour. More importantly, it reached out to the Peace Corps, a voluntary organization funded by the American government, to place Kerry and Kate Sullivan in Uiaku for two years to assist the tapa business. Trained accountants, the Sullivans provided Maisin Tapa Enterprises with a stability that would have been nearly impossible for villagers to achieve on their own.

Meanwhile, Cortesi orchestrated an overseas publicity campaign promoting tapa and the Maisin cause, including museum exhibits in Berkeley, Philadelphia, and New York; marketing research; and building connections between Maisin Tapa Enterprises and overseas buyers. Maisin tapa was featured in brochures, catalogues, and websites, usually accompanied by a capsule description of the people and their battle against loggers. Worried that the market for tapa wall-hangings would be too limited, Cortesi and his allies (including myself) conferred with various businesses to consider spin-offs such as tapa hats, handbags, and book covers. This met with limited success, but Cortesi pursued another possibility that might prove more lucrative in the future: the licensing of Maisin tapa designs. In 1997, Greenpeace Germany licensed a design to use on coffee mugs and t-shirts. For a time, Cortesi was involved in hot negotiations with the clothing giant Patagonia to license tapa designs for a new fashion line, but unfortunately this fell through.

I found that a great deal of tapa was being produced in the villages when I visited in 1997 and 1998. There was also an impressive degree of innovation. Much of this was subtle, involving small design changes, more small one-panel tapas that were easier to market, and experimentation with dyes to produce sharper blacks and reds. Other changes, however, were radical. A number of men now designed tapa, although none seemed willing to undertake the hard labour of beating. My old language teacher, Gideon Ifoki, had developed not only into a fine artist but a skilled innovator, producing attractive tapa cloth hats and ties. Some Maisin were developing ways of rationalizing the process of producing tapa to make it more efficient. One household in Ganjiga, for instance, created a kind of factory line, with different people assigned to beating, drawing the design, and filling in the red on a steady flow of tapa cloths. Some traditionalists worried that designs were straying too far from customary norms, observing that some tapa makers were combing through magazines and pattern books for ideas. A number of people used crayons to design cartoon-like figures on tapa, usually accompanied by political slogans and biblical quotations. These were not for sale but adorned the walls of the MICAD building and some houses. Upon my departure in April 1997, Gideon surprised me with a beautiful tapa with a bright cartoon of Bart Simpson on a skateboard surrounded by traditional tapa designs to give to Jessica for her upcoming seventh birthday.

While the tapa sales and the cash injected by visitors resulted in a sudden rise in the prosperity of the Maisin villages, particularly Uiaku, no one became wealthy. Most of the money was quickly dispersed along exchange networks and spent on store-bought food, clothing, transportation fees, and other consumables rather than put in bank accounts. In any case, the surge didn't last long. By the time of my next visit in June 2000, the Painting a Sustainable Future campaign had petered out. Cortesi had left Greenpeace to work on environmental issues in Indonesia and the Peace Corps volunteers had finished their two-year contract. The fundamentals kicked back in. Faced with the problems of irregular and expensive transportation, no control over market prices, and the failure of some purchasers to pay for the tapa they received, Maisin Tapa Enterprises was moribund, and individual tapa sales, mostly to artifact shops in the towns, slowed to a trickle.

Although unusually intense, the short-lived tapa project is instructive not just of the challenges of integrating conservation with sustainable development in peripheral areas but of reconciling the demands of the market economy with deeply held Melanesian values. Every villager I spoke to was delighted by the money that outsiders brought to the community, either directly or through tapa sales. However, this was coupled by strong discontent with how things were actually working out. Some people whispered that the partners were getting far more out of the arrangement than others, pocketing more than their fair share of the profits that the cloth fetched overseas. Most discontent was directed inwards, upon the Maisin themselves. Each time that Maisin Tapa Enterprises made the rounds of the villages, complaints arose in its wake that people were not being treated fairly. Many felt that they were not given as much opportunity to sell their cloth as others. Rumours spread that the managers of the cooperative tended to favour their own relatives and perhaps had sticky fingers, skimming off profits for their own use. At times the griping and gossip grew so intense, I felt that the main accomplishment of the tapa initiative had been to stir up a hornets' nest. This was perhaps unfair. Gossip and complaint are normal in the context of a political system based on consensus and the morality of reciprocal balance, *marawa-wawe*.

The tapa project stirred up another conflict of values that proved just as stubbornly difficult. As I noted earlier, outside sponsors were attracted to tapa cloth not only because it was "Indigenous" but also because it was produced by women. Around the same time as the collaborative model between environmentalists and Indigenous peoples emerged, development agencies ranging from small NGOs to the giant World Bank increasingly earmarked funds to promote "women and development." In part, this initiative was motivated by a sense of justice. It was widely held that women held subservient positions in "traditional" societies, and there was lots of evidence that men were usually the main beneficiaries of development projects. There were additional pragmatic considerations. In most developing countries, women provide the glue holding families together. Very often they contribute more labour than men in support of their households. Beyond this, at least in the eyes of potential donors, women were considered to be more responsible and more likely to use scant financial resources to further their children's education or purchase medicine, while men might waste the same funds on gambling, alcohol, or prostitutes (Douglas 2003). In Melanesia, "church women's wings and village women's groups ... provide women's main opportunities for training, leadership, solidarity, networking and wider experience beyond the village and even beyond national border" and thus have provided the venue for numerous local development projects (Douglas 2000:5). In the case of the Maisin, however, the Anglican Mothers' Union was largely ignored by the outsiders, who instead focused on including women with men in ongoing projects and forming women's councils.[3]

Unfailingly respectful and polite, the partners working with the Maisin firmly insisted that women should have a prominent place in making decisions and enjoying the benefits of the tapa initiative. Just as politely, Maisin male leaders firmly resisted. The delegation to Berkeley, for instance, was originally supposed to include two women and two men. When four men showed up, the inevitable question from the audience was "Where are the women?" Leaders protested that women were unable or unwilling to take leading roles managing the business end of the tapa, yet they had little choice but to compromise if they wished further cooperation from the partners. Future delegations included women, although usually in the minority. Women were formally, although not effectively, given equal control over Maisin Tapa Enterprises, and women's councils were formed in Uiaku and Airara to meet with partners when they came into the area to discuss tapa-related projects. In 1997, I was amazed to find senior women sitting upon (rather than below and beside) the shelter platforms with their male counterparts during the various meetings I attended. They sat apart, for the most part silent, but a number made eloquent speeches about the importance of tapa sales as a means to promote development without destroying ancestral lands. This state of affairs didn't last long. By 2000, senior men again sat alone on the shelter platforms. I was then working on the early stages of organizing a delegation to visit Canada. When I told people it had to be half women, a number of men complained bitterly to me that I and the other partners were "interfering with the culture."

It was harder for me to get a sense of what the women thought. A few younger women (and men as well) were clearly happy about the changes, but most women, uncomfortable talking about political matters or for some other reasons, refused to share their opinion. It was clear that Uiaku was not on the brink of a feminist revolution. The women's council only convened when visitors requested a meeting. The Mothers' Union remained the only viable women's group. It was also enjoying a slight increase in membership, but still included only a small minority of mostly older women and limited its activities to shared meals and services and pastoral care for the sick and infirm. Senior women were among the most adamantly opposed to women joining delegations, and those who managed to go overseas could count upon tongue-lashings, particularly from their female in-laws. The main problem, I suspect, was that despite all the good intentions, the tapa projects did not do much to foster women's political clout. Indeed, they added considerably to their burden (cf. Douglas 2003). Women still remained responsible for most daily subsistence tasks. Not only were they beating considerably more tapa, they were doing the bulk of the work to provide food and housing for visiting activists, museum curators, and film crews. In many cases, their husbands, brothers, and fathers appropriated any cash earned from tapa, so women often saw few of the benefits. This all suggests to me that their resistance may have had less to do with cultural conservatism than resistance to being burdened with additional work.[4]

A third arena of controversy had to do with the symbolism of tapa itself. In the early 1980s, a few people had described the Maisin as "tapa people." By the late 1990s, this had become a mantra, encouraged by the various art exhibitions and visual prominence of tapa in the anti-logging media campaign. Tapa "posters" with slogans like "Keep out of Maisin lands" adorned several houses. As with profits and the political equality of women, the elevation of tapa as a political symbol created both outward and inward tensions. Although not new, rumours multiplied that other groups in Collingwood Bay and Oro Province at large had "stolen" *wuwusi* along with tapa designs to profit from the boom. A more focused concern, discussed at length at several meetings I attended, was that outsiders were reproducing and profiting from tapa designs in various media and forms without compensating the Maisin. For years, Maisin had complained about various groups in Papua New Guinea using their tapa designs for clothing, publications, and tourist promotions without compensation. For the first time, however, I now heard the word "copyright," reflecting a growing global discourse concerning the legality of the appropriation by educational, museum, and commercial enterprises mainly in Western countries of intangible Indigenous art styles and designs (Geismar 2013).

Maisin could do little about the problem of outside appropriations except complain. Internal tensions were another matter. The elevation of tapa as a symbol of Maisin unity directly paralleled the new politics of land and teetered on the same fault lines. Land, as we saw in Chapter 3, is passed on within lineages. Yet when Maisin speak of land, they attribute ownership to clans. Clan migration histories are important in large part because they constitute inalienable claims to land based on conquest and order of arrival in Collingwood Bay. In 1986, I recorded competing stories told by clan elders of how their ancestor had discovered *wuwusi* and were the first to abandon rough bush barks for the smooth texture of the new tree. Like clan histories, such stories laid claim to ownership. Similarly, *evovi* emblems worn on traditional costumes define clans, not the Maisin as a whole. Community projects, from the time of the earliest cooperative movements, have required overcoming such clan divisions. When they elected to approve logging in 1982, Maisin leaders publicly declared that the forest would no longer be clan territory but shared. When a consensus against logging was formed, the same declarations were made and tapa emerged as the symbol of the new unity. Yet land and tapa remain Janus-faced symbols, simultaneously representing Maisin divisions into clans and clan federations and their common identity as the joint conquerors and owners of the land (cf. Hermkens 2013:324–38).

Bridging these tensions was the key challenge faced by the Maisin Integrated Conservation and Development organization—MICAD—to which we now turn.

MICAD

What began as a normal market day on the Uiaku mission station in March 1997 broke into a flurry of activity as men began to converge on the area, some carrying heavy hardwood logs and others a large portable winch. Under the careful supervision of Sylvester Moi, MICAD's chairman, teams of young men dug deep holes and then manoeuvered the winch to lift and set the massive posts down. The atmosphere was festive, with the men singing and trading barbs with each other as women shouted jibes from the market stalls. It was indeed a moment for celebration. The Maisin were erecting their very first two-storey building. Once completed, it would house the satellite telephone just donated by Sister Yasuko and powered by a solar panel contributed by another NGO. It would also serve as the headquarters for MICAD itself. There was one sour note. People from other villages had been invited to contribute materials and labour for the new office building. Sylvester became increasingly worried when they failed to show up. The splendid new office building and phone had been located in Uiaku by agreement of all the village representatives on MICAD, he told me. It was the most central location and, with neighbouring Ganjiga, the largest of the communities. Everyone had agreed, but now it appeared he had more work to do to convince the other villages that it really had been the right choice.

MICAD was the joint creation of Maisin leaders and outside partners, in particular Greenpeace and Conservation Melanesia. Its immediate origins lay in the landowners' refusal to cede control over the forest in the mid-1990s. The emergency, perhaps for the first time, brought together all of the Maisin villages in large political rallies, including even remote Uwe, lying far to the north and possessing no commercially valuable stands of timber.[5] The model of integrated conservation and development being introduced nationally around the same time gave this political movement form. That form was recognizably Western and democratic. Working closely with Conservation Melanesia, MICAD developed a constitution laying out procedures for electing officers and their duties and responsibilities to the community. While Maisin saw the need for a unified front to stave off attempts by individuals or whole villages to sign contracts with loggers, the partners perhaps had the greater need for a formally constituted political organization. Indeed, it is hard to see how the partnerships could have continued without the invention of MICAD or something similar. MICAD's constituted authority included the power to negotiate projects with outsiders, make arrangements for food and accommodation for visitors, and handle profits from tapa sales and the telephone, along with direct grants, for the benefit of the Maisin people as a whole. Without MICAD, the partners would have had to negotiate virtually everything they did directly with individual villagers, adding enormously to their expenses as well as the difficulty of getting projects up and running.

During my fieldwork in the late 1990s, I was curious to learn more about MICAD. The various partners I had spoken to talked about the organization as a kind of government, albeit one that was still finding its feet. My curiosity stemmed in part from my historical research into the cooperative movement of the 1950s and 1960s. How did the Maisin view MICAD? Did they see it as a return of the old cooperative movement, only now on a much greater scale? Or did it represent something entirely new, a true break from the past? Because I had "family" in Uiaku, I was treated somewhat differently than other partners. Still, I now paid an accommodation fee to my clan sister as set by MICAD for visitors. MICAD had a large presence in Uiaku. I attended workshops and meetings and interviewed the leaders at length. I also spent much of my time with people in several villages, getting their views on the organization and listening to the gossip.

I came away convinced that MICAD really did mark a major change in Maisin society. While the organization itself was shaky—more an ideal than established reality—it provided the Maisin with a new way of thinking of themselves, more as a kind of nation than as individual communities or simply as members of clans. This kind of development is by no means unique to the Maisin. "Micro-nationalist" movements have been common across Melanesia as people rethink and rework their notions of cultural and linguistic identity in the context of the multicultural states of which they are citizens (Foster 1995). At their more heady moments, some Maisin—particularly young men—talked defiantly of the Maisin rejecting the authority of the Papua New Guinea government entirely, of building up local businesses and infrastructures that would allow them complete autonomy. I doubt that many Maisin shared this illusion, but certainly the integrated conservation and development movement contributed to a new sense of their identity as Maisin and increasingly fostered a politics focused upon unity across the region rather than based at the village level.

Important as such changes were, I also found much that was familiar in the ways the Maisin actually dealt with MICAD. This is perhaps inevitable when you consider that MICAD was essentially a volunteer, part-time organization. It had no paid staff and through most of its years has lacked the budget even to hold the twice-yearly meetings of the board as required by its constitution. All the leaders and village representatives in MICAD were at the same time "ordinary" villagers in the sense that they spent most of their days engaged in subsistence activities, taking care of their households, and meeting their obligations to extended kin and exchange partners. Much of the time, the office building on the Uiaku mission station was locked and empty. MICAD had an impressive organizational charter with elected officers administering six "departments," representation from all villages as well as women, and so forth. Yet I was reminded of the talk I had heard when I first arrived in 1981 of various committees that didn't seem to meet and work days that only happened periodically. My sense was that MICAD existed less as an organization and more as a mode of organizing in response to a need, such as a request from an outside partner to set up workshops or an impending threat to Maisin lands.

I heard lots of talk about MICAD, talk that followed the patterns of political discourse we examined in the last chapter. Assessments were deeply informed by the key value of equivalence. While most villagers I spoke to took pride in MICAD's role stopping the "theft" of Maisin land, it did not take long before the talk became critical. People everywhere (including some MICAD leaders) complained that the organization did not fairly share projects and the money they brought in. Such criticisms were especially acute the further one moved from Uiaku, which was accurately perceived as receiving the lion's share of benefits. For Maisin living in Sinapa or Airara, the MICAD office building was proof of their subservient role in the organization, and they let it be known that unless things improved they might pull out. It didn't help that all of the MICAD's executive lived in Uiaku and Ganjiga (Hermkens 2013:307–08). Within Uiaku and Ganjiga, criticisms focused more on the leaders who were widely suspected of taking advantage of their positions to skim money or secure other benefits. Such suspicions were not misplaced. MICAD leaders tended to be heavily represented on overseas delegations, to visit Port Moresby frequently, and to take other perks. When asked about the lack of representation of Airara and Sinapa on the MICAD board, some Uiaku people voiced a familiar complaint, made as well about church stewardship, that the eastern villages did not put in their share of labour and funds and thus didn't deserve a larger voice. Others, more diplomatically perhaps, likened the relationship to that of *Kawo* and *Sabu* clans: living near the original settlement site of Gorofi from which the Maisin dispersed, Uiaku and Ganjiga acted as older brothers "caring for" their junior siblings in the *Sibo* (deep water) villages who, in turn, owed them respect.

MICAD existed unsteadily in the tension between the need for an authority that could speak for all of the Maisin and the cultural expectation of equivalence between individuals of the same rank, clans, and villages. In MICAD's formative years, it was the work of community leaders to navigate that space, to build and maintain consensus despite the contradictions. No one played a more significant role than Sylvester Moi, who until his death in 2003 served as the director of MICAD. Sylvester's life reads like a history of the Maisin in the twentieth century. His father had been a mission teacher and founder of the first cooperative in Uiaku. As an infant, Sylvester was fostered to the Jogun clan in Ganjiga, who are *Sabu*. When his adopted parents died, he returned to his own *Kawo* clan of Gafi but retained ties to Jogun. He was among the first generation of Maisin to go to high school. After receiving medical training in Papua New Guinea and New Zealand, he worked as a medical orderly at the Panguna copper mine on Bougainville Island until fighting broke out. Sylvester's family settled with him in Uiaku, making gardens and contributing to exchanges, thus establishing his reputation for "generosity." He was also a skilled orator. However, his greatest skill lay in quiet diplomacy. Making use of his split identity as *Sabu* and *Kawo*, belonging to two villages, Sylvester spent many evenings quietly visiting elders, making use of his extended kin networks to establish bonds in all of the Maisin communities. He was equally effective as a cultural broker, comfortable working with outsiders. No one worked harder to convince partners to visit and engage with people in all of the communities or to make sure that the benefits of MICAD were shared equally. It is a measure of Sylvester's sensitivity to the cultural value of equivalence, as much as political astuteness, that he declined to join overseas delegations after the first trip to Berkeley.

Building and maintaining consensus in a politically egalitarian society is enormously difficult even when limited to a single village. The ambitions of MICAD, of course, were much greater. Like any big man, Sylvester was subjected to constant scrutiny and gossip. He was an obvious target for sorcery attack from jealous rivals. Although he joked about this with me, he did leave the village for extended periods of time when the pressure got too intense. I have no doubt that many Maisin attribute his early death to sorcery. It is a testimony to his leadership, along with the other founders of MICAD, that the organization continued after his death and, as we'll see in Chapter 7, provided the model for a wider alliance of southern Collingwood Bay people.

THE LAND

I had long wanted to visit a small lake near the little mountains that form a backdrop to Uiaku and Ganjiga. I first heard of it years earlier from Cuthbert

Itati, a *Kawo* elder who told a dramatic story of treachery and violence. Cuthbert broke into tears as he related how his Simboro clan massacred its junior *Sabu* soon after migrating to Collingwood Bay. Their blood formed the waters of the lake. Villagers said that when you call out the name of your ancestor, the slain rise to the surface in the form of huge crocodiles, their heads still marked by *gameti* war paint. Anne's clan brother, Ross Kania, agreed to take me. It took much longer to walk to the lake than I anticipated. We crossed through gardens, secondary bush, grasslands, and deep primary forest before arriving at a huge tree overhanging the waters. It was a spooky place, but I saw no crocodiles. I did see many wonderful things all the same: verdant gardens, shimmering expanses of deep green *kunai* grass, massive flanges spreading out from giant ficus trees. And birds, so many birds! As we came up to the edge of the forest lining the grasslands, I was astonished to witness a huge flock of prehistoric-looking hornbills nesting in the branches of the trees. As we made our way home in the gathering darkness, hundreds of fruit bats filled the air as they came down from the mountains to feast on insects in the gardens.

While that walk in March 1997 gave me great pleasure (as well as painful blisters), it had a practical purpose. I was keenly interested to learn about the Maisin's motivations for opposing logging, one of which I assumed was a desire to safeguard the rich environment upon which they depended for so much. Unlike my earlier work, this was an exercise in applied anthropology. I offered to write up a report for MICAD and Conservation Melanesia on my findings and to make recommendations to help their efforts. I attended community meetings and workshops, administered a survey, formally interviewed leaders about the campaign, and joined in the local gossip, visiting most Maisin villages. I also spent time in the Conservation Melanesian office in Port Moresby, reading their studies of the land and ocean environment of southwestern Collingwood Bay and getting to know the staff and some of the biologists and lawyers they consulted with.

It became clear as my work progressed that the image of the Maisin as "primal conservators" that appeared in much of the media promoting their cause was somewhat misleading. Maisin leaders and ordinary folk alike repeatedly declared that their ancestors had "conquered the land." Their key motivation in opposing the various development ventures proposed for their area was not conservation per se but stopping the theft of resources they rightly owned. They likened themselves to warriors of the past. Indeed, young men promised that should barges appear bearing logging equipment, they would be met with spears, clubs, and shotguns. Symbolizing this determination, Maisin delighted in greeting delegations visiting the villages in a customary way that I had only heard of in the early 1980s—with warriors, bodies blackened with

193

Figure 6.4 Stó:lō-Maisin exchange, June 2000. As their dinghy approaches Ganjiga beach, the Stó:lō delegation receives a traditional welcome from dancing "warriors." Sonny McHalsie (standing) responds with a Stó:lō gesture of peace. (Photo by J. Barker)

soot, dancing along the beach before hurling spears at the boats bearing the visitors. While the spears deliberately missed their targets (and were in any case fake), the greeting was suitably alarming and made a lasting impression even as the guests were led across the beach and feted with green coconuts, speeches, a feast, and traditional dancing.

It is tempting to see the partnership between Maisin "warriors" and foreign conservationists as a marriage of convenience. Certainly, the tensions ran along fault lines that suggest an unstable bargain. Members of Conservation Melanesia worried that the message of the inherent good of preserving the environment for future generations was not getting through. One person speculated that the anti-logging campaign had triggered a kind of "cargo cult" mentality, which she interpreted (wrongly) as a desire to get something for nothing. Others worried that some Maisin saw the partnership as a means of extorting benefits by not too subtly suggesting that if more money didn't come into their pockets they would turn to the logging companies. For their part, villagers also worried that they were being taken advantage of. The surveys of marine and land flora and fauna, mapping of clan boundaries, and talk of creating a conservation preserve triggered worries that the conservationists might be engaged in their own theft of Maisin land. As we've seen, the attempts of outside groups to promote women generated complaints of interference in Maisin culture. More generally, many villagers quietly wondered at, and to some extent resented, the obvious wealth of the outsiders.

Yet if the idea of Maisin as "primal conservators" is misleading, so too is the opposing image of them as hard-nosed pragmatists manipulating others for material advantage. Both of these stereotypes amount to ethnocentric projections that obscure Maisin experience and cultural orientations. Based on my research and familiarity with Maisin ways, it struck me that their reception of environmental activists in the 1990s had a familiar ring to it. The way they talked about the newest outsiders resonated with more familiar relationships: *Kawo* and *Sabu*, older and younger siblings, and parents and children. These are all asymmetrical relationships in which unlike things are exchanged, denoting the superiority of one party over the other. Ideally, the superior partner "takes care" of the junior who, in turn, "respects" (*muan*) their superior, bringing the relationship into reciprocal balance (*marawa-wawe*). Of these various cultural models, the *Kawo/Sabu* was the most salient. Recall that in Maisin traditions, *Sabu* are the hot-headed warriors whose emblem is the spear (*ganan*) while *Kawo* "take care" of their juniors by forming alliances with outsiders and bringing "peace" by holding feasts; thus their emblem is the drum (*ira*). Cuthbert's story of how his ancestors massacred their *Sabu* clans was powerful precisely because it denied that essential relationship. For Cuthbert and many others, the existence of the lake was a reminder of the ever-looming possibility of "bad living," of the upending of the social order, *tauk ramara sii*.

Maisin spoke about the long-departed Anglican missionaries and newly arrived activists in much the same terms (Barker 2004a, 2014). I didn't hear anyone specifically liken the activists to *Kawo* or older siblings, but then much of culture is acted rather than spelled out in words. As "strangers and friends," anthropologists are in a position to spot social patterns less visible to those for whom they are lived. One such pattern we've examined throughout this book is the near constant demand for reciprocal balance. The more Anne and I were accepted into Maisin society, the more frequent the requests we received for gifts. Among themselves, Maisin often gossip about someone being "greedy" or having too much, and they praise those who are generous to others. With people one is not particularly close to, requests can come in the form of "trying luck" with no realistic expectation of return. But the closer the relationship, the stronger the moral imperative of equivalence. Thus, while the demands and complaints Maisin made against MICAD and Conservation Melanesia reflected real tensions, the fact that they were so openly expressed signalled that villagers were coming to accept these organizations within the moral fabric of their community. They treated them as they would treat any Maisin who failed to measure up to their reciprocal obligations (as most people do). In my report, I advised Conservation Melanesia to listen patiently to the concerns and accusations. While they required appropriate action, the open voicing of criticisms reflected growing acceptance, not rejection.

And what of Maisin attitudes towards the environment in general and the rainforest in particular? During the 1980s, I don't recall hearing villagers talk about conservation. Yet it was obvious each time I accompanied Maisin friends into the bush that they appreciated the beauty and richness of their lands. The language of conservation was new, but Maisin picked it up quickly. In part, this was because the environmentalists provided people with a new and flattering view of themselves as living in a "rich" place where food was plentiful and "free" as opposed to the towns where those without money went hungry. Maisin who had recently retired from careers in the town took up the chorus, praising the peace and safety of the villages and the beauty of the country. Yet the talk of the richness of the environment also resonated with values already present in the community. As I made my way through the villages, I heard considerably less talk of "poverty," replaced by an insistence, particularly from younger people, on creating sustainable development that allowed a steady income to local people while preserving the forest. At the end of our visit in 2000, Jess took a bundle of letters written by the school kids to be shared with her class back home. Almost all included lovely drawings: tapa designs, villages houses, favourite pets, but mostly trees, plants, animals, and birds found around the gardens, in the grasslands and the deep forests.

We left Uiaku feeling inspired and hopeful for the Maisin people. Yet there were reasons for concern. The Peace Corps volunteers had left, threatening the survival of the tapa cooperative, and other partners were already shifting their attention to projects elsewhere in the country. The Maisin's triumphant victory in the National Court in 2002 capped the end of an intense period of interactions with the forces of globalization that left huge changes in its wake and, yet, had not altered a fundamental problem. None of the development schemes had panned out into viable businesses. Meanwhile, logging companies continued to eye the rich timbers of Collingwood Bay. The question now was whether the Maisin consensus against logging would be sustained once the spotlight shifted elsewhere.

THE MAISIN DECLARATION (1995)

WE, THE LEADERS OF THE CLANS AND SUBCLANS of the Maisin-speaking people of Collingwood Bay, Oro Province, Papua New Guinea, hereby declare:

That, we enjoy plentiful food and materials for shelter that nature provides from the land and the sea;

That, we take strength from and enjoy great pride in our traditional culture including the clan structure, traditional medicines, ceremonies, and the tapa art form unique to our people;

However, we do not only wish to live as our ancestors did. We seek to maintain our heritage but also to improve our lives and the lives of future generations. We therefore require better opportunities for education, health care, and transportation to name a few. The Government has failed adequately to assist us in developing these opportunities. We require money, information, training, and technical support to develop ourselves.

THEREFORE, WE DECLARE:

That, because we understand that large-scale logging and agriculture will not assist the Maisin people in realizing their aspirations but on the contrary undermine them;

That, to assure a source of cash income which will benefit the entire Maisin community and assure the protection of our natural and cultural resources;

That, to maintain control of our destiny in the hands of our own people;

The community will explore, and invites the collaboration of interested parties in supporting, appropriate alternative sources of income such as expanded markets for tapa, village-based tourism, and community-based sustainable forest management.

FURTHERMORE, WE DECLARE:

That, insofar as the forest environment of the traditional Maisin lands provides a home for the game that is our food, a source for the pure water that we drink, a site for the cultivation of our gardens including the tapa trees uniquely suited to the soils of our region, and protection against the ravages of flooding;

That, insofar as this land was inherited from our ancestors and that we intend to pass it on to future generations;

That, insofar as we are aware of how other peoples of Papua New Guinea have been taken advantage of by logging interests, who have

197

repeatedly exploited landholders' ignorance, taking all the goodness out of their place and leaving it barren;

We firmly and unanimously stand opposed to destructive large-scale industrial logging, and to agricultural activity that entails the clearing of large areas of forest, in any part of the lands traditionally held by the Maisin people.

Hellow

my name is Wendy·Bunari. Im a girl. I am 13 years old. I come from Uiaku village in the colling wood bay, Papua New Guinea. I attend uiaku Primary School and I am in grade five my teachers name is John Bendo. We have 31 children in our class. Now I want to tell you about my our Rainforest. At that rainforest we have plenty birds and many colourful birds. And plenty of bird of pardise. And for rivers we have plenty of water falls. And some times we use to go up make camps near the rivers. And we have different types of animals. We got plenty of high mountains and we use to go under the mountains and our father's use to climbs the mountains. Some times we use to go up the forest and have picnic for one week and come back to our place. And we all love our rain forest. Thats why we don't want logging to come in our place. Now Ill talk about my garden. In my garden I planted peanuts, corns and sugar cane. most I planted kaukau, taro and pumpkin. At school we lent mathematics, english and Combine subject. My favourite subject is Mathematics. Thats all. Thank you very much hope to hear from you soon. Wendy. Bunari

This is about our forest.

Figure 6.5 Wendy Bunari's letter, 2000. In July 2000, students at the Uiaku Community School wrote letters and drew pictures of their homes for Jessica to share with her classmates in the United States. Wendy's comment about going under and over the mountains is a reference to the Maisin origin story. (Photo by J. Barker)

Notes

1. The Summer Institute of Linguistics (SIL) is a branch of the Wycliffe Bible Translators International, one of the largest missionary organizations in the world. The SIL works cooperatively with established churches and local people to provide basic linguistic research on unwritten languages with the aim of furthering biblical translation. Given its vast number of vernacular languages, Papua New Guinea has long been a primary target for the SIL. While its volunteers receive advanced training in linguistics, their aim is to organize and provide expert advice to local people ("national translators") who eventually carry out the actual work of writing Bibles in their own languages.

2. See Chapter 1, note 5.

3. Mothers' Union chapters in Uiaku date back to the late 1940s and have a long history of supporting the local church as well as their own social activities. Membership has tended to be small and limited to older women. In the 1990s, the Mothers' Union included several of the most skilled and prolific tapa artists. Although ignored by outsiders, the Mothers' Union greatly expanded its ranks during the tapa boom, using their funds for travel to provincial and national gatherings and to purchase a dinghy (Barker and Hermkens in press).

4. See Hermkens (2013:311–20) for a detailed account of women's experiences during this period and local responses to the various overseas trips and partners.

5. Sylvester Moi explained that since the ancestors of the Uwe Maisin once lived in the Uiaku area, they retain a claim to the land.

CHAPTER 7

ANCESTRAL LINES

In June 2007, Anne and I returned to Uiaku for a month's stay. Anne had prepared a project to record the life histories of Maisin women as a way of probing the changing experiences and outlooks of women over three generations. For the first time, I came without a definite project in mind. I had just completed the final draft of the first edition of *Ancestral Lines* and wanted to talk to villagers about the book. But even more than this, I wanted to catch up with old friends and get a sense of changes in the village. As it turned out, both of us got more than we bargained for. A year earlier, the first-born son of George and Mary Rose Sevaru, my hosts in 1986, had been murdered by *raskols* in Port Moresby where he worked. This tragedy had been compounded by the deaths of two big men from the same clan, one of whom was my old friend Rufus. George had organized a ceremony to lift mourning from his clan's hamlet. One of the most respected of *Kawo* leaders, he had drawn on his networks within and far beyond the village to stage what would be one of the largest events in recent Maisin history. Relatives from across Papua New Guinea were pouring into the village. These included several people we had known as children or heard about from other villagers. The presence of these returning kin allowed Anne to explore the experiences of the Maisin diaspora as well as village residents while I made the best use I could of this opportunity to witness a major ceremony up close.

We were saddened by the passing of many of the people who had shared their lives and stories with us a quarter century earlier, but thrilled to be back. We were once again living on the station, this time in the house built for the SIL translators. It was a bush house, but had the "high tech" luxury of a solar panel, allowing us to recharge batteries for our cameras and enjoy a dim electric light at night (although the millions of insects it attracted diminished the pleasure!). The village looked much the same. Yet we soon noticed changes: English and *Tok Pisin* intermixed in daily speech with Maisin; more steel pots and pans in the kitchen shelters; an increasing use of store-bought foods, partic-ularly rice, flour, and cooking oil; a well-attended twice weekly market in the station shelters. Several houses had solar panels, and ghostly lights shone in corners of the village after dark. Above all, we noticed that the population had increased. Groups of teenaged boys and girls roamed the village paths in the evenings. The size of the congregation at the Sunday service swelled when a seemingly endless line of children were led up to the church from the beach shelters, where they attended Sunday school, to be blessed by the priest.

There was a flurry of activity in preparation for the ceremony. George's clan mates had cleared and planted an immense garden behind the station specifically for the event, and gardens had been enlarged elsewhere. Young men were busy erecting shelters for the many guests expected to arrive soon. Large quantities of locally caught fish and bush pig meat were being smoked in the village. Women made frequent visits to the gardens to bring food to feed the workers. As the big day approached, the pace of work picked up and there was mounting excitement. Groups of women bearing heavy loads of garden produce and firewood, hunters with bush pigs strung across their backs, young men with bundles of sago, and canoes bearing live village pigs were greeted with boisterous conch shell trumpets, children rattling sticks in outrigger canoes, and shouts of "*oro kaiva!*" (the traditional greeting call used throughout Oro Province). Meanwhile, visitors from town arrived on dinghies bearing sacks of rice, sugar, flour, tinned fish, and other store goods. The piles of food gradually mounted under the houses. The day before the scheduled cere-mony, a score of canoes sailed in from Wanigela bearing relatives of George's clan. They too brought gifts, most notably stacks of clay cooking pots which are as much a signature product of the Wanigela people as tapa is for Maisin.

Managing the many parts of this huge event took tremendous skill, patience, and energy. As a *Kawo* and church leader, George commanded much respect. What he could not do, however, was command others to do his bidding. Every stage of the ceremony required seemingly endless discussion and negotiation among the senior men to assure consensus. They, in turn, directed the younger men and women to do much of the physical work. It was clear that there was widespread support for the ceremony, but complications incessantly arose. I learned that it had already been delayed once, and now there was concern that unless it took place within a few days, the garden produce would rot and the whole process would have to begin from scratch. As it was, the ceremony was postponed by a week as George and other senior men discussed each and every detail at length.

Many of these complications were purely practical matters: for example, gauging whether enough firewood had been gathered. Yet there were more persistent issues. A few people quietly expressed suspicion about George's motives. This was not a surprise; given the ethos of equivalence that runs through reciprocal morality, envy is an expected response to any major undertaking. Yet most of the complications arose directly from confusion as to the purpose of the ceremony. At first, I assumed that the ceremony was an enlarged version of the end-of-mourning ritual described in Chapter 4. Indeed, several people assured me it was. George corrected me on this. The ceremony was to thank the Wanigela people who had carried his son's body back from Port Moresby and then to the beach to be transported to Uiaku. Their arms and shoulders would be rubbed with pig grease, a customary way that Maisin thank allies for their service. At that point, the hamlet plaza would be open for dancing and other celebration. This raised the first complication. When they received their invitation, several of the recipients insisted that since they were kin folk they neither deserved nor wanted the honour. This was not acceptable to George and his kin, who would be greatly shamed to not go through with the ritual. The matter had gone back and forth for months and was still unresolved. A second set of complications revolved around the presence of a memorial shelter in the clan plaza that had been erected following the deaths. Containing tokens of the deceased, the plan was to tear it down and burn it to mark the end of mourning. George insisted this was traditional practice, but many villagers I spoke with felt uneasy, worried that the ghosts of the deceased were attracted by the shelter and, worse, might be angered by its destruction.

On the day of the ceremony, another potential crisis arose. A group of young men had gotten drunk and high on marijuana in the bush during the night. They got into a fight, with one young man receiving a life-threatening gash from a machete. As we patched him up as best we could and arranged for a dinghy to take him to the Wanigela medical post, we wondered about the repercussions. Yet the ceremony took place more or less on time. With villagers and visitors watching from shaded spots under the houses, the priest conducted a memorial service. Several people, including myself, then walked to the centre of the plaza to speak of our memories of the deceased. The memorial items were publicly burned and the shelter torn down. During the evening, the visitors were quietly fed.

The rubbing of pig grease was scheduled for the next morning, but the Wanigela men continued to insist that it would be inappropriate for them to be so honoured. George was equally insistent. The discussion dragged on through most of the day until enough visitors had relented for both sides to save face. Given its significance, the ritual was amazingly subdued. Quietly, young men walked up to the shelter bearing a bowl with cuts of pig fat. They rubbed this

Figure 7.1 Memorial feast food exchange, 2007. Women add to mounting piles of (from left) sago, yams, sweet potatoes, bananas, and taro. (Photo by A.M. Tietjen)

on several men's shoulders as we silently watched and then provided a bowl of water and towel for the recipients to clean themselves. And that was it. With no further ado, the hamlet was now "open."

The following morning, we heard the conch shell trumpet and hurried over to the village. As we watched, women carried loads of taro, bananas, and sweet potatoes, dividing them into separate piles—a material "thanks" to the visitors that accrued to the hosts' prestige as a demonstration of their productivity, hard work, and generosity. The job of carefully dividing the raw food so that each of the visiting families received an equal share was given to young married men of the clan. Late in the afternoon, after the last canoes had departed, young people resplendent in tapa, shells, and feathers arrived in the plaza. Over the next few days, people gathered late in the afternoon, their numbers mounting as the hours passed until two facing lines of paired dancers snaked across most of the hard earth clearing. Returning home, we fell asleep to the mesmerizing echoes of rhythmic drums and rising and falling chants as the dancing continued late into the night.

Like many smaller ceremonies I had witnessed, the memorial combined elements of old and new, local and introduced. It even had a master of ceremonies—a retired Maisin businessman who introduced each act using a battery-run megaphone. Yet most of the elements were familiar, from the church service to the destruction of the deceased person's possessions. And all were in a way wrapped up in the most customary form of all, an intertribal feast organized by a *Kawo* leader in the plaza of his hamlet. I was reminded that in a society built upon reciprocal relationships and consensus, collective activities requiring months of preparation and dealing with the personalities and desires of scores of people will necessarily be somewhat improvisational. Each ceremony is familiar and each is unique. A second thing that struck me was that, unlike most of the rituals I witnessed during the anti-logging campaign, this was an entirely Maisin affair. We were the only outside witnesses (although assured repeatedly that we were family). As relatives poured in from across the country to participate, however, we were reminded that the Maisin community is not limited to the villages of Collingwood Bay but has expanded into a very broad network that, in turn, is reshaping not just local practices but Maisin culture as a whole.

One last thing that Anne and I noticed with concern: other than the dancing costumes, there was little tapa. None was made during our visit and, astonishingly, none was given to the guests.

THE LAND

Tapa manufacturing wasn't entirely absent from Uiaku on this visit. Our old friend Gideon had been experimenting for some time with new tapa products: bags, hats, and even neckties. He gave us a gift of handsome tapa document folders, his latest innovation. But for the first time, we did not hear the distinctive sound of wood mallets striking anvils or see a line of women's *embobi* hanging from clotheslines. When I asked Mildred and others about this, they explained that the water levels had risen in the gardens and *wuwusi* wouldn't grow.[1] Tapa was still being made in the eastern Maisin villages of Airara and Marua. Gideon secured his pieces from there and a few villagers got bark from relatives to bring back home and pound, but the decline in tapa making was profound.

During November 2007, the situation got considerably worse. A severe tropical storm— Cyclone Guba—gathered strength in the Coral Sea between Papua New Guinea and Australia. Although the cyclone didn't make landfall, it caused torrential rain and high seas on the northeast coast. Lowlands across the entirety of Oro Province were flooded, bridges washed away, and villages threatened by landslides, leaving a death toll of 149. Located on sandbars, the Maisin villages were entirely unprotected. Houses were undermined and lowland bush behind the villages flooded for kilometres inland. Miraculously, no one was killed. Yet there was no denying the extent of the disaster. The gardens were destroyed, buried under a layer of debris and fine silt, cutting off the local food supply other than surviving stands of sago. Relief efforts started immediately, with the Papua New Guinea government taking the lead in supplying food relief to the stricken areas, including Collingwood Bay. Some villagers left the area to live with relatives in town. Those who remained depended on shipped-in food supplies for much of a year until local gardens could be re-established, and prayed that there would not be another storm.

The people of Collingwood Bay had experienced cyclones before, most recently in 1974 when a storm destroyed much of the government station at Tufi. Cyclone Guba, however, was on another scale altogether. Single storms cannot be attributed specifically to global climate change, but there is strong consensus amongst climate scientists that as the planet warms, weather events become increasingly extreme and dangerous. The cyclone also provided stark evidence of how vulnerable low-lying regions are to the rising sea levels predicted in most climate change models. Many Maisin talk about moving their villages inland to higher grounds, both to protect themselves from flooding and to cope with the pressures of an increasing population. But the closer one gets to the mountain wall, the greater the danger from landslides and flash flooding along the rivers. Cyclone Guba changed the course of the Vayova River that separates Uiaku and Ganjiga and created a lake behind part of the village. People adapted by rebuilding their houses on the shifting sandbar, while retaining the relative positions of clan hamlets.

Climate change may well prove the greatest challenge to Maisin people in the future, but it is not the only one. Chief among these is the ever-pressing need to find ways of earning money. Even before the victory in the National Court in 2002, the attention Maisin were receiving from environmental activists was waning. The tapa cooperative collapsed with the departure of the Peace Corps volunteers, taking with it access to international buyers. Tapa makers returned to a situation of carting boxes of tapa to towns in hopes of selling to the artifact shops or in the open markets. Although Collingwood Bay remained roadless, access to the outside world improved during this period when Lutheran Shipping began a weekly boat service between Alotau on the eastern tip of Papua New Guinea and the city of Lae on the north coast. A splendid dock was constructed at Sinapa to accommodate the boat, and movement of Maisin between town and villages increased markedly. My impression is that the availability of the boat service has also increased the flow of remittances, in cash and goods, from working relatives in the towns to the village. Yet during our visit in 2007, our friends felt more isolated than ever. Repeating a refrain one hears in many parts of the country, they described Uiaku as a "last place," pointing to the closing of the Wanigela airstrip, the erratic flow of government funds to the elementary school, and the near absence of any means of making money locally, among other evidence of decline.

Given such frustrations, it is not surprising that some villagers continue to place their hope in companies proposing large-scale development projects for the area. Those hoping to make money from the rich natural resources of southern Collingwood Bay keep coming despite the National Court ruling banning trespass in the region. In 1996, prospectors began searching for mineral deposits in the Wowo Gap, the mountain pass between southern Collingwood Bay and the upper Musa basin. They have since returned annually, locating large deposits of nickel. Although this is a remote area far from villages, some Maisin claim partial or full ownership by virtue of clan migration histories and thus would expect royalties and jobs, as would Musa peoples. The longer-term effect if an open pit mine were constructed—apart from the threat it would pose to the ecology of the vast Musa wetlands—would be the possible construction of a road through virgin rainforest to Collingwood Bay and the dredging of the shallow water to allow barges to dock. Meanwhile, other companies continue to eye the rich forest resources inland from the Bay, tempting landowners with promises of replacing the trees with massive commercial plantations of oil palm, cashews, or acacia (a fast-growing tree used to make wood chips). In a repeat of the events of the 1990s, in 2004–05 individuals claiming to represent landowners signed a contract opening lands around Wanigela to logging. In 2009, Maisin learned that another alleged landowning company had signed a long-term lease covering the entirety of southern Collingwood Bay. Word quickly spread that the agro-forestry project, which would replace 34,350 hectares of primary rainforest with commercial oil palm, had been approved by both the national and provincial governments. At Christmas, a barge landed three tractors and a team of operators with camping equipment. They claimed they had come to restore the Wanigela airstrip, but soon revealed their real purpose by widening the road to the beach and creating a jetty and log pond, destroying garden land and one of the clay pits from which Wanigelan women get clay for their traditional pots. A few months later, more workers arrived, accompanied by an armed escort. Rumours swelled that a barge was headed to Sinapa.

In 2009–10, Collingwood Bay seemed destined to follow a well-established pattern not only in Papua New Guinea but in the neighbouring Solomon Islands and Vanuatu as well. On the basis of agreements of dubious legality, logging companies have targeted easily accessible timber resources, sometimes resorting to force when met with local opposition. While lease-leaseback arrangements have been around for a long time, Papua New

Guinea authorities significantly reduced their scrutiny of proposals in the early 2000s. In short order, millions of hectares of forest land amounting to some 10 per cent of the country were leased to development companies promising to convert them to money-making commercial plantations. Although local people formally retained customary ownership, in practical terms the agro-forestry projects collectively amounted to a massive transfer of land and resources into private hands—or, as one observer bluntly described it, a "land grab" (Filer 2011).

Agro-forestry projects tend to divide communities. This is no doubt what the loggers who invaded Wanigela in 2009 were counting on. Instead they were met with well-organized opposition. Despite seemingly endless internal conflicts, MICAD did not collapse after the National Court victory of 2002 but instead expanded its reach. Assisted by Conservation Melanesia, Maisin leaders reached out to neighbouring language groups along southern Collingwood Bay to negotiate a general policy on development and conservation. The Collingwood Bay Conservation and Development Association (CCADA) came into being in March 2005 as clan leaders from across southern Collingwood Bay gathered to sign a memorandum of agreement. In response to the developments in Wanigela, the CCADA convened a meeting of clan leaders in February 2010 to hear from the proponents of the development project with the aim of forming a consensus. At the same time, opponents notified their worldwide network of supporters of events in Wanigela, raising funds to bring lawyers and other experts to the meeting. Three local clans boycotted the meeting. Still, the consensus of the 500-plus people who attended couldn't have been clearer: absolute opposition to the development projects. A joint communiqué was issued "under the authority vested in the Traditional paramount chiefs" (that is to say, *Kawo* leaders), stating, among other things, "we the traditional owners of our land will be masters of our own destiny and will determine on our own terms the best options for developments we want for our people" (Gangai 2010).

Despite the meeting, the loggers continued with their work, adding an armed retired police officer to fend off protests and intimidate villagers. CCADA and its allies continued to appeal to the media and government agencies. In July 2010, provincial police arrived to arrest two Asian managers. This brought work to a halt, but most of the workers remained camped on the grounds of an abandoned plantation on the slopes of Mount Victory. The opponents now hired lawyers and returned to the National Court, protesting the violation of the 2002 ruling and seeking the dismissal of the lease-leaseback agreements. In May 2015, they won. The judges ordered the loggers to leave the area immediately.

As of November 2015, loggers remain encamped near Wanigela.

ANCESTRAL LINES

Telling stories is a common human trait. It is hard to resist the temptation to turn the Maisin experience into a story either of victory—the plucky Indigenous tribe that faced down an international logging company and won—or equally of impending tragedy given the myriad threats to their forest and way of life. Yet it is important to resist, not only because life is rarely as simple as such stories presume but also because in telling them we may fail to fully appreciate what the Maisin experience has to teach us.

Cultural anthropology began as an endeavour to document human cultures, particularly small-scale Indigenous groups widely expected to vanish under the juggernaut of Western colonial expansion. Natural science provided the main inspiration, with cultures treated as analogues of species destined to evolve or be replaced. This master narrative proved false. Human cultures are not biological species, and Indigenous peoples, while brutalized by the spread of colonial powers and their successors, have proven remarkably resilient (Davis 2009). Anthropology retains a core interest in the exploration of human diversity and commonality, but it too has changed in fundamental ways. Our disciplinary goal is no longer to document "disappearing worlds" but *this* world. For many years now, most ethnographic research has been carried out in recognizably "modern" settings: city neighbourhoods, hospitals, classrooms, sports, businesses, and so forth, albeit all around the world. I've been privileged to experience a community living a life that approximates the classic anthropological stereotype. Remote as they may appear in terms of where and how they live, however, the Maisin are every bit as much a part of the modern world as my neighbours in Vancouver. Like all of us, they have a distinctive cultural biography that defines their character within the human family; they are connected to other peoples directly and via the global system; and as members of the global community, they face common challenges.

Much of this book has been concerned with the cultural biography of the Maisin people. Drawing upon the metaphor of the making of a piece of tapa cloth, we have observed how cultivating and exchanging food and labour forms a pattern of economic activity based on the principle of reciprocity; we have traced the lines of moral values and relationship that shape gender, social organization, and passage through the life cycle; we have explored how spiritual beliefs and practices fill in the spaces of experience and give them vitality; and we have witnessed how Maisin put their values and orientations into practice as they deal with the inevitable conflicts that periodically rock all communities. These are the ancestral lines that give Maisin culture its distinctive character. Like the designs on tapa, Maisin culture draws upon its past in shaping its present. Also like tapa designs, the patterns are innovative: constantly changing, familiar and yet different, as the society encounters new challenges and experiences historical change.

The Maisin and their ancestors were always connected to neighbouring groups, yet the arrival of government officers and missionaries in the 1890s ushered in a whole new world of connections that fundamentally challenged and continue to challenge ancestral ways and values. For a century, Maisin have negotiated the difficult moral waters between the collective values of reciprocal exchange and the individualism of cash and commodities; they have engaged in a long conversation between the tangible spirituality of spirits and sorcerers and the abstract doctrines of Christianity; and they have struggled to reconcile the long slow work of consensus with the urgency to make hard decisions affecting the community's future. In the same accelerating process, connections have spread outwards, drawing Malaysian loggers, environmental activists, film makers, museum curators, and anthropologists to Collingwood Bay. Exquisitely designed tapas, originally intended as skirts, decorate walls in far corners of the world. Maisin delegations have visited major cities to promote the principles of conservation, Indigenous rights, and sustainable development. It is quite possible that a decade or so from now, plywood used for a Chinese apartment development or the palm oil in the margarine you're eating will have originated from Maisin lands.

And that brings us to the common challenges. The Maisin are very much part of our modern world. Yet they represent a way of life with far deeper roots in the human past than the politico-economic system that now engulfs the globe. It was by no means an easy way of life, but one that formed a relatively stable balance with the rest of nature. The ideals of integrated conservation and development came from the outside, but MICAD found success in the anti-logging campaign in no small part because it resonated with deeply held local values about the land. Maisin and others in Collingwood Bay who have rejected the quick money promise of logging and mining projects struggle to find alternative ways of earning money from distant, rich, and powerful outsiders so that they can have some of the things most of us take for granted: well-funded schools, decent medical care, and relief when natural disasters strike. In the complex system Andrew Walsh (2013) characterizes as the "global bazaar," people like the Maisin have very limited bargaining power and few products to offer up to the marketplace. Yet their dilemma is ours as well. We like the nice things we purchase cheaply that draw on the exploitation of natural resources and labour in the Global South. Troubling news of abuses leaks out, but for most of us it is out of sight, out of mind. However, the scientific consensus on global climate change leaves no room for doubt and increasingly little room for complacency. In the aftermath of the Industrial Revolution, humans have spewed massive amounts of carbon into the atmosphere, creating a greenhouse effect leading to global warming and increasingly violent storms like Cyclone Guba. While we must reduce our dependence on hydrocarbons, we also need to preserve our forests which absorb carbon from the air (Gore 2006). The diminishing forests of the tropic zone are worth vastly more to the human race left in in place than cut down. They are key to our survival. As they fight against terrible odds to preserve their ancestral lands, Indigenous people like the Maisin are doing the world a huge and largely unacknowledged favour.

In the years since Cyclone Guba, the gardens behind the Maisin villages have slowly recovered. *Wuwusi* is growing again, and friends who have recently visited Uiaku report hearing the rhythmic sounds of tapa beaters echoing through the village. Consignments of beautifully decorated cloths are back in the artifact shops and marketplaces of Port Moresby. Maisin studying in schools and working in towns have created Facebook pages, several featuring lovely tapa designs and their owners in traditional dress. End-of-mourning ceremonies, bride wealth prestations, and first-born initiations—each one familiar and different—provide occasions, along with church celebrations, to feast, exchange gifts, don tapa and other decorations, and renew social ties. Commercial service to the Wanigela airstrip has ended, but the weekly boat continues to ply the coast, easing the movements between town and village. Last year, Collingwood Bay received cellular coverage, a communication revolution that has overtaken the rest of the country. Several cell phone owners keep vigilant watch for barges on the waters of Collingwood Bay, quick to report the appearance of logging equipment to their kin in the towns who, in turn, relay the message to their worldwide supporters. They are far from the only ones. Small remote communities around the world have taken courageous stands to preserve their ways of life and guard our shared environment. The world has much to learn from them.

NOTE

1 Anna-Karina Hermkens (2013:75) reports that little tapa was being produced in Ganjiga in 2001. Her informants attributed this to a creeping weed that suffocated *wuwusi* saplings and malicious magic that was killing the trees. I suspect that an additional factor may have been that the *wuwusi* plantations had not yet had enough time to recover from the enormous quantity of tapa being beaten in Ganjiga and Uiaku just a few years earlier. Tapa production in Airara remained strong in this period.

REFERENCES

Addo, Ping-Ann. 2013. *Creating a Nation with Cloth: Women, Wealth, and Tradition in the Tongan Diaspora*. Oxford: Berghahn.

Akin, David, and Joel Robbins (Eds.). 1999. *Money and Modernity: State and Local Currencies in Melanesia*. Pittsburgh: University of Pittsburgh Press.

Barker, John. 1979. Papuans and Protestants. A Sociological Study of the London Missionary Society, Methodist, and Anglican Missions in Papua, 1870 to 1930. M.A. thesis. Victoria: University of Wellington.

Barker, John. 1985. Missionaries and Mourning: Continuity and Change in the Death Ceremonies of a Melanesian People. In *Anthropologists, Missionaries, and Cultural Change*, ed. Darrel L. Whiteman. 263–94. Williamsburg: College of William and Mary.

Barker, John. 1986. From Boy's House to Youth Club: A Case Study of the Youth Movement in Uiaku and Ganjiga Villages, Oro Province. In *Youth and Society: Perspectives from Papua New Guinea*, ed. Maev O'Collins. 81–107. Canberra: Department of Political and Social Change, Research School of Pacific Studies, Australian National University.

Barker, John. 1987. Optimistic Pragmatists: Anglican Missionaries among the Maisin of Collingwood Bay, Oro Province. *Journal of Pacific History* 22: 66–81.

Barker, John (Ed.). 1990a. *Christianity in Oceania: Ethnographic Perspectives*. Lanham: University Press of America.

Barker, John. 1990b. Encounters with Evil: The Historical Construction of Sorcery in Maisin Society, Papua New Guinea. *Oceania* 61: 139–55.

Barker, John. 1992. Christianity in Western Melanesian Ethnography. In *History and Tradition in Melanesian Anthropology*, ed. James Carrier. 143–44. Berkeley: University of California Press.

Barker, John. 1993. We are "Ekelesia": Conversion in Uiaku, Papua New Guinea. In *Christian Conversion: Historical and Anthropological*

Perspectives on a Great Transformation, ed. Robert Hefner. 199–230. Berkeley: University of California Press.

Barker, John. 1996. Village Inventions: Historical Variations upon a Regional Theme. *Oceania* 66: 211–29.

Barker, John. 2001. Dangerous Objects: Changing Indigenous Perceptions of Material Culture in a Papua New Guinea Society. *Pacific Science* 55: 359–75.

Barker, John. 2003. Christian Bodies: Dialectics of Sickness and Salvation among the Maisin of Papua New Guinea. *Journal of Religious History* 27: 272–92.

Barker, John. 2004a. Between Heaven and Earth: Missionaries, Environmentalists, and the Maisin. In *Pacific Island Societies in a Global World*, ed. Victoria Lockwood. 439–59. Englewood Cliffs: Prentice-Hall.

Barker, John. 2004b. Films and Other Trials: Reflections on Fieldwork among the Maisin, Papua New Guinea. *Pacific Studies* 27: 81–106.

Barker, John. 2005a. *Kawo* and *Sabu*: Perceptions of Traditional Leadership among the Maisin of Papua New Guinea. *Research in Anthropology and Linguistics* Monograph 6: 131–37.

Barker, John. 2005b. An Outpost in Papua: Anglican Missionaries and Melanesian Teachers among the Maisin, 1902–1934. In *Indigenous Peoples and Religious Change*, ed. Peggy Brock. 79–106. Leiden: Brill.

Barker, John. 2007. Taking Sides: The Post-Colonial Triangle in Uiaku. In *The Anthropology of Morality in Melanesia and Beyond*, ed. John Barker. 75–91. Aldershot: Ashgate.

Barker, John. 2012. Secondary Conversion and the Anthropology of Christianity in Oceania. *Archives des sciences sociales des religions* 157: 67–86.

Barker, John. 2014. The One and the Many: Church-centered Innovations in a Papua New Guinea Society. *Current Anthropology* 55 (Supplement 10): s172–81.

Barker, John, and Anna-Karina Hermkens. In press. The Mother's Union Goes on Strike: Maisin Women, Tapa Cloth and Christianity. *Journal of Australian Anthropology*.

Barker, John, and Franklin Seri (Eds.). 1995. *Maisin Buk: Stories in the Maisin Language*. Unpublished manuscript.

Barker, John, and Anne Marie Tietjen. 1990. Female Facial Tattooing among the Maisin of Oro Province, Papua New Guinea: The Changing Significance of an Ancient Custom. *Oceania* 60: 217–34.

Barton, F.R. 1918. Tattooing in South Eastern New Guinea. *Journal of the Royal Anthropological Institute* 48: 22–79.

Bashkow, Ira. 2006. *The Meaning of Whitemen: Race and Modernity in the Orokaiva Cultural World*. Chicago: University of Chicago Press.

Bloch, Maurice, and Jonathan Parry (Eds.). 1989. *Money and the Morality of Exchange*. Cambridge: Cambridge University Press.

Bonshek, Elizabeth. 1989. Money, Pots and Patterns: The Percy Money Collection of Bark Cloth and Pottery Held at the Australian Museum. M.A. thesis. Brisbane: University of Queensland.

Brosius, J. Peter. 2003. Voices from the Borneo Rain Forest: Writing the History of an Environmental Campaign. In *Nature in the Global South*, ed. Paul Greenough and Anna Lowenhaupt Tsing. 319–46. Durham: Duke University Press.

Burridge, Kenelm. 1960. *Mambu: A Study of Melanesian Cargo Movements and Their Social and Ideological Background*. New York: Harper and Row.

Burridge, Kenelm. 1969. *New Heaven, New Earth: A Study of Millenarian Activities*. New York: Schocken.

Burridge, Kenelm. 1975. The Melanesian Manager. In *Studies in Social Anthropology*, ed. J. Beattie and G. Lienhardt. 86–104. Oxford: Clarendon.

Burridge, Kenelm. 1979. *Someone, No One: An Essay on Individuality*. Princeton: Princeton University Press.

Cannell, Fenella (Ed.). 2006. *The Anthropology of Christianity*. Durham: Duke University Press.

Carrier, James G. 1981. Labour Migration and Labour Export on Ponam Island. *Oceania* 51: 237–55.

Carrier, James G., and Achsah H. Carrier. 1989. *Wage, Trade, and Exchange in Melanesia: A Manus Society in the Modern State*. Berkeley: University of California Press.

Chignell, Arthur Kent. 1911. *An Outpost in Papua*. London: Murray.

Chowning, Ann. 1979. Leadership in Melanesia. *Journal of Pacific History* 14: 66–84.

Comaroff, Jean, and John Comaroff. 1991. *Of Revelation and Revolution: Christianity, Colonialism, and Consciousness in South Africa*. Chicago: University of Chicago Press.

Comaroff, John L., and Jean Comaroff. 1997. *Of Revelation and Revolution: The Dialectics of Modernity on a South African Frontier*. Chicago: University of Chicago Press.

Crowther, Gillian. 2013. *Eating Culture: An Anthropological Guide to Food*. Toronto: University of Toronto Press.

Dakeyne, R.B. 1966. Co-operatives at Yega. In *Orokaiva Papers*. New Guinea Research Bulletin No. 4: 53–68. Port Moresby and Canberra: New Guinea Research Unit.

Davis, Wade. 2009. *The Wayfinders: Why Ancient Wisdom Matters in the Modern World*. Toronto: House of Anansi.

Dinnen, Sinclair. 2001. *Law and Order in a Weak State: Crime and Politics in Papua New Guinea*. Honolulu: University of Hawai'i Press.

Dorney, Sean. 2000. *Papua New Guinea: People, Politics, and History Since 1975*. Sydney: ABC Books.

Douglas, Bronwen (Ed.). 2000. Women and Governance from the Grassroots in Melanesia. State, Society and Governance in Melanesia, Occasional Paper 00/2. Australian National University. http://ips.cap.anu.edu.au/sites/default/files/women%26governance3.pdf. Accessed August 20, 2015.

Douglas, Bronwen (Ed.). 2003. Women's Groups and Everyday Modernity in Melanesia. *Oceania* 74(1/2).

Durkheim, Émile. 1915. *The Elementary Forms of the Religious Life*. London: George Allen & Unwin.

Egloff, Brian. 1979. *Recent Prehistory in Southeast Papua*. Canberra: Department of Prehistory, Research School of the Pacific, Australian National University.

Errington, Frederick, and Deborah Gewertz. 1987. *Cultural Alternatives and a Feminist Anthropology: An Analysis of Culturally Constructed Gender Interests in Papua New Guinea*. Cambridge: Cambridge University Press.

Errington, Frederick, and Deborah Gewertz. 2004. *Yali's Question: Sugar, Culture, and History*. Chicago: University of Chicago Press.

Evans-Pritchard, E.E. 1937. *Witchcraft, Oracles, and Magic among the Azande*. Oxford: Clarendon.

Ewins, Roderick. 2009. *Staying Fijian: Vatulele Island Barkcloth and Society Identity*. Honolulu: University of Hawai'i Press.

Filer, Colin (Ed.). 1997. *The Political Economy of Forest Management in Papua New Guinea*. NRI Monograph 32. London and Port Moresby: International Institute for Environment and Development, National Research Institute.

Filer, Colin. 1998a. *Loggers, Donors, and Resource Owners*. Vol. 2. London and Port Moresby: International Institute for Environment and Development, National Research Institute.

Filer, Colin. 1998b. The Melanesian Way of Menacing the Mining Industry. In *Modern Papua New Guinea*, ed. Laura Zimmer-Tamakoshi. 147–78. Kirksville: Thomas Jefferson University Press.

Filer, Colin. 2011. New Land Grab in Papua New Guinea. *Pacific Studies* 34: 269–94.

Foster, Robert J. (Ed.). 1995. *Nation Making: Emergent Identities in Postcolonial Melanesia*. Ann Arbor: University of Michigan Press.

Frampton, Joanna Margaret. 2013. A Grammatical Description of an Oceanic Language in Papua New Guinea. M.A. thesis. Dunedin: University of Otago.

Frankel, Stephen, and Gilbert Lewis (Eds.). 1989. *A Continuing Trial of Treatment: Medical Pluralism in Papua New Guinea*. Dordrecht: Kluwer.

Gangai, Adelbert. 2010. *Collingwood Bay Community Consensus: We Will Be Masters of Our Own Destiny*. Unpublished manuscript.

Geertz, Clifford. 1973. *The Interpretation of Cultures*. New York: Basic Books.

Geismar, Haidy. 2013. *Treasured Possessions: Indigenous Interventions into Cultural and Intellectual Property*. Durham: Duke University Press.

Gell, Alfred. 1993. *Wrapping in Images: Tattooing in Polynesia*. Oxford: Oxford University Press.

Gibbs, Philip. 2005. Political Discourse and Religious Narratives of Church and State in Papua New Guinea. State, Society, and Governance in Melanesia, Working Paper 2005/1. Australian National University. http://ips.cap.anu.edu.au/sites/default/files/05_01wp_Gibbs.pdf. Accessed August 20, 2015.

Gibbs, Philip. 2006. Papua New Guinea. In *Globalization and the Re-Shaping of Christianity in the Pacific Islands*, ed. Manfred Ernst. 81–158. Suva: Pacific Theological College.

Gnecchi-Ruscone, Elisabetta. 1991. Power or Paradise? Korafe Christianity and Korafe Magic. Ph.D. dissertation. Australian National University.

Gnecchi-Ruscone, Elisabetta. 1997. Changing Feasts: Church Days as Transformation of *Vasái*. In *Cultural Dynamics of Religious Change in Oceania*, ed. T. Otto and A. Borsboom. 23–32. Leiden: KITLV Press.

Godelier, Maurice. 1986. *The Making of Great Men: Male Domination and Power among the New Guinea Baruya*. New York: Cambridge University Press.

Godelier, Maurice. 1999. *The Enigma of the Gift*. Chicago: University of Chicago Press.

Golub, Alex. 2014. *Leviathans at the Gold Mine: Creating Indigenous and Corporate Actors in Papua New Guinea*. Durham: Duke University Press.

Gordon, Robert, and Mervyn Meggitt. 1985. *Law and Order in the New Guinea Highlands*. Hanover: University Press of New England.

Gore, Al. 2006. *An Inconvenient Truth: The Planetary Emergency of Global Warming and What We Can Do About It*. Emmaus: Rodale.

Gregory, C.A. 1982. *Gifts and Commodities*. London: Academic Press.

Haviland, William A., Harold Prins, Dana Valrath, and Bunny McBride. 2013. *Cultural Anthropology: The Human Challenge*, 14th ed. Independence: Cengage Learning.

Hefner, Robert W. (Ed.). 1993. *Conversion to Christianity: Historical and Anthropological Perspectives on a Great Transformation*. Berkeley: University of California Press.

Herdt, G.H. 1981. *Guardians of the Flutes: Idioms of Masculinity*. New York: McGraw-Hill.

Hermkens, Anna-Karina. 2007. Church Festivals and the Visualization of Identity in Collingwood Bay, Papua New Guinea. *Visual Anthropology* 20: 347–64.

Hermkens, Anna-Karina. 2013. *Engendering Objects: Barkcloth and the Dynamics of Identity in Papua New Guinea*. Leiden: Sidestone Press.

Jacka, J.K. 2015. *Alchemy in the Rain Forest: Politics, Ecology, and Resilience in a New Guinea Mining Area*. Durham: Duke University Press.

Jorgensen, Dan. 2005. Third Wave Evangelism and the Politics of the Global in Papua New Guinea: Spiritual Warfare and the Recreation of Place in Telefolmin. *Oceania* 75: 444–61.

Jorgensen, Dan. 2006. Hinderland History: The Ok Tedi Mine and Its Cultural Consequences in Telefolmin. *The Contemporary Pacific* 18: 233–63.

Joyce, R.B. 1971. *Sir William MacGregor*. Melbourne: Oxford University Press.

Kahn, Miriam. 1983. Sunday Christians, Monday Sorcerers: Selective Adaptation to Missionization in Wamira. *Journal of Pacific History* 18: 96–112.

Kahn, Miriam. 1986. *Always Hungry, Never Greedy: Food and the Expression of Gender in a Melanesian Society*. Cambridge: Cambridge University Press.

Keesing, Roger. 1975. *Kin Groups and Social Structure*. New York: Holt, Rinehart and Winston.

Keesing, Roger. 1984. Rethinking Mana. *Journal of Anthropological Research* 40: 137–56.

Kirch, Patrick. 2000. *On the Road of the Winds: An Archaeological History of the Pacific Islands Before European Contact*. Berkeley: University of California Press.

Kirsch, Stuart. 2006. *Reverse Anthropology: Indigenous Analysis of Social and Environmental Relations in New Guinea*. Palo Alto: Stanford University Press.

Kituai, August Ibrum K. 1998. *My Gun, My Brother: The World of the Papua New Guinea Colonial Police, 1920–1960*. Honolulu: University of Hawai'i Press.

Kooijman, Simon. 1972. *Tapa in Polynesia*. Honolulu: Bishop Museum Press.

Lange, Raeburn. 2005. *Island Ministers: Indigenous Leadership in Nineteenth Century Pacific Islands Christianity*. Canterbury: Macmillan Brown Centre for Pacific Studies.

Lawrence, Peter. 1984. *The Garia: The Ethnography of a Traditional Cosmic System in Papua New Guinea*. Manchester: Manchester University Press.

Lepowsky, Maria. 1993. *Fruit of the Motherland: Gender in an Egalitarian Society*. New York: Columbia University Press.

Lindstrom, Lamont. 1993. *Cargo Cult: Strange Stories of Desire from Melanesia and Beyond*. Honolulu: University of Hawai'i Press.

Lohmann, Roger Ivar (Ed.). 2003. *Dream Travelers: Sleep Experiences and Culture in the Western Pacific*. New York: Palgrave Macmillan.

Lutz, Catherine, and Jane Lou Collins. 1993. *Reading National Geographic*. Chicago: University of Chicago Press.

Malinowski, Bronislaw. 1922. *Argonauts of the Western Pacific*. New York: Dutton.

Malinowski, Bronislaw. 1954. *Science, Magic, and Religion*. Garden City: Doubleday.

Marshall, Mac. 2013. *Drinking Smoke: The Tobacco Syndemic in Oceania*. Honolulu: University of Hawai'i Press.

Mauss, Marcel. 1990 [1925]. *The Gift: The Form and Reason of Exchange in Primitive and Archaic Societies*. London: Routledge.

May, R.J. 2004. *State and Society in Papua New Guinea: The First Twenty-Five Years*. Canberra: Australian National University Press.

Mayo, Lida. 1974. *Bloody Buna*. Garden City: Doubleday.

Meigs, Anna S. 1984. *Food, Sex, and Pollution: A New Guinea Religion*. New Brunswick: Rutgers University Press.

Monckton, C.A.W. 1922. *Taming New Guinea*. New York: Dodd Mead.

Moore, Clive. 2003. *New Guinea: Crossing Boundaries and History*. Honolulu: University of Hawai'i Press.

Moresby, John. 1876. *Discoveries and Surveys in New Guinea and the D'Entrecasteaux Islands*. London: Murray.

Morgan, Lewis Henry. 1877. *Ancient Society*. New York: Henry Holt.

Narakobi, Bernard. 1980. *The Melanesian Way*. Boroko/Suva: Institute of Papua New Guinea Studies and Institute of Pacific Studies.

Neich, Roger, and Mick Prendergast. 2005. *Pacific Tapa*. Honolulu: University of Hawai'i Press.

Newton, Janice. 1982. Feasting for Oil Palm. *Social Analysis* 10: 63–78.

Pagden, Anthony. 1982. *The Fall of Natural Man: The American Indian and the Origins of Comparative Ethnology*. Cambridge: Cambridge University Press.

Pratt, Thane K., and Bruce M. Beehler. 2015. *Birds of New Guinea*, 2nd ed. Princeton: Princeton University Press.

Ray, Sidney H. 1911. Comparative Notes on Maisin and Other Languages of Eastern Papua. *Journal of the Royal Anthropological Institute* 41.

Read, K.E. 1959. Leadership and Consensus in a New Guinea Society. *American Anthropologist* 61: 425–36.

Regius, Helena. 1988. Em Bobi Tutu: A Study of the Making of Tapa Cloth among the Maisin People in the Oro Province. Diploma thesis. Waigani: National Arts School of Papua New Guinea.

Robbins, Joel. 2004. *Becoming Sinners: Christianity and Moral Torment in a Papua New Guinea Society*. Berkeley: University of California Press.

Robbins, Joel, and Naomi Haynes (Eds.). 2014. The Anthropology of Christianity: Unity, Diversity, New Directions. *Current Anthropology* 55, supplement 10.

Robbins, Joel, Pamela J. Stewart, and Andrew J. Strathern (Eds.). 2001. Charismatic and Pentecostal Christianity in Oceania (special issue). *Journal of Ritual Studies* 15(2).

Ross, Malcolm. 1996. Contact Induced Change and the Comparative Method. In *The Comparative Method Reviewed: Regularity and Irregularity in Language Change*, ed. M. Durie and M. Ross. 180–217. Oxford: Oxford University Press.

Sahlins, Marshall. 1972. *Stone Age Economics*. Chicago: Aldine.

Scaglion, Richard. 2004. Legal Pluralism in Pacific Island Societies. In *Globalization and Culture Change in the Pacific Islands*, ed. Victoria S. Lockwood. 86–101. Upper Saddle River: Pearson/Prentice Hall.

Schieffelin, Edward L. 1976. *The Sorrow of the Lonely and the Burning of the Dancers*. New York: St. Martin's Press.

Schieffelin, Edward L., and Robert Crittenden. 1991. *Like People You See in a Dream: First Contact in Six Papuan Societies*. Stanford: Stanford University Press.

Schwimmer, Erik. 1969. *Cultural Consequences of a Volcanic Eruption Experienced by the Mount Lamington Orokaiva*. Eugene: Department of Anthropology, University of Oregon.

Schwimmer, Erik. 1973. *Exchange in the Social Structure of the Orokaiva.* London: C. Hurst.

Schwimmer, Ziska. 1979. Tapa Cloths of the Northern District, Papua-New Guinea. *Pacific Arts Newsletter* 9: 6–11.

Smith, Michael French. 1994. *Hard Times on Kairiru Island: Poverty, Development, and Morality in a Papua New Guinea Village.* Honolulu: University of Hawai'i Press.

Stephen, Michele. 1995. *A'aisa's Gifts: A Study of Magic and the Self.* Berkeley: University of California Press.

Strathern, Marilyn. 1988. *The Gender of the Gift: Problems with Women and Problems with Society in Melanesia.* Berkeley: University of California Press.

Street, Alice. 2014. *Biomedicine in an Unstable Place: Infrastructure and Personhood in a Papua New Guinean Hospital.* Durham: Duke University Press.

Strong, W.M. 1911. The Maisin Language. *Journal of the Royal Anthropological Institute* 4: 381–96.

Suzuki, David, and Holly Dressel. 2002. *Good News for a Change: How Everyday People Are Helping the Planet.* Toronto: Stoddart.

Sykes, Karen. 2005. *Arguing with Anthropology: An Introduction to Critical Theories of the Gift.* London: Routledge.

Synge, F.M. 1908. *Albert Maclaren, Pioneer Missionary in New Guinea.* London: Society for the Propagation of the Gospel.

Teilhet, Jehanne. 1983. The Role of Women Artists in Polynesia and Melanesia. In *Arts and Artists of Oceania*, ed. S.M. Mead and B. Kernot. 45–56. Palmerston North: Dunmore.

Tietjen, Anne Marie. 1985. Infant Care and Feeding Practices and the Beginnings of Socialization among the Maisin of Papua New Guinea. In *Infant Care and Feeding in the South Pacific*, ed. Leslie Marshall. 121–35. New York: Gordon and Breach.

Tietjen, Anne Marie. 1986. Prosocial Reasoning among Children and Adults in a Papua New Guinea Society. *Developmental Psychology* 22: 861–68.

Tietjen, Anne Marie. 1989. The Ecology of Children's Social Support Networks. In *Children's Social Networks and Social Supports*, ed. Deborah Belle. 39–69. New York: John Wiley & Sons.

Tietjen, Anne Marie. 2006. Cultural Influences on Peer Relations: An Ecological Perspective. In *Peer Relationships in Cultural Context*, ed. Xinyin Chen, Doran C. French, and Barry H. Schneider. 52–74. Cambridge: Cambridge University Press.

Tietjen, Anne Marie, and Lawrence J. Walker. 1985. Moral Reasoning among Men in a Papua New Guinea Society. *Developmental Psychology* 6: 982–92.

Trompf, G.W. 1994. *Payback: The Logic of Retribution in Melanesian Religions.* Cambridge: Cambridge University Press.

Tsing, Anna Lowenhaupt. 2005. *Friction: An Ethnography of Global Connection.* Princeton: Princeton University Press.

Turner, Terence. 1993. The Kayapo Resistance. *Perspectives in Biology and Medicine* 36: 526–45.

Turner, V.W. 1974. *Dramas, Fields, and Metaphors.* Ithaca: Cornell University Press.

Tuzin, Donald F. 1980. *The Voice of the Tambaran: Truth and Illusion in Ilahita Arapesh Religion.* Berkeley: University of California Press.

Wagner, Roy. 1967. *The Curse of Souw: Principles of Daribi Clan Definition and Alliance in New Guinea.* Chicago: University of Chicago Press.

Waiko, John Dademo. 1993. *A Short History of Papua New Guinea.* Melbourne: Oxford University Press.

Wallace, Anthony F.C. 1956. Revitalization Movements. *American Anthropologist* 58: 264–81.

Walsh, Andrew. 2013. *Made in Madagascar: Sapphires, Ecotourism, and the Global Bazaar.* Toronto: University of Toronto Press.

Wardlow, Holly. 2006. *Wayward Women: Sexuality and Agency in a New Guinea Society.* Berkeley: University of California Press.

Weiner, Annette B. 1988. *The Trobrianders of Papua New Guinea.* Fort Worth: Harcourt Brace Jovanovich.

West, Paige. 2006. *Conservation Is Our Government Now: The Politics of Ecology in Papua New Guinea.* Durham: Duke University Press.

Wetherell, David. 1977. *Reluctant Mission: The Anglican Church in Papua New Guinea, 1891–1942.* St. Lucia: University of Queensland Press.

Williams, F.E. 1928. *Orokaiva Magic.* London: Oxford University Press.

Williams, F.E. 1930. *Orokaiva Society.* London: Oxford University Press.

Worsley, Peter. 1968. *The Trumpet Shall Sound: A Study of "Cargo Cults" in Melanesia.* New York: Schocken Books.

Young, Michael W. 1971. *Fighting with Food: Leadership, Values and Social Control in a Massim Society.* Cambridge: Cambridge University Press.

Zimmer-Tamakoshi, Laura. 1997. "Wild Pigs and Dog Men": Rape and Domestic Violence as "Women's Issues" in Papua New Guinea. In *Gender in Cross-Cultural Perspective*, ed. C. Brettell and C. Sargent. 538–53. Englewood Cliffs: Prentice-Hall.

Zimmer-Tamakoshi, Laura. (Ed.). 1998. *Modern Papua New Guinea.* Kirksville: Thomas Jefferson University Press.

INDEX